GW00683510

Other publications by Van Haren Publishing

Van Haren Publishing (VHP) specializes in titles on Best Practices, methods and standards within four domains:
- IT management,
- Architecture (Enterprise and IT),
- Business management and
- Project management

These publications are grouped in series: *ITSM Library, Best Practice and IT Management Topics*. VHP is also publisher on behalf of leading companies and institutions: The Open Group, IPMA-NL, PMI-NL, CA, Getronics, Pink Elephant.

Topics are (per domain):

IT (Service) Management / IT Governance	Architecture (Enterprise and IT)	Project/Programme/ Risk Management
ASL	Archimate®	A4-Projectmanagement
BiSL	GEA®	ICB / NCB
CATS	TOGAF™	MINCE®
CMMI		M_o_R®
CobiT	**Business Management**	MSP
ISO 17799	EFQM	PMBoK®
ISO 27001	ISA-95	PRINCE2®
ISO/IEC 20000	ISO 9000	
ISPL	ISO 9001:2000	
IT Service CMM	SixSigma	
ITIL® V2	SOX	
ITIL® V3	SqEME®	
ITSM		
MOF		
MSF		

For the latest information on VHP publications, visit our website: www.vanharen.net.

Capacity
Management
A Practitioner Guide

Colophon

Title:	Capacity Management - A Practitioner Guide
Series:	ITSM Library
Author:	Adam Grummitt (Metron, UK)
Publisher:	Van Haren Publishing, Zaltbommel, www.vanharen.net
Editors:	Jan van Bon (Inform-IT, chief editor)
	Annelies van der Veen (Inform-IT, editor)
ISBN:	978 90 8753 519 3
Copyright:	© Van Haren Publishing 2009
Edition:	First edition, first impression, July 2009
Design & layout	CO2 Premedia bv, Amersfoort-NL

For any further enquiries about Van Haren Publishing, please send an e-mail to:
info@vanharen.net

Foreword

When I was asked to write the Foreword for this book I was honored. I will attempt to explain why.

Adam Grummitt is a Gentleman and a Scholar, and an unsung hero in the field of capacity management in the wider IT service management space. Of course, to those who specialize in capacity management, he has long been a recognized expert (guru, luminary—select your favorite word) and someone whose advice and guidance many of us have been very fortunate to benefit from.

Together with Hans Dithmar and Brian King, the main contributors to the first ITIL 'module' on capacity management, the Metron team and Adam were (and are) the 'go to' subject matter experts. For over twenty years (to my knowledge) Adam has been quietly involved in capacity management, as practitioner, speaker (at various Computer Measurement Group (CMG), itSMF, Masterclasses and other events) and the company he helped to found (Metron) has specialized in capacity management.

His expertise, however, is much wider than capacity management, as you will soon realize when reading this book. Adam has finally done what he has promised: he and the supporting team of editors and reviewers have written the definitive book on capacity management.

Those familiar with the wider issues of capacity management will not find surprises (though they will definitely learn from the expert!), but the wider community will soon discover many important concepts and ideas that aren't available elsewhere that will make a real impact on their day to day operations.

In my view, capacity management is the most important of the ITIL functions and processes; this explains why the original module was well over 200 pages and was often described as a brick! This book is a fine and worthy successor – Adam and the many contributors and reviewers provide the detail and depth needed for practitioners to fully understand the topic.

This book ensures that some of the vast knowledge and experience from several of the world's leading experts is now available for all of us to use for a very long time.

And this is why I am honored to write this Foreword; one of my own personal heroes has, with his colleagues and reviewers, produced a work that will deservedly have its place on the bookshelf of any serious ITSM expert.

Brian Johnson

Author of ITIL V1 Capacity Management, co-founder of itSMF, Honorary Life Vice-President itSMF.

Acknowledgements

We like to thank the team of experts that have been involved in the development of this publication. Above all we acknowledge their never-ending enthusiasm and commitment.

First of all we wish to thank author Adam Grummit for gathering best practices on IT capacity management, using his own huge knowledge and experience, existing literature and information from peers. We also thank him for seriously considering all 700 issues of the reviewers and for his persistence in improving the quality of the manuscript. This has enabled us to develop a true best practice on IT capacity management.

We also wish to thank our international review team of experts who have contributed their huge experience and knowledge. They provided encouragement, criticism and useful new ideas, to ensure that the book reflects the very best practice. Their expert help has been invaluable.

The review team:
- Nick Bakker, Capacity Management expert at Getronics, NL
- Frank Bereznay, Capacity Planning Manager at Kaiser Permanente, USA
- Gabriele Biondo, Trust In People – DHL, NL
- Edouard Boris, Director of Service Engineering Europe, Yahoo, France
- Stephane Duperrex, Senior Associate – Capital Group Corporate International, Switzerland
- Irwin Friedman, independent Capacity Management consultant, USA
- Prof. Javier Garcia Arcal, Universidad Antonio de Nebrija, Manager of ITIL Best Practices at Oesia Networks, Spain
- Mike Hogg, ITIL Business Capacity Manager, NHS Account, CSC UK
- Kevin Holland, Head of Service Quality Improvement at NHS Connecting for Health, UK
- Neil Jabri, Availability, Capacity & IT Continuity Manager at Nestlé, Switzerland
- Ron Kaminski, Director of Capacity Planning & Performance at Harrah's Entertainment Inc., USA
- Tomoyuki Kawano , Managing Director of IIM, Japan
- Mike Ley, UK Computer Measurement Group (UKCMG)
- Gert Luyten, Senior manager Global Outsourcing Services at CSC, Belgium
- Tuomas Nurmela, Technology Manager at TietoEnator Processing & Network Oy, Finland
- Tony Oliver, Capacity and Availability Management at RWE IT, UK
- Bipin Paracha, Practice Head at Wipro Consulting, Wipro, India
- Gavin Pomfret, independent Capacity Management expert, UK
- Tony Verlaan, Capacity Management expert at Getronics, NL

We are also extremely grateful to the UKCMG and CMG and members of their boards for their contributions to the quality checking process. UKCMG is the UK chapter of the international Computer Measurement Group (CMG), see www.ukcmg.org.uk and www.cmg.org.

On the author

Adam Grummitt, MA (Cantab), C Eng, MIEE, CITP, MBCS

Adam has been playing with computers since graduating from Cambridge way back. Doing research in mass spectrometry[1] he used the first Digital PDP-8 in the UK and early IBM mainframes. He has since been an analyst, designer and programmer for end-users, software houses and a consultant. He has worked in a variety of computer applications, from scientific engineering and aircraft design to medicine[2], law, technical publishing and retail. He was a founding Director of Metron in 1986, which was an early partner in UKCMG, ITIL and itSMF UK. He is currently chairman of UKCMG and on an executive sub-committee of itSMF UK. He gives papers and workshops on capacity management practice at numerous international IT conferences and is a well-known speaker at many chapters of CMG.

The author thanks all those in Metron, past and present, who have helped in the development of its capacity management material over the years and in reviewing early drafts of this book. In particular, Mike Garth, who first introduced the author (and many others) to formalized capacity management and who demonstrated powerfully just how effective it can be with a top practitioner.

The author would also like to acknowledge the support of all kin and kith over the years; above all his wife and, in the crafting of this book, his daughter's attempts to improve the style and grammar and his his son's efforts to improve the structure and logic (both somewhat in vain!).

---

1   Interpretation of mass spectographic ionisation efficiency curves by deconvolution methods using Fourier transforms assuming Maxwellian distributions, AEI MSI 902 proceedings 1968

2   Real time record management in general practice, Int. J. Bio-medical computing (8) 1977

Contents

Foreword V

Acknowledgements. VII

Introduction XI

1 Context for capacity management 1
    1.1   Setting the scene. 1
    1.2   Introduction to capacity management. 4
    1.3   Capacity management in IT service management 8
    1.4   Capacity management and ITIL 11
    1.5   Capacity management maturity 15
    1.6   Demand management 18
    1.7   Roles for capacity management. 19
    1.8   IT service management drivers 20
    1.9   Basic concepts and terminology 20

2 What: What is capacity management 23
    2.1   Objectives. 23
    2.2   Definition of capacity management practice (CMP) 24
    2.3   Main terms and definitions. 25
    2.4   Basic concepts of capacity management 30
    2.5   Scope of coverage 32
    2.6   Capacity management versus general ITSM process flow 42

3 Why: Benefits of capacity management 47
    3.1   Primary benefits 47
    3.2   Operational benefits 48
    3.3   Management benefits 48
    3.4   Business benefits 49
    3.5   Costs 49
    3.6   Cost-benefit analysis. 50

4 How: Practice of capacity management 53
    4.1   Capacity management data flows 53
    4.2   Capacity management activities 54
    4.3   Capacity management control 90
    4.4   Inputs, outputs and deliverables 90
    4.5   Relations with other practices. 94

5 Who: Roles and perspectives on capacity management 99
    5.1   Customer perspective 99
    5.2   End-user perspective. 100
    5.3   Provider perspective 100

	5.4	Employee perspective	102
	5.5	Management perspective	103
	5.6	Project management perspective	105

6 Get there: Planning and implementing capacity management 107
	6.1	Plan for capacity management	107
	6.2	Design CMP	108
	6.3	Deploy capacity management	113
	6.4	Compliance issues	117
	6.5	Organizational change	117
	6.6	Pitfalls and problems	119

7 Be there: Managing the capacity management practice (CMP) . . . 127
	7.1	Operational management	127
	7.2	Positioning the CMP in processes	128
	7.3	Measurement and reporting	129

8 Improve: Optimizing the capacity management practice (CMP) . . . 133
	8.1	Critical success factors	133
	8.2	Key performance indicators	133
	8.3	Risks and countermeasures	135
	8.4	Self assessment	136
	8.5	Gap analysis	138

9 Leverage: Tools 141
| | 9.1 | Requirements for a capacity management tool | 141 |

Epilogue 147

Appendix A. Basic concepts for IT service management 149
Appendix B. Terminology and definitions 167
Appendix C. Checklists 175
Appendix D. Capacity Plan 191
Appendix E. Knot ITIL 211

Sources 213
Index 216

Introduction

This book is intended to provide information complementary to that about capacity management as provided within ITIL V2 and V3. The book can be read either from start to finish or selected sections may be used for reference. In particular, various checklists and templates are provided as a starting point for readers to 'adopt and adapt'.

The intent of this book therefore is to augment the ITIL books by providing more specific detail on capacity management. Thus it assumes the reader has an awareness of the ITIL descriptions and so knows 'what to do' and wants to know a bit more about 'how to do it'.

There are numerous books (and white papers) available on the subject of capacity management. They tend to fall into three classes. There are the mathematically oriented ones that discuss the underlying principles of queuing theory and related statistical techniques. There are the business oriented ones that discuss the philosophy of governance and process management. Finally there are the pragmatic ones with discussions of practical experience with particular domains or the latest new 'hot topic'.

The papers on theory can very quickly develop into a mathematical treatise with equations and algorithms for the few. The papers on process definition can very quickly develop into an unending set of checklists of guidelines and project management that can give middle-management a bad name and lose the interest of the experienced practitioner. The papers on current experience tend to be very site and domain specific and age rapidly.

This book tries to give a reasonable appreciation of capacity management from all three perspectives. It takes an understanding of IT service management (ITSM) processes as a starting point and expands on the specific issues raised when implementing or improving capacity management practices. It introduces elementary arithmetical approaches to analyzing data.

The main objective of this book is to ensure that a realistic, practical and pragmatic approach is adopted, where timescales, effort, priority and money play as much a part as process dataflow diagrams. It is worth remembering that some experts summarize the Information Technology Infrastructure Library (ITIL) simply as 'documented common sense' and ISO/IEC 20000 as 'auditable common sense.' Of course the common sense in question may be based on many years of practical ITSM experience.

How to Use this Book

This book is intended to provide the reader with some general background and a little technical detail as regards the practice of IT capacity management. It is assumed that the reader has an understanding of IT infrastructure and may well have read the relevant parts of the IT Infrastructure Library (ITIL). No matter which version of ITIL (V2 or V3) has been read, the material amounts to some fifty pages of general description of the activities involved in capacity management. If the reader has read the capacity management requirements identified in the ISO/IEC 20000 standard, they will appreciate that it is a three page summary of the expected deliverables of the practice. This book extends the description of the practice to around 200 pages and goes into a bit more practical depth, more in keeping with the excellent, original 200 page module in ITIL V1[3].

The target audience is anyone involved with capacity management, whether as a practitioner or as a manager or working in related areas and seeking a better understanding of it. It should be recommended reading for those in any ITIL activity as well as developers, testers, customers (ITIL's term for end-user managers paying for the IT service) and service level agreement creators. The book provides general descriptions of all the related activities and deliverables as well as many checklists going into some detail of tasks and data involved. Thus the book could be read from start to end but it is anticipated that for many readers the most value will lie in the checklists in the appendices, using them as draft templates for internal use. It is entirely within the spirit of ITIL, and most authorities on the subject, that the reader chooses at will whether to adopt or adapt any part of this book. Take it or leave it. That was true of the first version of ITIL and is still true today, despite many false prophets debating the precise interpretation of some of the contradictory descriptions within ITIL.

The book is structured into nine chapters.

The first chapter provides an introduction to capacity management practices in the context of IT service management and chapter two expands on its background.

Chapter three reviews the benefits gained by adopting the practice of capacity management.

Chapter four is the longest chapter and outlines the activities, inputs, processing and outputs involved in capacity management.

Chapter five summarizes different perspectives of capacity management.

Chapter six discusses implementation issues.

Chapter seven outlines the management of the capacity management practice and chapter eight its optimization.

Chapter nine considers the requirements and options for related tools.

The remaining chapters are essentially appendices, and contain a lot of useful information and checklists.

Appendix A provides the basic concepts for IT service management, and is the common philosophy for all books in the Practitioner Guide series. It is important that anyone not fully aware of the differences between processes and functions reads this Appendix to avoid conceptual errors in the embedding of capacity management in their organization. ITIL and IT service management are most often related to process-based approaches, and capacity management can follow that approach. capacity management in itself, however, clearly is a function (or 'practice'), an organizational capability, using people, processes and technology to accomplish its goals. This Appendix explains the approach to make that work.

Appendix B lists the acronyms, models, frameworks and standards used and a personal glossary.

Appendix C contains checklists which should prove useful as a starting point for any site to review its own capacity management practice.

Appendix D contains a template for capacity plans and a simple, sample capacity plan.

Appendix E offers an alternative approach and wording of the six basic processes in IT service management.

At the end of the book you'll find a few useful reference sources and an index to keywords and their location within the book.

1 Context for capacity management

This chapter introduces the concepts of capacity management and how they are typically reflected in real life. It introduces some basic concepts and terminology of capacity management to pave the way for the rest of the book.

1.1 Setting the scene

Capacity management is a well-established practice that has been used in information and communications technology[4] (ICT, or IT) for several decades. In most large enterprises today, IT plays an increasingly significant part in the business. The focus is moving towards reducing both capital expenditure and operating costs and make more use of existing assets. Capacity management is a key component in helping organizations to optimize costs and also reduce carbon footprints by consolidation techniques. It can also impact on datacenter management at the level of contracts or even real estate management such as the construction of required new buildings.

IT solutions are implemented on mainframes, distributed systems on UNIX, Linux, Windows or thin clients or combinations thereof. Applications are developed that interact with the users in the business areas to help the enterprise succeed in its business goals. The applications may be developed in-house, off-shore or bought in as 'Commercial Off The Shelf' (COTS) packages. These applications are typically composed of interactive transactions to achieve particular results such as invoices, orders, database updates and so on. Developers tend to think in terms of the software development life cycle (SDLC) and applications with projects to develop them. The SDLC covers requirement definition, analysis, specification, coding, testing and pilot implementation. Once the application is in production, it then tends to be considered as ready for operations to take responsibility for it. It is worth remembering that many in IT are involved with development and testing and not much aware of ITSM or ITIL. In the same way, many involved with ITSM and ITIL are not much aware of the software development life cycle which has its own management philosophy and typically works under the control of projects rather than the implementation of infrastructure processes.

Operations people tend to think in terms of groups of applications used by particular groups of users and refer to them as services. The capacity managers have to ensure that the services run on suitable equipment so that the desired level of service is achieved. This is usually described in terms of availability (such as 7x24 at 99.99% uptime), continuity (such as a proven disaster recovery capability), performance and capacity (so many transactions per peak hour with a certain response time from end-to-end in terms of servers and networks) and maximum capacity (so much headroom for spare capacity to cater for special peaks in traffic). This is moving into the area of capacity management, which is usually taken to include all the activities to ensure the

---

4   Throughout this book, we use the term IT to indicate information and communication technology (ICT) as well as information technology.

performance of a service and the capacity of the infrastructure to support it. Thus it incorporates performance monitoring and analysis, capacity planning and related liaison with development, testing, service level management, business areas and more.

In essence, the challenge is to find the equipment necessary to meet the ever increasing demands of the business and then to ensure that the inevitable bottlenecks are minimized and the costs of providing the service are also minimized. This requires demand management in the sense of controlling and prioritizing requests as well as monitoring of performance and throughput to ensure an understanding of the relationship between the business application and the resource demands placed on the infrastructure.

All of the IT infrastructure is involved, from the space in the data center to the routers in the network. Over capacity and lightly used servers, especially on X86 platforms, are a focus for improvement to the benefit of both budgets and sustainable IT. Data center facility capacity management is a growing aspect as servers become higher density placing greater demands on air conditioning, as well as moves towards consolidation and green 'sustainability'. In practice, many practitioners will focus on the higher cost servers and the systems that support heterogeneous applications rather than a single workload. Thus a lot of this book will consider the impact of mixed workloads on larger servers. However, most of the practices described can be applied to distributed systems, networks, storage farms, data warehouses, or other IT solutions.

1.1.1　Lean, mean and green capacity management

In lean, tough times of need for competitive advantage, it is important to adopt a focused approach to core activities in all IT practices. In times of mean, frugal economic measures, it is essential to focus on those practices that are effective and yield practical deliverables. In enlightened times of sustainability, it is also an advantage to find solutions that appear to satisfy the criteria for 'greenness' – even if some of the benefits are debatable. In practice, the most pragmatic 'lean mean green IT service management solution' is to promote the same core activities that have been established over the years for effective capacity management.

The 'more' to be done usually means, these days, more applications in more services on more servers for more users of more critical business requirements. This means trying to automate as much analysis and reporting as possible to be applied to increasing numbers of machines, both real and virtual. The 'less' available usually means less available resources on all fronts. This includes all financial budgets, as well as reducing numbers of data centers and their staff, reducing spare capacity and headroom, consolidating servers, virtualizing machines with probably less specialist staff for all the work on both the infrastructure and all the related development projects.

However, the 'more' has to be related to what is actually achieved now (in a business sense) and the 'less' has typically to be assessed in financial terms for any 'overhead' costs involved in the provision of the infrastructure and services. This is also a time of increased outsourcing, off-shoring or otherwise off-loading some of the IT services. This may be done via a managed service provider (MSP) who may offer software as a service (SaaS). Whichever approach is adopted, the traditional needs within capacity management for baseline definition, workload characterization, business driver identification, application sizing, demand management, monitoring, analysis, forecasting and modeling are all involved.

In lean, mean times there is an increased desire to try to make the most of current investment, to identify any spare capacity and assess just how much more traffic can be accommodated without undue loss of service level. Virtualization of Windows servers, instead of merely grouping a number (like ten or twenty) of highly under-utilized servers to a single or mirror pair of larger servers, is moving towards more significant consolidation ratios like twenty or forty to one. With higher utilization levels, contention becomes a dominant consideration and performance degradation for virtual machines has to be assessed in the light of workload priorities, quotas and service level agreements. Also, as more significant services are virtualized, the overhead incurred and performance impact of an extra layer of software can become more evident.

Centralizing, virtualizing and consolidating machines give a company more opportunity to have an effective energy management policy by reusing the heat generated. The machines may occupy less physical space but may require more air conditioning and clear space around them, so the total green saving is debatable. The policy towards write-off or reuse of the old equipment will largely determine the green benefit. In theory, virtualization, consolidation, auto-provisioning, workload management and dynamic workload balancing (such as VMotion) allow companies to turn off machines at low demand periods. Potentially, combined with grid or cloud/sphere computing, these could offer the ultimate in greenness by only using power and machines when you really need them.

The net result is that there may or may not be fewer machines using more or less power. There may be better services on fewer machines, or contention may lead to degradation in the service. But in all cases, there is a need to find the costs and performance benefits of the current and proposed configurations to justify the levels of expenditure planned in the light of business demands. This balancing act is at the heart of capacity management and is as much a requirement in a well-managed IT environment as ever.

In order to optimize on the 'hardware costs versus capacity' and the 'user requirements versus service level' balances effectively, often it is necessary to have a quick technical audit of current capacity management practice (CMP). Many sites have fewer performance analysts and capacity planners than in the past, yet looking after more servers for services that are ever more business critical. The capacity management team (CMT) is often stretched in different directions by the competing demands for the IT expertise that is necessarily resident within the team. There are fire-fighting demands for optimization, tuning, debugging and detailed 'project work' (usually arising from development demands, test labs or pilot trials). These all compete with effort required to achieve the ITIL description of good infrastructure practice.

Many sites have an attitude to CMP that is derived from a long history of a datacenter glasshouse – silos and ivory towers tend to be the key words. But sites with large investments in major UNIX super-servers, or even so many hundreds of smaller UNIX servers and thousands of Windows servers, are rediscovering the IT planning infrastructure ideas that have served the mainframe so well for so long. The focus and metrics are of course different. The amount of analyst time per application, service or server is much reduced. But the need to balance 'supply versus demand' and 'capacity versus cost' remains the same.

Thus the lessons are clear. In current times, the need is to make the most of the resources already in place, both in terms of computer hardware, software, licenses and support staff and expertise. All the activities undertaken by the CMT need to be reviewed. Long periods set aside to maintain some esoteric reporting regime for a long-stable application could be dropped. Coding corrections to some complex Excel solution developed some years ago by a previous analyst for a particular solution could be dropped in favor of a solution that is now available within some proprietary tool already in place. Excessive reports to an intranet with lots of tables of figures that are out-of-date, on irrelevant metrics or even inactive servers and without any exception reporting could be reviewed.

Thus capacity management remains at the hub of IT service management (ITSM) practices, in summer and winter, economic expansion or recession. It provides the performance metrics and their interpretation to ensure that the IT service is meeting expectations, whether explicit in a service level agreement (SLA) or implicit just by identifying potential relative degradation if nothing is done.

1.2   Introduction to capacity management

This section is a brief summary introduction to the discipline of capacity management and establishes a common foundation for what follows. The headlines in the figures indicate some of the key aspects which will be expanded within this book. They are shown here in brief to indicate to new readers the sorts of issues involved. They are not comprehensive lists – these emerge later and in the appendices. Experienced practitioners will be more interested in later discussions on these topics. Those who are ITIL certified may well find this summary too simplified, but it is intended to establish a common foundation for what follows.

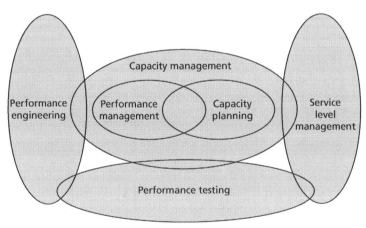

Figure 1.1 Capacity management and some related practices

Capacity management can be thought of as a combination of performance analysis and capacity planning with close links to related activities in performance engineering, performance testing and service level management (SLM), particularly in the area of service level agreements (SLAs). The practices shown in figure 1.1 indicate a degree of overlap and hence a need for defined interfaces and data flows across the boundaries. Like all good boundaries, there is a need for proper control of passage in both directions with agreed procedures for cooperation on both sides.

> ***The prime objective of capacity management*** *is the provision of a consistent, acceptable service level at a known and controlled cost. This requires the control of two essential balances: supply versus demand and resources versus cost.*

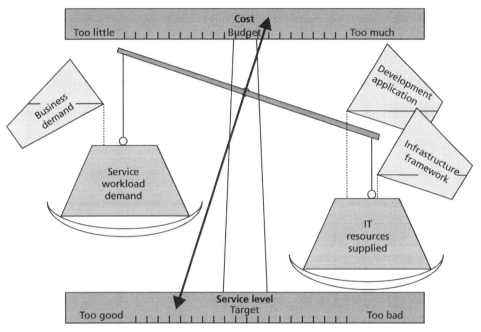

Figure 1.2 Capacity management balances

This balancing act is a continual practice as indicated by the continual changes due to the 'trickles' shown from demand management, application development and infrastructure framework requirements.

In order to maintain this practice, it is necessary to assess things in three views: what has happened in the past, what is happening now and what is likely to happen in the future. This is achieved by three main activities within capacity management: past performance trending, current performance analysis and future performance forecasting. A number of related activities are linked, such as shown in figure 1.3

The list of related activities and where they reside within departments will vary somewhat in different organizations, but again there is an inevitable overlap that will need control to ensure effective control of information.

The prime objective above can be extended and shown beside the list of key deliverables as in figure 1.4.

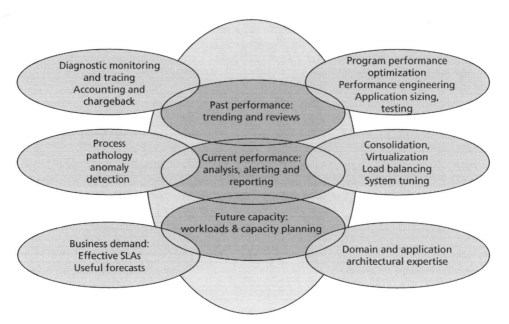

Figure 1.3 Capacity management and related activities

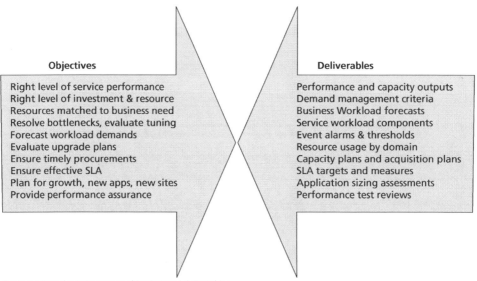

Figure 1.4 Capacity management objectives and deliverables

The objectives and deliverables shown in figure 1.4 do not match line for line, but there is some degree of correlation between the two. These lists are expanded and discussed in later chapters. The practice of capacity management is essentially at three levels, covering the business view, the service view and resource or component view. These are known as business capacity management (BCM), service capacity management (SCM) and resource/component capacity management (R/CCM). The performance and capacity inputs and outputs are many and various.

The inputs are from a wide variety of sources, ranging from business plans and IT budgets to operational statistics. The data captured and collected is maintained in a capacity database (CDB) and used by the capacity management information system (CMIS). The outputs range from performance reports and capacity plans to guidelines for SLAs and event management thresholds.

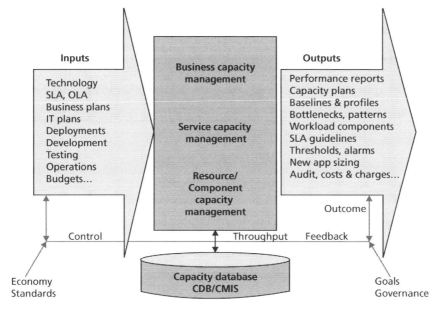

Figure 1.5 Capacity management inputs and outputs

Note that where there is not a useful SLA in terms of performance requirements, it is often useful to coin an internal operational level agreement (OLA) which determines an approximate overall performance requirement, such as 'not more than twice as bad as the current level'.

The sub-practices of business, service and resource or component capacity management involve a number of activities. These are actioned in concert but at different levels of perspective, granularity and time. The level of control to be achieved depends on the organization and the business need for IT. IT resources may be controlled on a minute, hourly or daily basis, IT services reviewed on an hourly, daily or weekly basis and business demands assessed on a monthly, quarterly or annual basis.

The CDB contains large amounts of data from a wide array of sources.

Note that quality assurance (QA) and testing of applications (typically in a test lab) should provide useful input to capacity management. Also the liaison with business should be aimed at deriving relevant metrics for the work to be done, plans for its likely changes and key performance indicators (KPIs) to assess its success. relational database management systems (RDBMS) such as Oracle and SQL Server are major components of many applications. Application instrumentation ideally yields relevant transaction statistics, maybe in the format suitable for application response

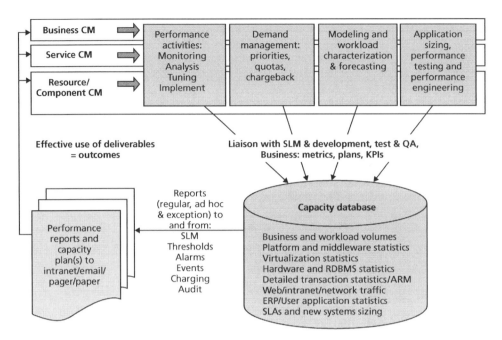

Figure 1.6 Capacity management activities

measurement (ARM) application program interface calls. enterprise resource planning (ERP) solutions such as SAP, Baan, Oracle Financials and Peoplesoft are examples of typical packaged applications.

1.3   Capacity management in IT service management

Most IT providers think in terms of providing services (IT service delivery, ITSD) and managing the provision of those services IT service management (ITSM). capacity management is a key aspect of this.

Capacity management is described in most frameworks for ITSM. Prime examples are the Microsoft Operations Framework (MOF), the Application Service Library (ASL) and the Information Technology Infrastructure Library (ITIL).

In ITIL capacity management is presented as a process. In version 2 of ITIL ('ITIL V2'), it is included as one of five service delivery processes. Version 3 of ITIL ('ITIL V3') expands on the business aspects and lifecycle of IT services. It restructures the ITIL V2 processes with capacity management described largely within a book entitled Service Design. However, although some of the terminology has changed and a few extra activities identified, the outline description of capacity management is much the same in the two versions. Although there are references to capacity management as a *function* and as an *activity* in each of the five ITIL V3 books, the Service Design book largely refers to it as a *process*. In this book we will show how capacity management can be perceived as a function in an organizational context, and how it relates to dimensions of process, organization, and technology. For practical reasons we will use the term **capacity management practice (CMP)** to indicate all activities involved with capacity management, and **capacity management team (CMT)** to indicate the staff with a commitment to fulfilling capacity management activities. Appendix A addresses the distinctions between functions, processes and practices in some detail.

Capacity is perceived as one of the core attributes of service quality (see figure 1.7), ideally to be found in service agreements. Like most other service attributes, capacity is influenced by applications as well as systems. That is, the demands for, and usage of, capacity are affected both by the application itself as well as the system it is running on. However, whereas the influence of functionality on service delivery in general is largely determined by the application coding, the influence of capacity in general is largely determined by the system (being the hardware/network/facilities infrastructure that applications run on). Capacity management can be applied to all areas of IT and the weighting of factors can vary, such as the capacity of VOIP communication depending on business usage rather than application factors.

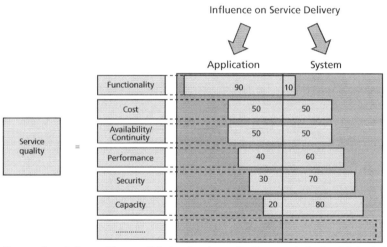

Figure 1.7 Capacity is one of the core attributes of service quality (figures are indicative of their relative contribution, not result of research)

In essence the CMP covers the well known activities of **performance analysis** and **capacity planning** with links to **performance engineering, performance testing** and **service level agreements.** Performance analysis is mostly concerned with production systems, shorter time-scales and detailed data. Capacity planning tends to be longer time-scales with more aggregated data. Performance engineering is mostly concerned with building good performance into the service design and development stages. Performance testing should be part of quality assurance and be done in conjunction with conformance testing, typically in a test lab. Service level agreements ideally contain key requirements for performance and capacity.

Capacity management can be applied at three levels; technology, service and business. These correspond to the interests of the optimum management of resources or components (primarily technology units), the services they support and the business requirements that they are intended to meet. These are described as three sub-processes in ITIL.

Capacity management is applicable to most financial, commercial, industrial, retail, public and non-profit organizations with IT systems designed to provide production level services. It began in the 1970s in the centralized world of mainframes and their datacenters. Initially it was a specialist activity for systems programmers who understood the technical issues to do with the performance of a mainframe and who learned to apply this technical understanding in conjunction with a business understanding of the supported application transactions

In those days there may have been a **capacity management team (CMT)** of performance analysts and capacity planners supporting a single machine (or possibly a small number of machines).

Nowadays, the same functions are required, but applied to a much greater number of machines. As a result, the same team's efforts are typically spread across so many hundreds or even thousands of machines. The solution architecture is often more complex in that there may be many levels or tiers involved with pools of machines at each level. So although there is less time available per machine and each machine may have a different role with specific workload profiles, the discipline remains technically similar. However, there is now the added burden of gaining understanding of and focusing on business criticality issues, as the applications have become more mission critical as well as more numerous. Furthermore, as there is often less technical appreciation of the relevant factors and less time to understand the normal behavior of any one machine, so there is more need to automate the practice as much as possible and to avoid the most extreme dysfunctions.

*The **essential task** of capacity management is to look at the current performance of a service, identify any bottlenecks, understand the workload placed on it and the underlying business drivers that may affect future traffic. The next task is to assess the workload growth history and define potential future scenarios, then to map that workload demand on to the existing resource configuration to assess likely future performance. This needs to take into account the likely future resource configuration in the light of improved device service times. The final task is to predict the impact of any suggested changes to ensure maintenance of the required level of service.*

Thus capacity management is generally viewed as embracing both the activities involved in performance management as well as capacity planning. These tend to work in different timeframes and with different objectives but together help to establish the optimum balance between demand and supply as well as costs and resources.

Related activities typically include the establishment of a reporting regime, usually to pagers, email or intranets, to provide a reference point for all interested in the performance of the machines and the services running on them. This also helps with the assessment of new applications as they emerge, preferably in pre-production saturation testing before they are launched into production.

Although a CMT is often set-up in many enterprises, its role is not always clearly understood by those working in the business areas or the IT service infrastructure. It may be dominated by domain experts who represent the detailed technical resource expertise within the enterprise. So there is always a danger of the activities being focused on fire-fighting, in the sense of resolving current problems and panics, at the expense of planning to avoid them. This is often caused by project managers who tend to ignore non-functional requirements. There are many reasons for firefighting becoming dominant. One is the CMT's pleasure at becoming 'heroes'. But it would be better to try to find the gremlins causing the issues which are making it all go wrong.

Gremlins are well known. They are creatures, commonly depicted as mischievous and technically oriented. Their origins were with World War II airmen, claiming that gremlins were responsible for sabotaging aircraft. Grumlins are similar but smaller and more aggressive (check the author's surname) and are responsible for sabotaging the best endeavors of the CMT.

Grumlin #1 is borrowed from Murphy and states that 'anything that can go wrong, will go wrong'. This means that the CMT should look for program loops, memory leaks, missing indexes, fragmented discs, housekeeping schedules et cetera to avoid building forecasts based on a badly tuned system.

1.4   Capacity management and ITIL

The Information Technology Infrastructure Library (ITIL) offers a systematic approach to the delivery of quality IT services. ITIL was developed in the 1980s and 1990s by CCTA (Central Computer and Telecommunications Agency, now part of the Office of Government and Commerce, OGC), under contract to the UK government[5]. Since then, ITIL has provided not only a widely used framework, but also an approach and philosophy that is shared by the people who work with it in practice. ITIL has been updated twice, the fist time in 2000-2002 (V2), and the second time in 2007 (V3).
The ITIL approach has been widely adopted throughout the world in all sizes and shapes of organizations, and is the de facto framework for IT service management.

ITIL V3 uses the concept of a service lifecycle for the provision of IT services. There are five core books that describe the lifecycle. In order, these are Service Strategy, Service Design, Service Transition, Service Operation, and Continual Service Improvement. ITIL is technology independent, for example avoiding mention of specific operating systems, database platforms, or service management toolsets. The library provides information on concepts, processes, functions, activities, organization, methods, techniques, tools, implementation considerations, and measures. In V3, capacity management is viewed largely as part of the service design phase of the service lifecycle. In ITIL V3, a service has two dimensions, utility (functionality, what it does) and warranty (provisioning, how well it does it). Capacity management is described as a warranty

---

5   www.best-management-practice.com lists various documents produced by the OGC, including ITIL (for ITSM), PRINCE2 (for project management), Managing Successful Programmes (MSP for programme management), Management of Risk (M_o_R) and Portfolio, Programme and Project Offices (P3O). The Structured Systems Analysis and Design Method (SSADM) is in some references under www.ogc.gov.uk

attribute. Capacity management is described at a high level in some fifty pages, with content extracted from the orginal book in version one[6] and similar to a single chapter in version two.

Top level frameworks such as ITIL are usually introduced with numerous lower level details about processes, sub-processes, interfaces and required data flows. There is always a danger that the description of a reference framework can become viewed as a formal definition of recommended procedures and activities. Sometimes the mere formalization of a view of a subject from the top down introduces a structure that becomes an entity in itself. This has unfortunately happened with ITIL, with many people incorrectly believing that you must explicitly follow its recommendations. This is not the case. The ideas from ITIL should be 'adopted and adapted', tailored to meet the specific needs and circumstances of an organization. In fact, very few organizations have adopted the whole of ITIL; most adopt just a few areas of the whole library.

1.4.1   Processes, functions and activities

Because ITIL covers the full service lifecycle, there are a high number of subject areas, which ITIL calls 'processes'. There are twenty-six[7] of these, most of which have sub-processes. There are also subject areas that ITIL calls 'functions': e.g. service desk, application management, technical management, and IT operations management. Apart from these, ITIL also describes a lot of other practices that it calls 'activities'. These terms are discussed in some detail in appendix A1.

Most of what ITIL calls a 'process' does not follow the definition of what a process is (according to the definition presented in ITIL[8]). One solution to this is to consider the twenty-six ITIL 'processes' as twenty-six ITIL 'practices'. So capacity management in ITIL, which uses several real processes to achieve its aims, can be considered to be a 'practice', and not a 'process'.

In the early days, the organizational functions needed within IT were clear: Development and Operations. Since then Development has separated into functions for analysis, design, coding, and testing, before merging into software engineering and then splitting again. Operations has similarly split into functions such as systems management, network management, and desktop management.

For IT service management there is no need to create twenty-six functional departments, just because there are twenty-six ITIL practices described in ITIL. How practices are mapped within an organization is as variable as the organizations themselves, and the people within them. However, most sites will try to establish standards to reduce the variations.

---

6   The original book was written by Brian Johnson, one of this book's referees.
7   Estimates of this number vary, mostly in the twenties. The excellent IT skeptic (www.itskeptic.org) has shown the incon-
     sistency within seven ITIL V3 references containing 22 processes in all sources and 40 mentioned in at least one source
     (with 11 only in one). So the likely range is 22-29, depending on which sources you most respect.
8   ITIL V3 definitions are:
     • A process is "a structured set of activities designed to accomplish a specific objective. A process takes one or more
        defined inputs and turns them into defined outputs".
     • A function is "a team of people and the tools they use to carry out one or more processes or activities".
     • An activity is "a set of actions designed to achieve a particular result".

Grumlin #2 is that the great thing about IT standards is that there are so many to choose from.

Grumlin #3 is that on average, new standards last for eighteen months so that in any large enterprise there are typically five active standard definitions in various degrees of implementation in place for each aspect of IT and five to the power 'n' permutations for the 'n' regimes of standards defined.

Capacity management is viewed largely as part of the service design phase of the service lifecycle. ITIL does not mention information specifically required for capacity management such as performance data sources, virtualization levels, consolidation trends, utility computing, blades, parallel processing, multi-core processors, clustered technologies and so on. These architectures are very dynamic and their performance issues are very real and have to be addressed. Vendors of capacity management tools have a continuing challenge to ensure that they keep up with new architectures and new releases. Members of the CMT have a continuing challenge in keeping up with new technology.

So there is a need to consider such matters and that is usually achieved by reference to domain experts. They in turn attend conferences and read papers to keep up-to-date in this specialist area. Formal certification on general principles is a useful starting point, but the real education comes from sharing experiences with other experts in the field addressing today's practical issues. This is achieved for capacity management primarily by the **Computer Measurement Group (CMG)**. This organization was founded in the USA in 1975 when capacity management was sometimes known as computer performance evaluation. Related topics have been included over the years with various descriptions of ITSM, IT infrastructure planning (ITIP), performance engineering and capacity management. The CMG annual conferences and meetings in the USA, UK, Central Europe and other local and international chapters are a primary source for the latest approach to current topics. For more information about CMG see www.cmg.org. There are typically some 200 papers given yearly at CMG (and more in the international chapters such as the United Kingdom Computer Measurement Group, UKCMG) so there is a vast amount of material to review.

1.4.2   Key parameters

ITIL and other books talk of People, Process, Products (or Technology) and Partners as the key interrelated entities concerned with the establishment of an effective ITSM practice regime. This book extends the alliteration by adding Price and Planet.

Price ensures that the costs of providing the different elements of IT service management are taken into account, prioritizing the implementation of processes or functions that can achieve the largest benefit. A categorization of the importance of services to the business is often introduced to identify those that are 'mission critical', 'standard', 'specialist' and 'other' (or something similar, and sometimes called 'service tiering' with typical levels of gold, silver and bronze). ITIL is then applied in full for the mission critical services, with a reduced application for services that are less critical.

Planet implies care of the planet, in that IT services should be sustainable and green so that capacity management should limit the enterprise IT negative impact on the environment. Examples are less powerful processors for lightly utilized servers, consolidation of lightly utilized servers (maybe including virtualization), smart data archiving solutions, demand management to set quotas and remove false traffic peaks and so on.

Playfully, the alliteration of the six P's above (People, Process, Products, Partners, Price and Planet) can be even further extended. The main attributes of the people and partner entities include politics, policies and psyche. This is using the word 'psyche' to imply the impact of 'company culture' which often dominates ITIL implementation considerations (and sometimes described as 'ABC' considerations[9]). A company with poor results and increasing competition is likely to be frugal in all its thinking. A growing company with a critical IT service is liable to focus on maximum practical performance. Most companies lie in the middle, trying to get the balance 'just right'.

People is used in this case to include partners, policies, politics and psyche. The issues that affect process include projects, practice, plans, prognostications and procedures. Products can include platforms and proprietary tools. The main output from price concerns is the allocation of priorities with due consideration to issues affecting the price impact on the planet in terms of CO_2 emissions et cetera. See figure 1.8.

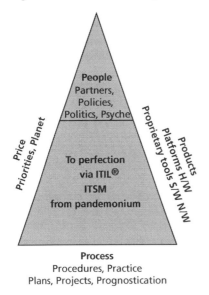

Figure 1.8 ITSM parameters

---

9   Paul Wilkinson has written about Attitude, Behavior and Culture as the vital, 'soft skill', key aspects for success in imple-
      menting ITSM practices.

ITSM parameters include:

- **People** – are the entity least inclined to conform to predefined process definitions; **partners** – involve relationships between people and so the complexity is exponentially increased with the numbers involved; **policies** are the declared objectives for the organization; **politics** are how these are interpreted; and **psyche** is the 'company culture' which sets an overall attitude framework.
- **Process** – is a set of prescribed activities using resources to transform inputs to outputs, i.e. 'what is to be done'; **procedures** – are the detailed instructions to carry out the activities of a specific process, i.e. 'who/how to do it'; **policy** – is the overall intention and direction of a service provider formally expressed by senior management; **practice** is what actually happens; **plans** are what is meant to happen; **projects** are the workloads arising from development and **prognostication** is the forecasting of business demand.
- **Product** – is often the clearest on the pricing issue (unless developed in-house), but perhaps not on the cost-benefit; typically based on **platforms** for hardware and software; with **proprietary-tools** for hardware, software, networks et cetera.
- **Price** – is the largest factor on pragmatic decisions, and control of it requires the allocation of **priorities** to business demand and resultant services; and **planet**, the consideration of sustainability and green issues.

All of these parameters influence capacity management practices (CMP).

1.5 Capacity management maturity

A common analysis of success in business suggests it can be ascribed to the following key elements, which are here interpreted in the adoption of ITIL:

- vision (ITIL offers a good framework to achieve IT and business objectives)
- mission (to implement ITIL practices)
- belief (ITIL will make IT service management more effective)
- strategy (define practices for consideration)
- tactics (select and define activities for planned action)
- operations (do it)

Process 'maturity' levels are often defined based on five levels (or six if inactivity is included), according to the Capability Maturity Model (CMM) or CMM Integration (CMMI) model as defined by the Carnegie Mellon Software Engineering, as illustrated in figure A.10 (Appendix A). A similar approach can be followed for capacity management maturity. The precise terminology associated with maturity levels varies in different presentations, but the levels described below are typical.

In capacity management terms (to be discussed in more detail later) the levels may be thought of as moving from simple monitoring through analysis to the three sub-practices of capacity management as described in ITIL. The related activities and tasks vary from simple monitoring of utilization through trending to capacity planning and corporate performance management with executive dashboards. Although the detailed interpretations of each of these levels and what they mean in terms of capacity management is open to debate, the following are reasonable indicators:

- **Level 0** – means that there are no activities or procedures of CMP in place.
- **Level 1** – implies an ad hoc response each time to any event with ad hoc or post hoc attempts to gather relevant information to address a capacity-related incident.
- **Level 2** – moves up to a reactive response based on precedent, with a basic measuring regime in place to gather core metrics such as utilizations for capacity and performance and uptime for availability.
- **Level 3** – moves up to a proactive practice established to minimize the potential events, with a capacity management database (CDB/CMIS) and resource or component capacity management (R/CCM) in place, some simple event management around performance alerts, basic utilization trend reporting and core metrics published to the intranet.
- **Level 4** – is where that practice can be measured for its effectiveness with an effective service portfolio or catalogue including meaningful performance objectives and capacity planning in place for service capacity management (SCM).
- **Level 5** – is where the practice is optimized, with business capacity management (BCM) in place and key performance indicators (KPIs) measured and optimized for the CMP itself.

An appreciation of leading enterprise sites indicates informally that only a very small percentage (the 'bleeding edge') is in the area of level 5. A larger but still small percentage (the 'leading edge') would be at level 4. The bulk of sites would place themselves somewhere within levels 2 and 3, maybe accounting for more than half of all sites. The remaining sites do little or only in an ad hoc manner at levels 0 and 1. See figure 1.9.

#	CMMI	ITSM	Capacity management	Task	%
6	Optimized	bITa	Business level	Dashboard CPM	2%
6	Measured	ITSM	Service level	SLAM Capacity plans Service catalogue	8%
6	Proactive	Center	Resource level	CDB Trends Web reporting	30%
6	Reactive	Tickets	Analysis	Utilization Uptime Some event monitoring	50%
6	Ad hoc	Help calls	Monitor	Ad hoc alerts Ad hoc investigations	10%

Figure 1.9 Capacity management maturity – showing the top 5 levels of CMMI and their relationship to capacity management and typical adoption in practice

Key findings from Gartner[10], using their own proprietary maturity model but with a similar overview, indicate that the users, customers, management and boards who express satisfaction with their IT services have a close correlation with the 'bleeding edge' or 'leading edge' sites. The best sites in practice work across the levels according to the priority of the service and have a spectrum of activity something like one of the bracket curves shown in figure 1.9 where the most effort is only applied to the key business critical services.

There is clearly a possibility of over-simplification in this approach. The level of maturity of solution applied to a service changes during its lifecycle. A long–running application that has few changes (maybe a payroll) requires little attention beyond monitoring resource level utilization. Maturity level is also impacted by the volatility of the business and the criticality of the service to the business. A major new application requires application sizing as early as practicable in its lifecycle and should continually be reviewed but typically less rigorously as time goes by.

Further, the definition of each level is subjective and some activities in different levels may be applied to any given service. Particular activities will be selected to meet the particular issues of the service. This is particularly true for a multi-tier solution with pools of machines at different levels being employed to provide the service. The degree of focus overall will depend on mission criticality of the service, but within each tier it may well depend on the cost of the machines.

The practical conclusion in most sites is to adopt a flexible approach as indicated by the dotted bracket lines in figure 1.9. This is a reflection of what actually happens in most cases; it is not the integrated solution that would ideally be proposed, it is more a pragmatic recognition of what is feasible in most sites. Most sites start with a performance monitoring regime across the board (as it is impossible to know which machine is likely to be next at risk). A standard service reporting regime based on R/CCM is usually adopted for the majority of services. This is typically delivered to an intranet, where the number of hits by users outside the capacity management team should become a matter of interest. Ad hoc reporting is typically used by the team itself to deal with new issues. Then for a selection of services, maybe mission critical, key and major production services, a capacity planning regime is exercised. This needs to be based on historic trends in terms of likely traffic growth and likely resource utilization levels. For the machines where there is a workload mix and a significant financial investment, formal capacity planning is performed using modeling techniques. Sometimes this will also be applied to a sample of other services or servers. This is true particularly where there are hundreds or thousands of servers of similar type doing similar jobs for a distributed solution. In that case, a categorization by market segmentation or customer type is usually defined, such as 'typical urban', 'typical suburban', 'typical rural' et cetera (where the location of a branch office indicates the likely population of users and hence related IT traffic and demand for services).

1.6   Demand management

A typical management edict for IT is to 'do more with less'. But typically there are more requests for work than resources. Demand management is commonly proposed as a way to understand and throttle demand from customers. It is important as requests for projects often outstrip the resource capabilities of service providers.

Demand management is described as a capacity management activity within service delivery in ITIL V2 with a constrained view of its scope (focusing on degradation of service due to unexpected increases in demand or partial interruptions to service due to hardware or software faults and establishing the redistribution of capacity in order to minimize the impact on business critical services). In ITIL V3 it is allocated to service strategy with a wider view of its scope and links with capacity management identified, but still focused on patterns of business activity and user profiles. In this book it is treated as a capacity management related activity and is interpreted as most practitioners use the term including both of the above as well as establishing longer term practices to deal with handling requests for new services, avoiding un-necessary peaks in workload, provisioning of resources, setting service priorities and quotas, chargeback and related activities.

The objective of demand management is to optimize and rationalize the demand for the allocation and use of IT resources. It covers the entire spectrum, from one extreme of over-provisioning without regard to cost to the other extreme of under-provisioning such that there is no headroom and hence capacity problems.

Effective demand management and capacity management ensures the timely provisioning and efficient allocation of IT resources at three levels:
1. forecasting business demands
2. applying IT strategy and assessing service trends
3. assessing and controlling resource or component utilization levels

At an IT component level, most large organizations have adopted capacity management by monitoring capacity and performance from servers, storage, networks, and so on. They have also used modeling and trending tools to predict future requirements. Fewer have successfully shifted the emphasis from day-to-day needs to a more proactive, business-centric view of future requirements. Effective capacity management must factor in future business developments, including step changes in demand that may arise from longer-term business initiatives or advances in technology. The future plans for the business in terms of growth or change are key to this. It is not always readily available outside the Board Room and so often some simple rules of thumb need to be applied by the CMT, such as 'if the current demand is X and the performance is Y, then the service needs to cater for 2X and the worst performance acceptable is 2Y'.

Delivering effective capacity management requires forecasting business demands, applying IT strategy and assessing service trends, and evaluating utilization of the current implementation. Key factors include:
• identifying which services are vital to the success of the business

- ensuring that these services are available as the business needs them
- improving efficiency by ensuring that resources are not over-provisioned

The key output is a capacity plan for IT resources that:
- facilitates successful management of IT assets
- monitors and communicates key performance indicators (KPIs)
- is able to evolve as business demands change

1.7   Roles for capacity management

Capacity management touches upon many very practical issues in day-to-day management of an IT service organization. Many of these are addressed in relation to financial management, service level management, operations management et cetera with input from the CMP. These are discussed in more detail in later chapters. In essence, the key role is the provision of decision support in the establishment of the optimum IT services at the minimum cost.

Decision makers from different departments of an IT organization have to make many decisions affecting cost, performance, availability and other service levels for the services provided to end users so that the enterprise can compete successfully in its marketplace. The decisions range across a number of areas including:
- application to be bespoke or packaged or 'Commercial Off The Shelf' (COTS)?
- development to be in-house, outsourced, off-shore?
- service to be outsourced or 'facilities managed'?
- centralized or distributed? Open or proprietary? Thick or thin clients?
- single tier or multi-tier? Pools of small machines or fewer large ones?
- clustered, coupled or multi-core processors?
- applications consolidated or virtualized or both?
- devices duplexed, triplexed or mirrored or striped?
- capacity 'right-sized' or 'safely-sized' or 'over-sized' or 'on demand' to meet local needs?
- hardware standby on fail-over, flip-flop, disaster site?
- storage retention period, classification of data (information life cycle management)

These are all complex issues to be resolved in the light of local factors, typically with significant IT budget implications, as well as major corporate impact. Capacity management can help provide the decision support infrastructure by establishing the instrumentation, metrics, analysis and reporting to aid these activities.

Managing a complex IT environment requires the analysis of many trade-offs. The wrong decisions will negatively affect IT performance and result in lost business opportunities. Businesses, vendors and customers demand accurate and timely information from IT, in order to enable real-time management of business processes and to satisfy governance requirements and regulations. Equally, finance management will expect the infrastructure to be sized correctly to meet the business objectives without overspend. IT is tasked to deliver new applications, support more users, process more data and implement new IT solutions with predictable and low total cost of ownership (TCO).

*The **role of capacity management** is to answer a variety of 'what if' questions, to evaluate alternatives and tradeoffs, to compare options and justify strategic and tactical decisions during all phases of the application and information lifecycle. Essentially to enable continuous, proactive performance engineering, performance management and capacity planning and so provide accurate and timely information that can be used to ensure the delivery of quality, cost-effective services to the business.*

New IT solutions, new applications and more users may also increase the contention for resources and the key balance lies in establishing the right amount of computing resource to ensure acceptable service delivery to meet the real current and projected future business demand. This balanced plan is likely to be also influenced by issues of cost, new technology and sustainability.

1.8   IT service management drivers

ITIL and ISO/IEC 20000 are currently the dominant default descriptions for IT service management (ITSM). Other drivers come in to play when considering the practices to be adopted within enterprises. Quality initiatives are encapsulated by total quality management (TQM) and ISO/IEC 9000. Audit requirements driven by SOX and Basel II and COBIT contribute to the need for defined IT processes. Process improvement lies at the heart of Six Sigma and continuous improvement. Business process re-engineering has paved the way for process definitions and Balanced Scorecards and the Capability Maturity Model (CMM) to refine process control.

The Office of Government and Commerce (OGC), in the UK, owns the intellectual property rights to ITIL. OGC have outsourced the management of ITIL to TSO (for publications) and APMG (for examinations). APMG have licensed several other exam institutes, including EXIN and ISEB.

Also, in the Netherlands, the ASL BiSL Foundation promotes professionalizing application management and business information management and improving the communication between these two IT management domains by spreading knowledge on their process models.
These describe structuring the management and maintenance practices of existing information systems on one hand (ASL – Application Services Library) and defining business information management practices on the other (BiSL – Business information Services Library).

1.9   Basic concepts and terminology

1.9.1   Basic concepts for IT service management

Capacity management, like other practices in the IT service organization, finds its roots in IT service management. Appendix A describes the basic concepts for IT service management. It deals with common terms and definitions, e.g. service, value, system, process, function, line, maturity, and organization. It also provides information about important questions for the structuring of service organizations:

• What is the difference between a process and a function?
• How can process management be organized?

- What are core processes in a service organization?
- How to construct a process model?
- How can functions be constructed in a service organization?
- How can maturity models be used for improvement?

These basic concepts apply to the rest of this book, and to the other books in the Practioner Guide series.

1.9.2   Jargon and acronyms

ITIL terminology is used throughout this book, using both ITIL V2 and ITIL V3 terms. This reflects what is in common usage at the time of writing and may well be for some time.

> *ITIL V2 described a **CDB** for capacity management database and a **CMDB** for configuration management database. V3 introduced the **CMIS** for capacity management information system and the **CIS** for configuration management information system. This book adopts the convention of referring to the **CMDB/CIS** and the **CDB/CMIS**. In the same way, V2 described a sub-process of resource capacity management and V3 renamed it component capacity management. This book refers to the activity of resource/component capacity management or **R/CCM**.*

Difficulties with jargon abound within ITSM. There is a risk that each organization develops slightly different approaches to, and interpretations of, related disciplines. **Performance engineering** can cover a variety of activities to try to ensure and improve the end result for a particular service. **Software performance engineering (SPE)** is usually taken to cover assessment of likely performance needs and resulting resource demands of new applications at an early stage in their development. **Performance assurance** is often used to describe the entire domain of development, testing and operations in the area of performance. It includes aspects of performance engineering within development, performance testing within quality assurance and service level management within service management as well as capacity management

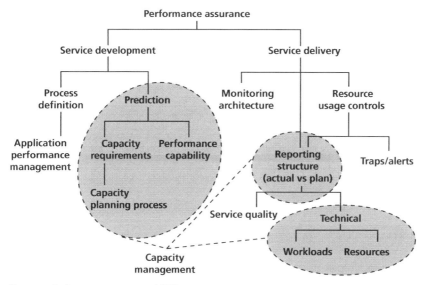

Figure 1.10 Performance assurance and CMP

itself. Capacity management is typically seen as a practice covering most of the technical aspects involved. This is indicated in figure 1.4, showing the overlaps between a performance assurance hierarchy (shown as a tree structure) and capacity management practice (shown in dotted circles).

How this is mapped out in terms of actual teams and functions varies significantly in differing organizations; figure 1.10 is intended to indicate the nature of the overlap rather than make any specific recommendations.

2 What: What is capacity management

This chapter describes the objectives of capacity management and provides some detail of capacity management practices. It then introduces more of the basic concepts involved and discusses the main terms and definitions, such as resource, service, performance, workload and so on.

2.1 Objectives

The **primary objective** for capacity management is to serve the needs of the business by ensuring that the organization understands and tracks demand and can maintain required service levels under both normal and contingency conditions both now and in the future within agreed cost constraints. The essential goal is to achieve the most cost-effective balance between business demand and the size and form of the IT Infrastructure needed to support it.

To put it another way, it means having the right resources, in the right place at the right time for the right costs to do the right work at the right speed to meet the right target for the right users to exploit the right performance to achieve the right results for the business.

The right work has to be assessed in demand management, gauging the priority and fluctuations likely so that the scaling limits of the current situation can be determined. This will be influenced largely by the business context. At one extreme, where downtime and poor performance is not an option, the strategic directive might be to enable the business to continue with its IT services at all times and at all costs. At the other extreme, the strategic directive might be to minimize IT costs to meet a reduced budget no matter what the impact is on IT services. In most cases, the situation is somewhere in between. In all cases, it needs the CMP to put numbers to the current situation and enable the directive to be met.

Arising from the primary objective for capacity management, are a number of **strategic objectives** at tactical and operational level. How these are mapped on to the local CMP and CMT varies across sites.

The **strategic objectives** for capacity management are to:
• ensure the right level of investment, resource and capacity
• match equipment to business need, supply and demand
• identify and resolve bottlenecks
• evaluate tuning strategies
• improve and report/publish performance
• 'right-size' or 'consolidate' or 'virtualize'
• evaluate upgrade plans to ensure accurate and timely procurements
• ensure effective service level management
• plan for workload growth, new applications, new sites
• avoid performance disasters and achieve performance assurance.

These can be further resolved to a tactical level. The **tactical objectives** of capacity management are to:

- identify relevant metrics for KPIs and resource usage
- establish thresholds for values and patterns of behavior for key metrics
- produce workload forecasts, including all workloads for all resources on all servers that are within scope and significance
- track actual usage against plan at resource and workload levels
- provide support to developers in producing capacity requirement forecasts for significant, new or changed applications
- provide financial information for the organization's budgeting activities based on predicted capacity requirements
- Keep informed and aware of new technologies that might impact on capacity

The **operational objectives** of capacity management are to:

- set and use appropriate performance criteria for components or resources (service levels and/ or utilization thresholds) to ensure that the tactical objective will be met
- cater for specific constraints such as lead times (internal and external), cost or service compromises, change management and forward schedule of change, shortage of environmental resources (floor space, power, air conditioning, et cetera)
- track all agreed configuration items throughout their lifecycle for all equipment – central and distributed
- liaise effectively with configuration management as the capacity database (CDB) and the configuration management database (CMDB) effectively share a common index, in that both need to manage a lot of information on the same assets

All of these objectives are laid out in the checklist in Appendix C.1 in a form suitable for audit and gap analysis.

2.2   Definition of capacity management practice (CMP)

There are a number of descriptions of this practice. A succinct and good one is:

> The **capacity management practice (CMP)** encompasses the provision of a consistent, acceptable capacity service level at a known and controlled cost.

ITIL states that capacity management is responsible for ensuring that the capacity of the IT infrastructure matches the evolving demands of the business in the most cost-effective and timely manner. It expands on the balancing acts involved, weighing costs against capacity and supply against demand. The former ensures that the processing capacity is cost justified and optimized. The latter ensures that the available resources match the demands made to meet the business need.

The balance chosen is necessarily context-driven and thus local to each enterprise: a rich financial institution involved with stocks and shares in London City or New York Wall Street transactions may decide that it is necessary to triplicate everything in order to minimize downtime which may cost millions, whereas an IT service supplier may try to deliver a service that closely matches imposed service level agreements underpinning contracts, with IT resource provision 'just in time' in order to maintain maximum profit.

> ***Capacity management aims*** *to understand the business needs, both present and future, and to map these onto services which will be required to achieve the stated goals. Capacity management must also provide a plan showing when, where and what resources will be needed to meet these service requirements. Without this forward-looking activity, there could be any number of unpleasant surprises, such as:*
> * *capacity and performance crises*
> * *unnecessary hardware expenditure*
> * *user dissatisfaction*

Capacity management is responsible for ensuring adequate capacity is available at all times to meet the requirements of the business. It is directly related to the business requirements and is not simply about the performance of the system's components, individually or collectively.

An important distinction to bear in mind in many sites is that there may be teams of people committed to the capacity management function for different domains, the capacity management team (CMT), but there is a separate issue of the practice of capacity management across the enterprise, the capacity management practice (CMP). The precise definitions vary across enterprises and even sites within them, with overlaps between projects, domains, architects, systems specialists, fire-fighting, process implementation and planning. Where the distinction between the team and the practice is particularly critical, the acronyms CMT and CMP are used.

2.3   Main terms and definitions

Appendix B provides a glossary of terms used as well as a list of acronyms and a list of key terms used. This section is intended to provide an initial 'walk-through' some of the main terms and definitions to establish a foundation for the following sections.

2.3.1   Resources

It is common capacity management jargon to say that a physical computer and network configuration supplies a limited set of resources, either directly as 'real' or indirectly as 'virtual', which can be utilized (or consumed) by the systems or applications that run on it. Resources include, but are not limited to:
* CPU time (utilization)
* memory occupancy (free pages)
* page space on disk (paging activity)
* file space on disk (spare file space)
* network bandwidth (network traffic)
* I/O throughput capacity (I/O activity)

2.3.2 Service

A service is a described set of facilities, both ICT and non-ICT, sustained by the ICT service provider to fulfill one or more needs of the customer, and to support the customers' business objectives. The customer perceives a service as a coherent whole.

Typically a (full) service is defined in terms of a group of specific applications on specific machines, real or virtual, designed to service the requirements of a particular business function. These full services can be decomposed into partial services, e.g. some application-specific services that 'use' network services, desktop services, or other generic services which are often shared by multiple customers. A service also calls for support services, such as service desk, service reporting and service requests (how to purchase or decommission the service).

ITIL V3 is expressed in terms of the lifecycle of a service. IT service management is the implementation and management of IT services to the quality that meets the needs of the business. Service level management is the practice responsible for negotiating service level agreements (SLAs) and ensuring that they are met and policed.

It is necessary to define a sensible measure for demand of a service to show its pattern of activity and behavior over time, either in terms of observed values of a useful metric in the past or predicted values for the future. This is usually presented using a single 'representative value' over a period for that metric, reflecting the value during a key period of busy activity, as shown in figure 2.1.

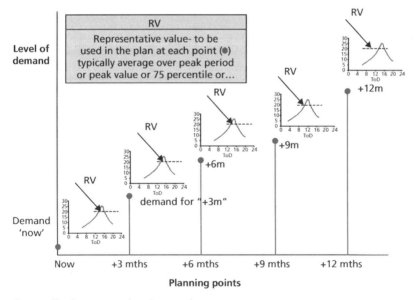

Figure 2.1 Showing representative values over time

Many graphs presented in capacity management are of this nature, in that a single line is often shown which is representing snapshot averages or other metrics over a period when there is a distribution of values involved. It is often the only practical way to show a pattern over a significant period of time. What should be remembered is that each point typically represents just an average or percentile value for a selected snapshot interval. And that any line drawn through the points is probably an approximation and if extended into the future should include an indication of the probability that the line is valid by showing confidence limits.

2.3.3 Performance and capacity

Performance and capacity are the two key issues for capacity management. Performance is essentially about the speed at which something can be completed and is typically measured as a response time. Throughput is the count of the number of such things completed in a given time. Capacity is the number of such things that could be completed in a given time and is the maximum throughput. Using a motorway analogy[11], the journey time is a measure of performance, the traffic flow per hour is a measure of the throughput and the 'gridlock' level of traffic is the maximum capacity.

The performance of a service is a key issue for most real applications. Particularly in the online industry such as news sites where users will not tolerate waiting and will quickly switch to an alternative site. Once the SLA has basic availability and continuity issues under control, the users are most likely next to express concern that although the service is 'up' it is not really functioning as the responsiveness of the application is so poor that the business can not be supported adequately. Some SLAs define this as 'slowtime' and include slowtime in unavailability. At this point in the discussion, it becomes clear that the use of a stop watch to try to collect information on response times is impractical. The concepts of services, applications and transactions emerge to define the workload and assess the throughput and response times in an objective and measurable manner. However, performance is not only a matter of responsiveness. If the application is poorly written or the logic annoying, then a user may well switch to another service supplier, no matter how quick the system is.

The capacity of a system is not simply the sum of the quoted capacities of all the devices in a given solution. It is the maximum throughput that a service can deliver whilst meeting SLA performance targets. It can be greatly reduced by the presence of a bottleneck device which saturates at lower traffic levels than other devices in the service. Spare capacity is not simply the 'idle' or 'unused' time; it is the measure of the amount of extra useful work that could be undertaken without detriment to the SLA performance targets.

2.3.4 Workload

The workload is the extent of a resource use in a defined period. It tends to be used to imply the throughput of work for particular groups of users or functions within the organization.
In the context of capacity management modeling, workload refers to a set of forecasts, which detail the estimated resource usage over an agreed planning horizon. Workloads generally represent discrete business applications and can be further sub-divided into types of work (interactive, timesharing, batch).

---

11   An analogy ably introduced and expounded by Michael Ley, a referee of this book.

Workloads may be categorized by users, groups of users, or functions within the IT service. This is used to assist in analyzing and managing the capacity, performance and utilization of configuration items and IT services. The term workload is sometimes used as a synonym for throughput.

The workload on a set of resources can be defined at whatever level matches the analysis required. For a single application server, it may be that the entire workload can be treated as a 'black box' with a 'system level' model showing how the resource behaves overall. If the server supports multiple applications, or if there is a need to separate the production work from system overheads such as back-up, then the workload needs to be 'characterized'. This is the technique of identifying how the workload on a server is split, for example by groups of users in different departments doing different work, or maybe simply by virtual machines. This is discussed in more detail in section 2.5.

2.3.5 Metrics

A metric is something that can be measured objectively to help manage or control what is going on. In order to assess the performance of a particular resource or device, it is vital that it is instrumented and reports on a range of metrics. The dominant examples would be the number of 'arrivals' at a device in a given period, the number held in a stack or queue waiting for service, the time each takes to be serviced, the total busy time of the device and related statistics. There have been many attempts to define standards for such metrics. These have ranged from the universal measurement architecture (UMA) to the application response measurement (ARM) initiatives[12] and also a variety of simple network management protocol[13] (SNMP) and management information base (MIB) definitions. Although each initiative has had its own devotees, none of these have achieved universal implementation. So capacity management has to accommodate a wide variety of metrics of different quality from a wide variety of sources. Most of these measures can only be obtained readily once the service (or a prototype) is running. As such, from the COBIT point of view, they are known as 'outcome measures'.

2.3.6 Data sources

There are three types of data that form the inputs for capacity analysis and modeling:
1. **Machine configuration details** – What kinds and models of host machines are present; what is their physical and logical configuration (processors, memory et cetera): where virtualization is involved what are the physical, logical and management parameters (in terms of the virtual machine view, the hypervisor view and the physical view) for the relevant domains, LPARS, VMs et cetera. Where there are, or have been, significant planned or actual changes to

---

12   The Open Group has defined the application response measurement (ARM) standard which describes a common method for integrating enterprise applications as manageable entities. It includes definitions for measures on application availability, performance, usage, and end-to-end transaction response time. Ideally, if widely adopted, ARM would allow users to extend enterprise management tools directly to conformant applications creating a comprehensive end-to-end management capability. It was preceded by a similar attempt at proposing a standard called the universal measurement architecture (UMA) which defined an open system for collecting and managing performance data in a distributed open systems environment but failed to achieve wide adoption.

13   Simple network management protocol (SNMP) is used in network management and administration systems to monitor network-attached devices for exception conditions as defined by the internet engineering task force (IETF). SNMP exposes management data in the form of variables which describe the system configuration and can be queried or possibly changed. The information on the managed objects resides in a standard format on a management information base (MIB).

configurations (upgrades, replacements, re-assignment of workload categories) it is very useful to also have this information as a time-line or event list.

2. **Machine performance data** – This is in the CDB/CMIS (which will contain resource-level information about the system utilizations and the different user-workloads which are present), augmented by any available application-level statistics. These are most likely to be transaction counts of some kind, and they may be provided by middleware such as Tuxedo or WebSphere or other business-logic. The usefulness of these is that they can provide a link between the low-level resource behavior (e.g. processor utilizations or I/O counts), and the high-level numbers coming from the final set of data.

3. **Service reporting statistics, and service forecasting quantities** – Since these are the drivers for capacity planning, access is needed to the following types of business numbers:
   - Reports of actual business activity. Examples are number of flights per day for an airline or number of teller transactions for a bank. This is required preferably on a historical basis that extends over at least one business cycle, and in just sufficient level of detail to distinguish the major workloads on the infrastructure: by service, and preferably in the same level of detail that is to be planned for. This data can be correlated with the levels of machine-activity in the historical baseline.
   - Descriptions of any critical scenarios (end-of-month or seasonal peaks, conjunctions of different workloads, current known shortcomings et cetera).
   - Forecasts of future levels – Realistically, these may be in different terms to the actual figures above and also volatile since they are the product of business planning. They will need to be translated into resource requirements where possible to understand the true impact. It is very useful to have some explicit idea of confidence levels attached to business forecasting
   - it allows sensitivity analysis to be performed at the hardware level. This is an area where communication skills are critical. The CMT needs to coach the business users to appreciate the significance of the forecast numbers they provide.

The main data sources for most metrics of interest to R/CCM are those provided by the operating system, RDBMS, any middleware and related statistics from hardware, software logs and catalogs and trails and traces as appropriate. For SCM, the focus moves to the application and how well instrumented it is and how much service oriented data it provides. For BCM, the focus moves up again to a higher level of aggregation and the application instrumentation again is relied on for as much information as possible.

2.3.7 Queuing

Queuing is where a service has a limited resource and customers seeking their requirements form an orderly queue to wait their turn. Forming orderly queues is part of the inherent characteristics of the Anglo-Saxon. Other parts of the world may not have the same word ('waiting in line' being a popular alternative) or even share the concept, but most computer systems rely on servicing queues in the best manner to help improve throughput.

Nearly all servers of any size and complexity will be hosting applications that are accessed by several (possibly very many) users simultaneously. As soon as there is more than one user, there is a finite probability that several users will attempt to gain simultaneous access to the same resource – the CPU or a particular disk, for example. In the simplest case, one will be executing, and the others will have to wait for it to finish. In other words, there will be contention for resources, and contention causes queues to form.

It is completely normal for queues to form in a multi-user server. This is how operating systems support multiple users – by organizing the various requests into queues and managing these queues as efficiently as possible. This has been a key part of operating system design from the outset in the early sixties, and designers are now very good at it.

The problems arise if the queuing within the multiple-user server becomes 'excessive'. The effect will be degraded performance and – potentially – the inability of the system to support the required workload within agreed performance targets. Typically, excessive queues are associated with long end-user response times and reduced system throughput.

Excessive queuing is often caused by a specific bottleneck device, and one of the key objectives of performance management is to identify such devices and to reduce or eliminate their negative impact on overall system performance, by means of appropriate tuning or the provisioning of additional hardware.

2.3.8 Model

A model can be described as:

> A **model** is a simplification of reality built for a specific purpose, preferably incorporating measurements that can be modified under the control of laws.

There is little point in building a model that takes more effort than the benefit derived from it. The degree of accuracy in the model and the acceptable tolerances in its fabrication are significant factors. But the purpose of a model is always the key factor. It is essential to know what questions it is intended to answer before creating it. Consider two models of an aircraft. One is for the aerodynamicist and is a balsa wood outline of the body to test in a wind tunnel. The other is for an ergonomicist and is a plywood mock-up of the cabin and instrumentation. Both models are totally different and both invaluable in their own right.

In the case of capacity management, different models can be used to assess different issues. The three most popular in practice are trends, simulation models and analytical models. A simple spreadsheet model may well be used to review the history of a given workload, using trend analysis to define a likely growth. A discrete event simulation model may be used to look at the dynamic behavior of a network. An analytical model may be used to assess current performance and predict future performance in the light of different scenarios. These techniques are discussed in more detail in section 4.

2.4   Basic concepts of capacity management

Capacity management is usually described as three sub-practices, at resource or component level (technology infrastructure), service level (delivery) and business level (management view). These levels can be described separately but in practice they overlap. Sometimes the distinctions correspond to the different timescales involved, in that the hardware view is typically fairly short term (down to hours or minutes) and highly granular. The service view is more likely to be looking at a higher level of aggregation of data and over a longer period of days and weeks. The business view introduces even more aggregation of data, as well as weighting of its significance, to yield interpretations of the data for longer term business assessment. However, all three sub-practices may be involved in addressing similar problems over similar timescales and the distinctions should not obstruct the resolution process.

2.4.1   Resource or component capacity management

Resource or component capacity management (R/CCM) focuses on the technology that underpins the service provisions. The **resource or component** sub-practice refers to the management of individual components of the IT infrastructure (corresponding to the configuration items (CI's) in the CMDB/CIS) and ensures that bottlenecks are addressed. This is traditional performance analysis and capacity planning and is the most popularly implemented aspect of capacity management.

Note that 'resource management' in the sense of human resources, people, personnel and their management or demand control is not within the scope of CMP.

Effective resource or component capacity management needs to capture and store all relevant utilization data for all components of the environment. Data capture agents and import of data from external sources ensure that the CDB contains all relevant performance data. Integral scheduling technology ensures the collection of all data whenever needed irrespective of the source of the data.

2.4.2   Service capacity management

Service capacity management (SCM) addresses the delivery of existing services that support the business. The **service level** relates to the management of the performance of production applications and ensures that Service Level Agreements are defined in a measurable manner and are then policed. This is the performance aspect of service level management which many leading enterprises are now addressing.

More and more, the focus for day-to-day capacity management is moving from individual resource or 'silo' views of the world to a service or application orientated perspective. The need is to assess current and future performance against SLAs and service level requirements (SLRs) across the service. 'application views' enable all the elements that comprise each of the supported services to be reported on as a single entity, with drill down to the individual resource areas as required. This focus is reinforced by service oriented architecture (SOA).

2.4.3   Business capacity management

Business capacity management (BCM) is concerned with current and future business requirements. The **business level** relates to business-IT alignment and ensures that the key business needs are met. This is sometimes known as corporate performance management and is at the leading edge of capacity management.

Open data import technology is required to ensure that IT and non-IT business data is quickly and easily imported and stored in the capacity management Database. Where this data is produced on a regular basis by the business, the collection and storage of the data needs to be automated guaranteeing its availability. Once in the capacity management Database it is available for analysis and reporting alongside all data collected for service and resource/component capacity management.

This enables the correlation of business data over time with observed resource utilization and also enables an effective 'feedback loop' to be established with the business: business users see the impact of their business on services, and of those services on resources or /components, leading to better quality business information being provided over time.

2.5   Scope of coverage

The scope of capacity management practice is indicated in figure 2.2, the capacity management pyramid.

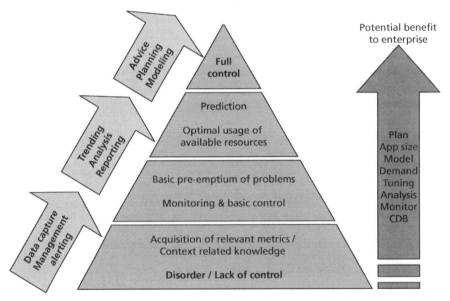

Figure 2.2 Capacity management pyramid – showing the path from chaos to control with the activities involved and showing the increasing potential benefit to the enterprise

The capacity management pyramid covers a variety of tasks which are introduced below to provide a basis for further discussion in chapter 4 of the detailed activities.

The scope of capacity management is described in ITIL with some V2 graphics that have become standard representations and enhanced in V3. Workforce resource management is not within the scope of capacity management as viewed by ITIL[14]. Although there are some common practices in terms of modeling techniques, the two are usually separated. Nonetheless workforce resource management is central for service providers to ensure that there is not poor delivery of service due to lack of personnel, or any slack in the availability of personnel is otherwise exploited.

Datacenter facility capacity management is a growing aspect of capacity management. With the technological changes of blades, virtualization etc. power and cooling demands per square meter are increasing. Many datacenters were built to older specifications and high density servers place high demands on floor loading and air conditioning. Many companies do not own the facilities and need supplier management to ensure capacity expansion and responsibilities are contractually clear.

An alternative traditional view of capacity management can be shown in figure 2.3. Note that, in the absence of a relevant contractual SLA, service level objectives (SLOs) are often defined internally by the CMT to provide a yardstick for measurements. This is typically a statement such as 'the current performance level must not degrade by more than 50%'. Also, note that the 'stress test results' shown in the figure imply all the results from any performance testing, volume/load, stress, saturation and soak testing. A further aspect is the use of the testing platform to establish the transaction flow for the main transaction(s). That is, the relevant calls it makes as it passes through the system.

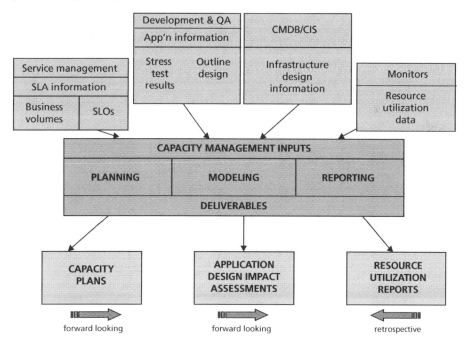

Figure 2.3 Capacity management inputs, practices and deliverables

---

14   There is a reference in ITIL to lack of human resources causing a delay in end-to-end response time, but that is probably based on operational problems on mainframes in the old days of operators mounting tapes.

In order to gain an understanding of what lies behind the myriad of commands, processes, I/Os within a computer system, it is a useful technique to identify workloads that can be used to simplify analysis. These are typically based on applications or users or services in some way.

2.5.1 Workload characterization

Workload characterization is the task of identifying the workloads within a system, usually breaking it down into workload components. That is, refining the workload into components that represent different aspects of the workload that need to be controlled separately in that they have different business drivers for growth. Also often categorized by key attributes such as its type (interactive, batch), priority (mission-critical) et cetera.

Workload characterization can be as simple or as complex as is required to meet the needs of the enterprise. It forms both the basis of performance reporting, whether by an application view of performance metrics across a number of machines or users or applications. It is the basis of deriving 'workload components' in a model of a multi-tasking multi-user machine. It is worthwhile to consider some real life examples to introduce the ideas.

In the case of Windows, for example, in many sites the Wintel servers are restricted to a single production application which can often be related to a small set of CPU processes that are continually running on that server. The business drivers for such systems are often essentially the number of concurrent users of that service. In order to gain a better picture of the true production workload on the machine, some sites will isolate all the known administrative processes into an 'overhead' workload (typically picking up on security, back-up, anti-virus, anti-spam, defragmentation processes and the like). This will leave a final workload component covering all the rest of the unallocated processes.

Virtualization of lightly used windows machines is a growing trend, which makes the machine essentially multi-tasking and the simplest approach is to treat each Virtual Machine as a separate workload component. In order to gain the whole picture, the information is usually gleaned from the hypervisor or virtualization machine monitor/manager as well as from the physical operating system itself. The required performance metrics are readily available from perfmon.dll reading the object counter information from the registry.

In the case of the mainframe, the concept of workload characterization has been in place for a long time. System programmers have been used to grouping applications into terms such as 'performance groups', 'service classes' and 'service report classes' to achieve much the same benefit. All the performance metrics are readily available as required, already allocated across these classes.

In the case of UNIX the usual approach is typically based on grouping users to reflect a departmental use of a machine, or grouping commands to reflect a particular application, or maybe a combination of the two to identify preferred views. The metrics are available to some degree, either by reading kernel counters (typically via 'devkmem') or by using standard UNIX utilities (typically 'sar', 'iostat' et cetera). However, not all the resource information is available per user and some mapping of I/O has to be done. In other words, the total number of logical block requests is known and the total physical I/O per device is known, but not the number of I/Os per device per command. Thus the performance analyst has to play a game called 'guess who did the I/O'. To do this well requires detailed knowledge of the mapping of files to devices. This is not always available, so typically simplified pro-rata assumptions are made.

A typical pair of workload characterization levels might be:
- level 1:
  - service classification relating service usage and hence resource usage to business lines
  - used to establish accountability, cost management, service and resource usage analysis by business function
- level 2:
  - technical classification to define online or batch, normal or contingency, accurate or inaccurate measures, firm or vague planned commitment
  - used to create workload forecast scenarios and input to resource management.

These categories can then be refined and exploited to establish workload limits such as:
- parameter 1: committed/uncommitted (firm workload)
- parameter 2: critical/noncritical (outage in disaster recovery (DR))
- parameter 3: online/batch (batch also meaning 'can be shifted to outside peak period', rather than simply a batch stream workload and so can be applied to back-up, archive, reorganize, management reports et cetera).

Use parameters 1 and 2 to construct combined workloads and create upper and lower bounds (UB and LB) for normal and contingency situations, thus:
- LBNORMAL is ALL COMMITTED
- LBCONTINGENCY is COMMITTED AND CRITICAL
- UBNORMAL is ALL
- UBCONTINGENCY is ALL CRITICAL

And use parameter 3 to separate online or batch workloads (again, where batch also means 'can be shifted to outside peak period', rather than simply a batch stream workload).

2.5.2 Business drivers

The concept of business drivers is essentially that of relating the traffic on a computer to the business requirement it is intended to satisfy. In a mature capacity management site, this information is available from a number of sources. The application itself records a log file in a time series format of significant transactions completed with key information. The user department maintains a file of workload information and the business management maintains a log of business metrics such as KPIs or business metrics of interest (BMIs). Ideally, some of this information is also incorporated in the configuration management database and the service catalogue which may help to prioritize services. All of these can then be reported on and analyzed with correlations and trends to help relate the business view to the service and resource or component level views.

Other terms for this are 'business forecast unit' (BFU) and 'natural forecast unit' (NFU). These are all terms the business uses to describe their workload that can be related to IT resource usage and may be different for different resource types. For example, business drivers may be orders placed, customer enquiries or web site hits. Measures may be maintained such that business volumes are recorded within application statistics, the SLA creation and review process or a BFU metric used for dynamic resources within the user area. The links to IT resources have to be identified and are variable, for example, disk space may reflect the number of orders placed, disk I/O the number of users and processor utilization the number of web site hits.

In many sites, however, this information is not so well defined and simpler assumptions have to be made. A frequent, practical parameter used is the number of concurrent users of a system. In the absence of that number, an even simpler assumption is based on the enterprise published overall figures for growth (whether based on turn-over, profit or any other financial measure). Thus the physical resource demands can be viewed in relation to the past business activity numbers and a trend based on the projected activity growth.

When meaningful BFUs can be defined, they:
- relate business volumes to service usage and hence resource usage
- require correlation between service and workload
- have inventories that are typically related to the following IT metrics:
  - user IDs
  - account codes
  - transaction IDs
  - job names
  - command names
  - process names
  - application instrumentation
  - self instrumentation
  - storage quota (mailbox size, personal data share)

The mapping of business drivers to applications and hence to resource demands is a skilled task involving an understanding of a number of different views of IT. It can be compared to a translator's task, although in this case it is mostly a question of jargon rather than language. Figure 2.4 makes the point. Consider 'transactions' for example. The end user will think in terms of a business action such as raising invoices. The system designer will think in terms of some application parameter such as 'creating invoice'. The programmer will think of a software object with interactions and calls to other objects, with activity arising from so many calls to each per transaction visit to the first object.

2.5.3 Service and server classification

There are major issues of scale in implementing capacity management. Firstly there is the number of services. Although there might be many hundreds defined, it is usually possible to categorize them into a few mission critical services and maybe fifty key services and the rest given a lower priority. Such numbers have to be manageable with a reasonable size of team committed to capacity management, such as five to ten full time employees (FTE).

Secondly there is the number of servers. There may well be many more instances than in the past, within a variety of platforms and solutions that are virtualized, multi-tier and have complex configurations with pools or clustered machines involved. To address this, in practice, many sites will also classify servers in order to treat each class appropriately.

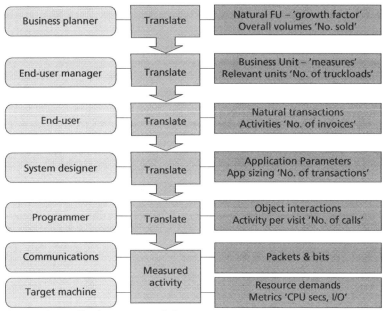

Figure 2.4 CMP workload – resource translation

This is highlighted by the major distinction that most sites still draw between the mainframe and distributed systems. The mainframe is centralized, with a limited number of distinct configurations. It is possible to monitor and report on everything as data gathering is well instrumented and interpretation well proven. Note that although the mainframe is often taken to mean machines from IBM running z/OS, z/VM, or z/Linux, there are other environments rightly thought of as mainframes. The original 'bunch'[15] of alternatives are mostly gone, but some solutions such as HP NonStop (originally based on Tandem), OpenVMS clusters including AlphaServers (based on VAX and Digital Tru64), Sun E25000 (derived from a Cray), and Teradata warehouses are all in the same mould in that there is a well established regime for large installations and well organized ITSM tools.

Distributed systems, on the other hand, have tens, hundreds or even thousands of servers involved with a huge number of combinations (despite standard builds). In this case, most sites try to establish norms, monitor exceptions from the norm and produce report exceptions (alarms). In this way, it is possible to minimize data gathering and processing by using an approach of summarization and selecting representative samples for trending and modeling.

The classification schemes vary but are typically by application (e.g. SMNP server, text processing, email or database software) or by business function (e.g. sales, stores). For each class a standard configuration is often defined. Then for each standard configuration, or band of server, rules of thumb may emerge in the light of experience and measurement, such as a 'medium branch server' will support 'n Notes users' or 'n Sales users'.

---

15 Burroughs, Univac, NCR, CDC and Honeywell were the bunch. Others in the list could have included DEC (now part of HP) and ICL (now part of Fujitsu).

Servers can also be usefully grouped according to their power rating. This can be based on public benchmarks such as Spec[16] or TPC[17] benchmarks. These numbers are useful guidelines to relative power of machines from the same supplier of the range and same architecture and using the same operating system et cetera. They are only used with great caution in any comparison across platforms.

The approach is one of selecting appropriate 'exemplar configurations'. These have to be one per category which is representative of its class (often the busiest). The exemplars are then used to track and trend growth (just like mainframes) and to identify norms. These can then be translated into application views of the data on all similar machines that can be readily automated into classified reporting regimes.

Relating capacity requirements to business drivers is necessary to plan for non-linear-trend factors and to justify investment and to assess operational quality requirements. As capacity management also has a deep view on the ways systems are managed, there is often some reluctance from co-workers to reveal complete data as the CMP may be viewed as 'unnecessary monitoring activity' and the CMT as a 'menace'.

Capacity planning for the 'top twenty' services (typically on multi-service servers) is required and is practical. It is simplified if there is a simple server/service mapping or simple virtual machine analysis. It is also simplified if there is a smaller number of larger servers, or if there is a rationalized hardware infrastructure and classification based on 'standard builds'.

2.5.4 Consolidation and virtualization

The move towards greater utilization of servers and more cost effective provision of IT services has led to increasing consolidation and virtualization.

Consolidation

'Consolidation' has previously been known as down-sizing or right-sizing. It can mean different things, depending on the entities being consolidated. Most people think initially of server consolidation and maybe moving workloads to a larger machine, possibly taking their disk farm with them. But the server itself may just be moved to a central location, or the disks may be added to a SAN. Also, the workloads may be moved to separate logical partitions on a larger machine, or possibly to virtual machines on a larger machine.

The performance metrics are there in each instance to help address possible scenarios and predict likely outcomes.

Virtualization

'Virtualization' is a buzzword used everywhere but with slightly different meanings depending on the context.

Separating the user or developer from the 'nitty-gritty' has been an integral part of computing

---

16   See the benchmarks on www.spec.org. SpecIntRate is a useful one for comparing the raw power of CPUs but others can be used to represent particular workloads.

17   See www.tpc.org and select a benchmark that is a reasonable representation of a typical workload of the type you are planning to support. Bear in mind that the actual production workload will be specific to your own applications.

since day one. Layers of abstraction have been added to coding. Disks have been directly attached and then via NAS then SAN. Memory has been virtualized for decades. But recent moves have tried to add processors, servers, services, networks and even data centers to the virtualization mix.

Let's consider some of these in turn.

Coding abstraction

Coding layers of abstraction have gone from machine code to assembler mnemonics to high level languages like COBOL to RDBMS languages or frameworks like ORACLE to object oriented languages and environments like Java and .NET and to automated application generators and coding generators like OmniBuilder.

In the past people have ascribed 'generations' to these languages but this gives a false impression. There are 'horses for courses' and depending on the situation any mix of any of these approaches may prove right. Although most new applications will aspire to the latest trend, most data centers still have a mix of languages of different generations in production use.

Disk arrays

RAID is now dominant. Although there are numerous logical definitions of levels (from 0, 1, 2, 3, 4, 5, 6, 7, 8, 0+1,10 et cetera) just a few are particularly prevalent. Directly attached storage devices are still popular and can yield optimum performance for dedicated applications. NAS is widely in use, largely because of the ease of implementation. SAN is also prevalent, especially where high performance is required alongside effective back-up and recovery.

Processors

There are a number of approaches to try to increase the effective power of a server. Processors can be closely coupled, loosely coupled in clusters or interconnected by special devices or buses in a mesh or a grid.

Clusters are part of this scene. They enable a number of servers to be linked and work in conjunction. They are typically established for the use of numbers of machines in a distributed processing environment with parallel processing, or for failover or for high availability load balancing. Thus pools of servers can be dedicated to a single service such as web servers, mail servers, database or file servers or applications with appropriate software to coordinate the servers and provide effectively a single large computing resource.

Multi-processors

Multi-processors are another route towards more power by adding more processors to a given server to exploit parallel processing or multiple threads across processors. The architectures for this have developed over the years. Initially, some were asymmetric, where one processor was the master and a number of others were slaves to it. This was replaced by symmetric processing which is now dominant but has limitations such that they are mostly around 4-16 and maybe 32 processors sharing a memory bus. Ways to increase further were defined as massively parallel processors (MPP) and non-uniform memory access (NUMA), which either use memory links or a crossbar switch to connect memories in a large matrix. Both remain as niche products but enable super-servers with 128 or more processors, although other techniques now achieve the same end. Now there is also a trend to stack more processors on a single chip, with dual core and soon multi-core. This may well be a reflection of the fact that the frequencies involved in current chips are now at very high levels and the challenges in production are being limited by various practical factors such as heat as well as electro-magnetic issues and cable lengths. So stacking more chips on the same chipset is adding an alternative axis for improvement.

Partitioning
Partitioning has a long and well established history. Early machines had physical partitions to isolate applications that were essentially static, although some operating systems allowed them to be changed if the relevant applications were in quiescent state. This led to the introduction of logical partitions or domains that allowed for multiple instances of operating systems on the same server. This proves useful in separating development and production, or allowing for different instances of operating system on the same machine, or with appropriate 'front-end' software, dynamic workload balancing across partitions. This is all now part of the super-server environment as well as the mainframe.

Processor virtualization
To virtualize is to 'decouple workloads and data from functional details of physical platform they are hosted on'. The approaches to virtualization tend to depend on where the microcode and software interrupts lie. Clearly there is the hardware level, the operating system and the applications. Most people are aware of hardware virtualization, where the operating system talks to a virtual layer which in turns talks to the hardware drivers, thus presenting an easier interface to the hardware for the operating system and known as para-virtualization, with hypervisors or virtual machine manager software to control the virtual machines. Software virtualization is where the application talks to a new virtualization layer representing the operating system rather than the operating system itself. Processor virtualization is achieved by hyper-threading where the O/S is led to believe it has more processor resource than it actually has.

Implementation of virtualization
Virtualization is a buzzword used widely with slightly different meanings depending on the context, but the use of virtual machines (VMs) to contain the workload of (previously) separate physical servers on a single server is key.

Separating the user or developer from the hardware limitations has been an integral part of computing since day one. Layers of abstraction have been added to coding. Disks have been directly attached and then via network attached storage (NAS) and then storage attached networks (SAN). Communications networks have evolved with local area networks (LANs) and wide area networks (WANS). Memory has been virtualized within operating systems for decades. But recent moves have tried to add processors, servers, services and even data centers to the virtualization mix.

Virtual operating systems and the use of hardware, software and virtual partitions has been in place for some time, with a rapidly growing range of options and terminology from the leading suppliers. The jargon and acronyms for each supplier are ever changing as new releases and new concepts emerge, but a general current picture is listed below (without expansion on the meanings or interpretations of each set of acronyms which are best viewed on the supplies' web sites):

- IBM with mainframes zSeries and z9 and use of LPARs, PR/SM, z/VM, z/OS, z/Linux; AIX with dynamic LPARs and micropartitions; and Linux pSeries and iSeries (OS/400, Linux)
- HP with Superdomes and a wide range of servers using nPars (logical) and vPars (virtual) and secure resource partitions
- Sun with UltraSparc or Intel/AMD servers and dynamic system domains, logical system domains and global zones with containers
- For Windows and Linux there are options from VMware (Virtual infrastructure), Microsoft (Hyper-V) and Open Source Xen

These all provide performance information on the VMs from their management systems.

The key elements of virtualization are often described as partitioning, isolation, encapsulation and hardware independence. Once the solution is adopted, it becomes an enabler for other features. Dynamic relocation of virtual machines across servers opens a route for dynamic resource scheduling (workload balancing), high availability (standby-nonstop) and consolidated backup (off-line).

In order to decide on the right mix of physical and virtual approaches, it is worth assessing where the market share has taken off. This is primarily in the consolidation of lots of extremely lightly used x86 servers that are typically dedicated to a single application service and have been widely distributed as part of the local autonomy boom over the last decade or so. As the costs of under-utilized equipment and the costs of support, management and maintenance begin to dominate, so there is a move towards consolidation, which can be made much easier by using virtual machines to reflect each local setup.

The virtualization of x86 architecture has been accomplished in mixtures of three basic ways: full virtualization, paravirtualization and hardware assisted virtualization. The borders between them are ever-changing.

Paravirtualization offers important performance benefits, but also requires modification of the operating system source, which may impact application certifications. Hardware virtualization offers benefits in that the hardware itself supports some of the virtualization. Full virtualization relies on sophisticated software techniques to trap and virtualize the execution of certain sensitive, 'non-virtualizable' instructions in software via binary patching. With this approach, critical instructions are discovered at run-time and replaced with a trap into the VM to be emulated in software. These techniques incur significant performance overhead which becomes a problem in the area of system calls, interrupt virtualization, and frequent access to privileged resources.

For machines running database applications or with significant traffic or with different sets of users running different tasks, some issues involved with virtualization begin to cause concern. Primarily, the issue of overhead, which depends primarily on how much physical IO is done and how many kernel interrupts etc cause changes of state in the CPU. A pure CPU loading will be low on overhead, but a practical SQL Server or Oracle application will have a significant overhead such that users will notice significant degrading in performance on virtualization.

Virtualization is widely adopted for consolidating lightly used servers, separating development, test, quality assurance, pilot and production systems. In some cases, it provides the opportunity for hardware upgrades to outdated operating systems. It provides a vehicle for easy roll-out of cloned player systems with a complete environment suitable for training or marketing. It has managed to establish a great reputation for reliability, fiduciary and integrity. Experiences have grown rapidly, with many sites having initially virtualized and consolidated by a typical 'density' factor of 10:1 (ten VMs to one physical machine). These have often still yielded remarkably light usage so that higher consolidation ratios can be actioned, with more analysis of the nature of the workloads per VM. As the power of the physical servers grows, so the techniques of traditional capacity management apply, with VMs being treated as workload components, but still requiring characterization. Assessment of virtualization in practice has also led to review of many VMs and retirement of outdated or unused solutions.

2.6   Capacity management versus general ITSM process flow

Capacity management is described as a process in ITIL but in this book it is considered simply as a practice. Capacity management requires knowledge of, or at least awareness of, particular technical skills to implement it rather than just pure project definition and project management techniques as for some other ITIL processes. Although tools can reduce the need for some detailed knowledge, the use of the tools is best exercised with understanding. Each site has to find its own balance of members of the CMT and sharing information with its domain and application architects.

Also, CMP involves various processes described elsewhere in ITIL (e.g. incident management is used to handle capacity incidents, change management is used to change capacity infrastructure), and it requires understanding of the underpinning technology. This book uses CMP to discuss the activities, and CMT to describe the team (whether nominated as capacity managers or not; full time or part time involvement). This is expanded in appendix A for those who want to consider the relationships between processes, functions, and activities.

2.6.1   Data archiving and information life cycle management

An important aspect of capacity management is that of formal data archiving under the aegis of information life cycle management control. There are potentially huge amounts of data captured, collected and stored in the CDB. There is long term value in much of it, but it can be summarized. A typical regime will keep all the most detailed data which has been captured at five minute intervals or less for a limited time of days or weeks when the data is essentially of a performance tracing nature. Then it will be aggregated into fifteen minute or hourly averages and retained for weeks or months. Then it will be aggregated into daily averages and retained for months or years and possibly then weekly averages only retained.

Theory of Constraints and capacity management

Theory of Constraints (TOC)[18] is an overall management philosophy. It is geared to help organizations continually achieve their goals. A system's constraint is "that part of the system that constrains the objective of the system." Goldratt states that: "In reality any system has very few constraints and at the same time any system in reality must have at least one constraint." He extended this approach to describe how to optimize steps, applications and operations largely within a factory environment, although it can also be applied to IT. End-to-end capacity management requires minimizing the performance bottleneck in the service chain in the light of the relative leverage factor. For example, amending the structure of a database query may be more useful than adding additional processors.

2.6.2 Capacity management and service lifecycle

The CMP ranges across the lifecycle of a service. Other parts of the enterprise are involved to differing degrees at different stages. Clearly for new services involving in-house development, there is a need for liaison with development and testing functions to ensure performance requirements are considered. As a service is implemented, interfaces with the service desk need to be established to identify performance issues. Throughout there needs to be an understanding of the business needs and expectations, which can be enhanced by establishing the relationship with business demand and service activity by trend analysis of new users, dormant users and leavers.

This can be summarized as in figure 2.5, showing the partners involved, the range of liaisons and the stages of the service as it moves from 'plan' to 'develop' to 'deliver' to 'improve'.

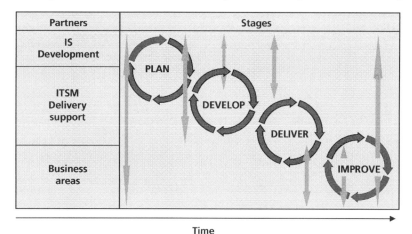

Figure 2.5 Iterative development of services

---

18   Introduced by Dr. Eliyahu M. Goldratt in his 1984 book entitled *The Goal*.

The essential points to notice in this figure is that each of the stages is iterative (and potentially with feedback loops from one to the previous). The partners involved at each stage tend to have differing levels of interest, but the key point is that all should be kept aware of each others' issues throughout the life cycle.

The lifecycle of a service can also be summarized as in figure 2.6. This shows the sweep of activities from development to 'productization' to service delivery.

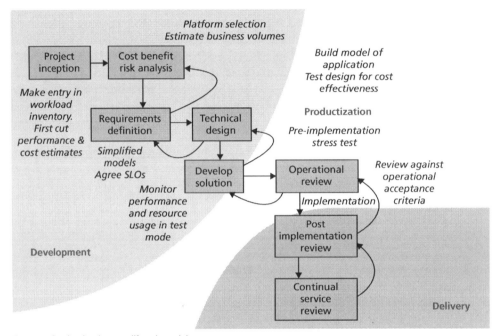

Figure 2.6 Service development lifecycle model

The iterative cycles within each stage are indicated as is the general flow from development through testing to delivery, with some of the main capacity management actions indicated.

The relationship between development and the service life cycle model on one hand and the IT infrastructure and ITSM on the other is a key issue in the establishment of the CMP. What is needed is a sensible balance between projects and practices.

Equally, there is a need for some use of forces to do work, requiring energy and generating momentum to effect some actions. These terms have all been described within mathematics and engineering for a long time, with the initial derivation of their relationships defined by Isaac Newton[19].

---

19   Newton's *Philosophiæ Naturalis Principia Mathematica* written in 1687 derived most of the laws of motion.

Various mathematical laws involved with capacity management will be introduced later. In order to set the scene, a few other laws are reviewed. Newton's laws of mechanics can be related to capacity management.

The first law states that things stay restful unless there is an external force applied to it (or in ITSM an organization can become stagnant without some catalyst such as a consultant for change).

The second law states that the rate of change of momentum of a body is proportional to the impulse applied to it (so that the larger the enterprise, the greater the force required to make a change to ITSM and the longer it takes, thus suggesting that long assignments of large capacity management evangelists are recommended).

The third law deals with the balance between equal and opposite forces, typically expressed in terms of actions and reactions (which encourages ITSM enthusiasts to find ways of working with those less keen, rather than against them; so that the deliverables are seen to be to the benefit of the organization).

3 Why: Benefits of capacity management

There are many benefits in adopting, implementing and enhancing effective capacity management. This chapter identifies some of them, as well as the costs and a few cost-benefit analyses and risk considerations.

3.1 Primary benefits

The primary benefit of capacity management is to provide the optimum balance of resource to meet the demands of business at a cost that ensures the appropriate service levels. This can be extended to a more complete checklist of primary benefits:
- improved quality service provision and cost justifiable service quality
- services that meet business, customer and user demands via integrated processes
- increased efficiency – cost savings
- deferred upgrade expenditure (cash flow)
- effective consolidation and virtualization (maintenance/licenses)
- reduced impact on the environment, by optimizing the IT infrastructure
- reduced costs of accommodation, energy consumption, raw materials
- planned acquisition (allowing time to negotiate discounts), introduction of new technology and meeting sustainability requirements
- reduced risk of poor performance
- fewer capacity/performance disasters (appreciated most by customers)
- fewer capacity/performance problems (appreciated most by users)
- more confident forecasts of performance
- application lifecycle enhanced (fewer performance disasters/abandoned apps)
- learning from previous experience with demonstrable KPIs

Each site will weigh these benefits differently, in the light of local circumstances, objectives and (bitter) experience.

The related capacity management activities are intended to provide these benefits by helping to:
- predict when the IT services will all fall apart leading to performance disasters and abandoned applications
- take action to avoid potential performance disasters in time
- provide early feedback as applications evolve or degrade
- have the right equipment in the right place at the right time
- avoid wasting money on redundant or unsupported equipment
- consolidate and virtualize servers effectively
- avoid wasting time on un-necessary interim upgrades or pointless tuning
- do it right first time
- optimize the IT infrastructure by studying new technology developments

In essence, all of the activities are designed to enable proactive performance and capacity management and all the benefits that such assurance brings.

In summary, capacity management is a 'Good Thing'. This is a reference to a classic slim volume entitled "1066 and all that" in which Sellar and Yeatman summarized 2000 years of confused schoolboy memories of English history into 124 pages. They also said that 'History is not what you thought. It is what you can remember".

This might well also be applied to ITIL capacity management, where ITIL summarizes many person-years of capacity management experience into 50 pages. Sellar and Yeatman sub-titled their book as "A Memorable History of England, comprising all the parts you can remember, including 103 Good Things and 5 Bad Kings". Perhaps Knot ITIL (Appendix E) describes "all the parts of ITSM you can remember, with 6 Good Things (core-processes) and 5 Required Teams (functions)".

3.2   Operational benefits

The primary benefits listed above may all have an effect on operations but specifically the main operational benefits lie in having a team dedicated to performing effective capacity management and so enable specific benefits to operations such as:
- more efficiency in operations as less capacity and performance issues
- less diagnostic skills required as the CMT address capacity issues proactively
- standardization benefits of demands, priorities and alerts
- less intervention required due to proactive capacity management
- less out-of-hours costs to cope with capacity or performance crises
- common tool means better exploitation and/or fewer bodies needed to drive it
- 'radar' to warn against possible potential problems
- smaller or greener footprint and less space or heat requirements with fewer servers
- smoother transition of new technology and better tuning of options
- improved awareness of 'out of support' issues and resultant planned actions

Operations and capacity management will share a lot of information and should establish a relationship that will lead to more effective ITSM.

3.3   Management benefits

Similarly, from a management viewpoint, the main benefits are probably seen as having effective capacity management from a governance point of view, but also explicitly:
- trustworthy IT services
  - customer trust directly reduces costs:
  - procedures can be simplified
  - budget can be allocated functionally rather than against unknown contingencies
- more control
- less degradation
- better information for decisions
- improved working relationships between teams (e.g. applications support, database support, network support, server support) as end-to-end capacity management requires good communication on performance and capacity between different functions
- benefits of more maturity, such as agility and business – IT alignment

In order to achieve all these benefits, management will have to liaise effectively with the CMT rather than assume it provides a merely technical function.

3.4   Business benefits

The business benefits will vary in interpretation in each site even more than the operational and management benefits but can be thought of under the following headings:
- cost reduction or control overall (despite cost of reporting tools)
- performance improvement
- flexibility and agility
- improvement to management of suppliers and delivery chains

The benefits of capacity management are most dramatically demonstrated when the discipline is not in place and is subsequently introduced. Sites have reported huge initial savings by objective assessment of proposed upgrades leading to the realization that, for example, 80% of the benefit of a proposed upgrade may be achieved by an alternative option at 20% of the cost. This is the traditional justification for the CMP and applies best to the case of a significant upgrade to a large machine costing a lot of money. However, it applies across all machines to some degree. The total cost of IT for most enterprises does not drop as the unit cost of machines drop. So the total expenditure remains the same or increases and the leverage in getting the optimum performance from those machines remains valid.

3.5   Costs

A typical set of cost headings is difficult to generate as budget headings and financial controls are so site specific, but a core checklist is shown below:
- procurement of required tools
- monitoring hardware, OS, applications
- CDB/CMIS for holding record of all capacity management data
- modeling tools for 'what-if' and statistics
- graphical reporting tools (web-enabled)
- project management as required
- staff costs including recruitment, training, accommodation et cetera
- development liaison and data flows
- QA load, soak and saturation testing data
- business liaison and attitude questionnaires

Each site will also find its own level of maturity for all of the practices discussed so that not all of the above costs are necessarily incurred in establishing capacity management.

3.6   Cost-benefit analysis

The current direct cost of a formal CMP within an organization is usually difficult to establish. Work undertaken in this area is often carried out as a by-product of other functions as well as the CMT. Any general time recording systems in use could only give figures for current activity in these areas if they have been identified as separate tasks. In sites and data centers where there are specific resources dedicated to CMP there are often limited levels of commitment and adoption.

Ultimately, the purpose of the CMP is to provide sufficient capacity to satisfy the needs of the business. The need is to match the computing infrastructure to the needs of the applications to achieve the business requirements. This discipline is increasingly needed, despite hardware price-performance improvements as the aspirations of end-users and resource demands of application software are increasing even more rapidly.

CMP has become highly visible in most corporations as e-commerce response times affect business transactions and the service level is manifested as web-based transactions. Equally, although modern severs may introduce smaller incremental upgrades and shorter time-scales for procurement, it still merits accurate sizing of demands for new procurements. New technology and how it is to be implemented to achieve sustainability is part of the challenge. The open competition between suppliers should allow even more benefit to be obtained from predictions of the likely impact of alternative procurement solutions. Also, the potential disruption and resource costs of every upgrade need to be reviewed before action.

Cost-benefit analysis is notoriously difficult in any discipline which is essentially directed towards providing an insurance against disasters, and offering a guideline for good practice and efficient operation.

The savings as a result of introducing performance assurance are not readily quantified on the basis of a 'per application' or 'per configuration' basis, as the previous efficiency of matching business needs to resources will vary widely from one site to another. Certainly, once established, few sites abandon the practice of formalized capacity management which is now widely adopted. The following notes indicate some of the factors in making financial estimates:

- **Performance prediction** – there are some extra costs per project as the procedures will be a new requirement imposed on the developers. The savings gained by performance engineering in terms of reduced development work in rewrites and maintenance are significant. There is also a major saving in avoiding corrective software development projects to resolve performance problems.
- **Performance testing** – depending on the level of previous procedures, some extra costs may be incurred due to the increased workload placed on QA conformance testing. Performance testing will extend the formality of benchmarking and may well incur extra costs in analysis and prediction. The savings are achieved through the earlier identification of problems and often substantial savings are possible because improved diagnosis and tools find errors and excessive consumption earlier in development when changes are cheapest to fix.
- **Performance assurance** – this area potentially adds extra costs in that a new discipline may have to be introduced at each service delivery site or data center. The costs of the staffing

and tools are highly variable depending on the extent of adoption. A 'typical' large computer centre might have a team of some two to five planners, with special areas of responsibility and expertise. The savings lie in the controlled acquisition of necessary upgrades.

- **CMP audit** – this is often a new activity requiring specialist expertise to liaise with all the other activities. The basic cost of the central function would be that of establishing the team, training it and providing appropriate tools. The savings lie in the integration of all the activities and the overall benefits of ITSM. The demand comes from a need to demonstrate compliance with various requirements

The costs identified above may turn out to be significant. But no site can survive without CMP, whether formalized or not, as no modern town can do without a (reactive) fire engine and (proactive) water hydrants to supply it. Formalizing the practice allows management to hold it to account and forces it to perform in the best interests of the company. Further, the savings and benefits in both financial and service terms will typically far outweigh those infrastructure costs.

Experience of introducing CMP into large organizations indicates that over the first few years of introduction there is likely to be a minimum average net saving in the order of 5%-10% on capital expenditure and operating costs, plus an unquantifiable (but possibly more significant) saving where systems have not been delayed (or cancelled) due to inadequate resourcing[20].

> "There is nothing more difficult to execute, nor more dubious of success, nor more dangerous to administer, than to introduce a new system of things: for he who introduces it has all those who profit from the old system as his enemies and he has only lukewarm allies in all those who might profit from the new system."
> Nicolo Machiavelli, The Prince, VI, 94.

In practice, some quantifiable data is available from a number of case studies. For example, the author worked at one site (that prefers to be anonymous for obvious reasons) which saved a million pounds on a proposed upgrade (on the wrong devices) which would have had insignificant impact on performance. And another site saved the costs of establishing a new performance assurance function in its first study. But these are difficult cases to refer to, as they imply criticism of those proposing upgrades before they are properly assessed. And, like keeping fit, the benefits of good practices are sometimes only demonstrable by stopping doing them.

Further, a major benefit lies in the guarantee of a known and controlled IT service, with the impact of proposed changes to workload or configuration being formally sized. In this way, the discipline provides insurance that performance disasters due to bad design or under-resourcing can be avoided at the same time as not overspending on equipment.

The unsurprising overall conclusion of this book is that it is feasible, desirable and cost-effective to establish a fully integrated CMP environment. The implementation, managing and optimization of the practice is considered in chapters 5-8, but key ingredients are establishing the right practice owner, budget champion and discipline evangelist. The last will be core members

---

20   See the papers referred to in 'Sources', section 'Useful Papers'.

of the CMT and will probably set the tone of the team in many ways, such as being energetic, good communicators, out-ward looking, business aware and altogether key to the business and IT relationship.

Again, paving the way for various laws of capacity management, consider those for thermodynamics. The three laws of thermodynamics can also be related to capacity management. Capacity management can use its energy to instigate better control of the infrastructure and improve insight in the relations between business demand, IT services and resources. To achieve this, the team needs to be good communicators and well energized.

The principle of the conservation of energy (the first law of thermodynamics) states that "The energy of a closed system remains constant during any process". So an enterprise considering CMP and related changes, needs to be open to change and establish an energetic CMT.

The second law is the conservation of entropy. Entropy is a measure of disorder, the more liquid the less ordered and the more entropy (for example, consider a glass of some alcohol with some melting ice). A pub can be viewed as an entropy pool. Perhaps what is needed to energize a lethargic CMT is the right amount of the right liquid to optimize entropy in the system. This may need a bit of practice.

The third law states that as the temperature of a body approaches absolute zero, so its entropy approaches zero. A restaurant serving a good chilled wine with seafood is also an entropy pool. Again, enough of the right liquid served at the right temperature can ensure a well oiled team.

4 How: Practice of capacity management

The practice of capacity management requires an understanding of the related activities and techniques involved. This chapter summarizes these and is an extensive chapter, as it describes the 'how' of capacity management.

This chapter also provides some simple examples of the statistics and mathematics that can be exploited to achieve the required objectives. These may seem trivial to some practitioners in that they only scratch the surface of a mathematical discipline but to others new to capacity management, we hope they provide a reasonably comprehensible introduction. Although CMP does not require the CMT to be mathematical or statistical experts, they should have a good basic appreciation of the techniques involved and how to interpret the results they get from spreadsheets and other tools.

> "Should I refuse a good dinner simply because I do not understand the processes of digestion?"
> Oliver Heaviside 1850-1925, Inventor of operational calculus

4.1 Capacity management data flows

To carry out CMP requires specific information from the following sources:
- **corporate** – e.g. mergers, acquisitions, down-sizing, centralization and consolidation
- **business units** – e.g. marketing campaigns, business forecasts, transaction rates, priorities, response requirements, seasonal workloads
- **technical design** – e.g. file organization, accesses, processes, communications needs
- **IT infrastructure (ITI)** – e.g. new technologies, computer types, devices, connectivity, communications
- **existing workloads** – e.g. current resource utilizations, transaction rates, patterns of usage/demand

There are numerous interdependencies between capacity management and the other ITSM practices, and these are also indicated in the checklists (see Appendix C2).

All the major practices have data flows required from capacity management and also provide data flows to capacity management. This applies in particular to management of availability, change, configuration, continuity, demand, events, finance, incidents, problems, releases, and service levels. Appendix C2 indicates the detail of the potential data flows in each direction.

Figure 4.1 is a sample data flow diagram for most of the activities within capacity management and linked to it, showing the relationships between the entities involved, the activities actioned and the data stores used. A suggested organization for local entities, and its relationship with other entities, is indicated. This will vary in practice from site to site. Since capacity management is by its nature a continuous practice, there is no necessary sequence of events.

Note that although the performance database and modeling database are shown as separate entities, this is just for graphical convenience. They are both parts of the CDB/CMIS which should also include the forecasting database and other relevant information not shown in this simple representation.

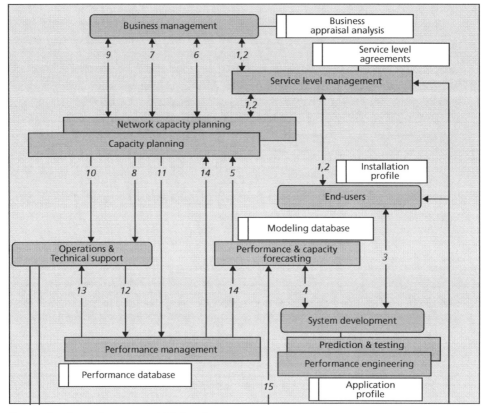

Figure 4.1 Sample capacity management data flow diagram

Legend figure 4.1: Note that single arrows represent information flows; double arrows represent activities of consultation and negotiation. Data stores are represented by the open boxes. Teams are shown in rounded rectangles and major practice groups shown in rectangles. This representation is an oversimplification of what often happens in practice, and it is a good practice to define the data flows (and flaws) in any CMP.

4.2   Capacity management activities

The main **iterative** activities are described in ITIL as monitoring of performance and utilization, analysis of abnormalities and bottlenecks, tuning recommendations to address them and implementation and tracking of those changes. The main **cyclic** activities identified are demand management, modeling, application sizing, storage in the CDB/CMIS and production of the capacity plan.

	The information flows are as follows:
1 2	Users, business and capacity planning agree on service level objectives for planned developments.
3	Business analysis and system design work takes place.
4	Systems are measured at the earliest possible stage in their development.
5	Modeling creates performance predictions for use by capacity planning.
6	Capacity planning reports to the business planning function on alternative action plans.
7	Appropriate action plans are agreed between capacity planning and business management.
8	The agreed action plans are passed to operations for implementation.
9	Revisions to the action plans are agreed between business management and capacity planning in the light of, for example, changes in workload forecasts.
10	Revised action plans are passed to Operations/ Development.
11	Capacity planning generates files of performance predictions, which are used by performance management to identify major deviations between actual and planned performance.
12	Performance management obtains performance data with the co-operation of computer operations.
13	Performance management responds to operations with details of tuning to maintain service levels.
14	Performance management reports to the modeling function on any major deviations from planned performance that are impacting on delivered service.
15	Forecasting obtains information about current service levels from computer operations.
16	Service level information of a less detailed nature is made available to users, who may then verify that they are receiving agreed service and may also revise their actual service level requirements.

Table 4.1 Sample capacity management information flows

Included in this area by implication (but not explicitly in ITIL V2 though introduced in V3) are:
- event management, alarms and alerts
- intranet status and exception reporting
- resource management and other performance- related activities

The list can be extended to include a number of other activities:
- monitoring, analysis, tuning, implement changes
- demand management (note described somewhat differently in ITIL V2 V3)
- modeling of workload forecasts and service components and resource usage
- application sizing, performance engineering and performance testing
- storage of data in the CDB and use of the CMIS
- liaison with problem management, service level management (SLM), development, testing, quality assurance, business users for demands, plans and key performance indicators (KPIs)
- generation of reports (regular, ad hoc and exception) to intranet and elsewhere
- setting and policing of capacity and performance thresholds and events
- charging for services and audit of ITSM

In practice, the tuning and implementation activities incorporate a necessary level of reporting. Depending on the application and organization, it may be regular reports or exception reports, to management, users or technicians, via the intranet, email or paper.

All the potential activities for the CMT should be quoted as part of a role description, or maybe part of a RACI[21] framework. The activities involved include the need to:

- ensure effective resource monitoring and CDB/CMIS integrity
- ensure adequate IT capacity
- recommend tuning and optimization approaches for existing capacity
- publish regular management and exception performance reports
- compare actual versus SLA performance and capacity targets
- address capacity issues
- produce timely regular and ad hoc business demand forecasts
- derive forecasts of workload component forecasts
- generate resultant capacity plans and recommendations
- maintain knowledge of future demand for IT services
- define need for hardware upgrades or consolidation
- size all proposed new systems and applications
- performance test of new systems
- assess impact of new technologies
- determine cost justifiable and measurable SLAs
- ensure that continuity/DR capacity requirements are met
- ensure that availability capacity requirements are met
- recommend resolution of performance related incidents
- recommend demand management stratagems
- ensure reliability and availability requirements incorporated
- assess changes and advise the change advisory board (CAB)
- perform ad hoc self-audits

The core practice has four main activities:

1. Creating a statement of requirements for capacity and producing a set of workload forecast scenarios (WFSs) via workload classification and integration algorithms that allow for factors such as capture ratio and peak load issues
2. Creating optional plans to satisfy the requirements based on current service-server mapping and likely options
3. Evaluating and optimizing on the best plan to ensure that all criteria are met:
   - under normal conditions
   - allowing for business continuity conditions (contingency)
   - within performance targets
   - within cost constraints
4. Establishing sensible thresholds for relevant metrics and tracking/ trending behavior:
   - warning – raise an alert – automated exception report
   - limit/critical – exceeding this will degrade performance
   - absolute – total capacity of the resource

---

21   RACI framework is an analytical approach used in business process management to identify the individuals involved in the execution of a process. RACI stands for the roles of the stakeholders involved: Responsible: does the work; Accountable: has the power to modify the business process ; Consulted: the involved for additional information; Informed: needs to be informed about the outcome of the process.

- typically established for processor performance, memory, disk storage capacity, disk performance and other resources within scope
  - typically reported on in regular, exception and ad hoc modes

The **essential tasks** of capacity management within these activities are to:
- derive detailed objectives arising from the corporate, business and IT strategies
- define and agree scope of CMP
- ensure the right level of IT infrastructure investment to:
  - ensure users are able to meet business demands
  - match the equipment to the need (configurations should be matched to workloads with adequate headroom and minimum excess)
  - optimize on infrastructure cost, aiming for sustainability
  - reduce the financial burden of redundant hardware where appropriate
- analyze data to identify and resolve/bypass performance bottlenecks and evaluate tuning strategies
- improve and report/publish performance and service levels achievements and issues
- optimize the resources available as appropriate within domains and 'end-to-end':
- 'right-size' or 'consolidate' or 'virtualize' as necessary
- delay procurements or purchase in bulk or at year-end where appropriate, giving consideration to upcoming technologies
- ensure accurate and timely procurements to:
  - minimize disruption and expenditure on a basis of formal hardware plans
  - size properly the impact of upgrades with known and targeted performance
  - plan for the introduction of new technology and products when cost effective or appropriate or required for sustainability to help preserve agreed SLAs
  - lever financial options (discounts and cash flow) by delaying procurements until really needed
- ensure effective management of service levels in terms of response time and throughput
- plan for workload growth, new applications, sites, acquisitions and upgrades
- size major new applications as soon as practicable, preferably at design phase
- avoid capacity or performance related incidents, problems and potential disasters
- liaise effectively with development, performance engineering, service level management, quality assurance and any other processes or functions which interface with CMP

Good capacity management includes consideration of the future power of hardware, which is still roughly doubling every couple of years or so as per Moore's Law[22]. Regular technology refresh and liaison with hardware vendors on their roadmap may impact on plans and affect issues such as space and power in the datacenter.

---

22   Moore's law is the empirical observation that the transistor density of integrated circuits (since they were invented in 1958) increases exponentially and doubles roughly every 18 months, but it is now commonly applied most computer hardware. The trend was first observed by Intel co-founder Gordon E. Moore in 1965. It has continued since and is expected to continue for another decade at least.

This practice has been discussed earlier mostly in terms of servers and their CPU and I/O performance. Other aspects need to be assessed, such as memory and disk space.

Memory metrics vary across operating systems as they work differently and provide different information. The possible metrics include free, available, committed and unreferenced memory, possibly with a hard page out rate reported. The typical planning technique used is based on simplified sizing, using a selected metric and then applying threshold exceptions (probably based on exponential trending). The old rules of thumb are changing as memory costs drop. Most configurations benefit in performance terms from having too much memory rather than too little or 'just right'.

Disk storage capacity assessment is not always as simple as might be expected. It can be difficult to define used and available capacity or to monitor them. There is a lack of a standard MIB format and measurement tools report different architectures differently. Numbers can be derived and controlled with workload management and resource management techniques. The hardware itself has raw capacity but it is then configured (mirroring, RAID5 et cetera) thus reducing the available effective capacity. The effective capacity is allocated to file systems, leaving some preset available effective space within the file systems. Space will be used or unused by files or databases and within files and databases. The 'available capacity' can be defined simply as the unused effective capacity, or unused within file system, or unused within databases or some combination of these. Often this is expressed in terms of 'spare days' before the daily growth is liable to exceed a predefined threshold. An extra layer of abstraction is added by the use of SAN. The SAN suppliers provide extra metrics within their own systems which can be used to assess the storage capacity issue.

Much of the discussion above is mostly single-server centric, as an easy way to introduce the concepts. However, most practical IT solutions are nowadays service centric, and most services are multi-tier with pools of physical machines per tier to support an array of virtual machines. Significant services merit performance assurance with models to characterize workloads and assess resources. This is supported by application views to reflect workload components and to track changes and trends. Meta-models can assess multi-tier solutions, given the ability to correlate workloads across tiers, and relate them to a business definition of quality of service (QoS), business metric of interest (BMI), KPIs or related drivers. This in turn needs the ability to characterize workload components by username, process name, service class, report class. See an outline of the business to resource mapping activity in figure 4.2.

4.2.1 Monitoring

Monitoring relies on measurement. Wikipedia describes measurement as the activity of assigning a number to an attribute according to a standard rule; the word measurement comes from the Greek 'metron', meaning measure, standard, rule or proportion.

The first pre-requisite for capacity management is the establishment of resource and application data capture and collection from all the defined target machines. A data collection strategy is essential to ensure appropriate cover across all selected servers and services rather than an ad hoc piecemeal approach. The capture of data requires the definition of what level of data is to be captured, at what sampling interval (or snapshot), over what collection period (or window).

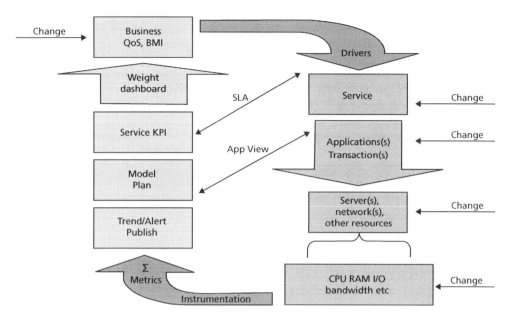

Figure 4.2 Business requirements to resource demand mapping

The sampling interval chosen depends on local factors. It is typically fifteen minutes which is a sensible period over which to accumulate performance statistics. It can be shorter for more dynamically changing systems or longer if less. Most data capture regimes will allow values from a few minutes to maybe an hour. Some will enable shorter time periods, perhaps more for tuning and real-time diagnostic purposes in real-time systems.

> The choice of sampling interval can sometimes be reduced to a debate on who has the shortest snapshot. The extreme example would be a system which captured data at the clock speed of the CPU. This would then be able to produce a vast report showing that the CPU was either busy or idle at every cycle. This is not of interest, so much as the average use over a sensible period of time to reflect patterns in user behavior.

For each metric, there should be attributes identified, such as thresholds for alarms and alerts as well as patterns for normal behavior. Furthermore, working instructions should also be generated to solve a violation or breach of any of the thresholds. Ideally, an indication of the quality of the selected thresholds would be reflected in the KPI's score.

The collection of data requires the definition of where the data will reside in a CDB/CMIS and how to ensure it gets there. This may be a distributed CDB/CMIS or federated or centralized and the data may be polled, pushed or pulled into the CDB/CMIS. Most sites exercise a standard basic level of monitoring across all significant servers or even all servers. Implementing such a regime usually requires a significant exercise in rolling-out an agreed agent or data collector and then ensuring that it becomes part of the standard build to ensure effective continuance of the activities.

Again, the number of metrics captured and the size of the resultant database can sometimes be reduced to a debate on who has the biggest number of metrics and the biggest CDB. Given the potentially huge volumes of data, it is wise to focus on those metrics that will actually be used.

It is also important to consider the data collection strategy with care, in order to avoid adding excessive overhead. It is not practical to run a trace on a machine other than for short periods for urgent diagnostic needs as the overhead is well recognized. The same argument can apply to data collection and parameters need to be set so as to avoid it becoming 'bloated'. It is usual to be able to select appropriate snapshot intervals at large increments for most purposes and be able to refine them dynamically to address specific issues. Similarly, often a core subset of key data may be collected and then a more comprehensive data set be added for specific issues. Other controls will include different granularities at different times of day, if the workload is not 7x24.

It is also useful to create and maintain a service assurance matrix (discussed in more detail in chapter 8. This is a list of the services and all components used by the service, the metrics monitored, thresholds, frequency of capture, and key commands/processes to check that the service is running. This provides a useful document for liaison with development and operations.

Monitoring relies on measurement. The importance of measurement was expressed by Galileo: "Measure what is measurable and make measurable what is not so".
Galileo Galilei 1564-1642

This was commented on somewhat later:
"When you can measure what you are speaking of and express it in numbers, you know something about it; but when you cannot, your knowledge is of a meager and unsatisfactory kind".
Lord Kelvin, 1824-1907

4.2.2 Analysis

This activity is where the analyst looks at the data gathered in the monitoring activity and looks for significant matters arising. Typically this involves looking at which devices or groups of devices of the same type are being most heavily utilized and thus causing potential bottlenecks. Also it involves looking for anomalies and abnormalities which might be affecting performance, such as those caused by issues like memory leaks, rogue users, administrative processes in production time, looping processes, viruses, missing indexes and all the other issues that can cause a machine to perform under target. A typical automatic analysis might look for suspicious resource consumption patterns (such as ever-increasing use of memory) and maybe significant correlations between all the major performance metrics and pick out the top ten processes, devices, users and other key factors. This sort of analysis has been called process pathology and its automatic detection is well described and promoted in a CMG paper by Ron Kaminski[23]

Some of the statistical issues raised are discussed in more detail in section 4.2.6.

---

23   See CMG proceedings on web www.cmg.org/proceedings . This link is to a huge vault of CMP information. In this case, select, for example, 2008 and Kaminski, or just search the site for 'Kaminski'.

Statistics

"There are three kinds of lies: lies, damned lies, and statistics". This quotation is usually attributed to Benjamin Disraeli, although similar phrases were used by others.

Another relevant quotation is from Andrew Lang:
"He uses statistics as a drunken man uses lampposts – for support rather than for illumination".

It is also from analysis of a typical period that the analyst can begin to understand the normal behavior for a system and establish meaningful performance thresholds for any event reporting and management system. 'Out of the box' threshold level values for most systems will either generate no alarms or nothing but alarms. They need to be set to reflect alarms only when they are meaningful without introducing too many false positives. Theoretically these levels may have been anticipated and defined in the project development stages, but this is not often the case.

A key issue is to identify the metrics to be used in assessing the performance of a given service or server. Usually the concern lies with the ability of the server to support the service to the required level at times of stress, namely peak periods. These need to be defined and then monitored and analyzed. A peak period definition typically covers a period of time of standard duration for which resource usage will be planned and reported. It is selected so as to represent demand on each day accurately, usually in the important part of the day for the service(s) as defined in SLAs for individual workloads or servers. The factors involved are the statistic used, period duration, time of day, time of week, time of month and point in the business/seasonal cycle. An example might be the peak hourly average (duration and statistic) within the critical SLA period (9-5) for month end balance (point in business cycle).

The statistic used is a local decision. There will be a distribution of values involved and so a representative value for that distribution has to be selected. That may be the average (mean), the most frequently occurring value (mode), the value that splits the distribution in half (median) or some percentile selected to include that percentage of values. These are discussed in section 4.2.6. The representative value may also be chosen to reflect a sensible granularity. Fluctuations in utilization minute by minute are not representative. Averages over a day are too smoothed (unless it is a 7x24 application that 'follows the sun'). Typically values such as the 'average over a peak hour' or the '75th percentile hourly average from the working month' are defined. Sometimes the choice of metric is determined by the package used; sometimes it is a decision that was taken a long ago. Often it is established within the choice of criteria for threshold determination, reflecting the degree of safety that the site feels is apt. Whichever approach is used, it should be applied systematically across the domains and be well documented within the caveats of any capacity plan.

The workload analysis needs to take into account issues such as non-concurrency of peaks, seasonality and capture ratios.

The peak issue is most easily explained by considering a mixed workload with different groups of users. The analysis of potential future workloads has to take a view on whether to allow for the likelihood of all the peaks of activity per group of users being concurrent (assuming they currently are non-concurrent). This is referred to as the policy on 'peaks of peaks'.

Seasonality in workload is described as the cyclic issues that affect a business and cause predictable fluctuations in workload. They may be seasonal in a variety of ways, such as the cyclic nature of some monthly financial transactions, or some weather related items such as the sale of umbrellas or the calendar related issues such as the sale of Christmas cards. Many businesses have well-known peaks in demand that exceed normal business by significant factors and they need to define an approach to the level of service acceptable for future peaks. Seasonality can be accounted for and statistically isolated from the underlying trends in workload (using Fourier[24] analysis) so that the future demands can be readily forecast.

Capture ratio is the term used to describe an instrumentation issue present on all computers. A typical operating system will provide two major logs of detailed information on the activity on the machine. One is a system view of the total demand placed on each device (such as total CPU utilization or total I/O per disk). The other is the view per user (or command or process) that logs the activity allocated to that user (or command or process) to an accounting file. These records are typically written on completion of the session or job from accumulated 'snapshots' of activity taken whilst the process is active. Characterizing a workload by, for example, grouping all the users into a few defined classes (and using a 'remainder' to collect all the 'uninteresting' users) should yield a total resource utilization that can be compared with the system view. However, there is usually a difference. In better operating systems this is usually only a few per cent. It is due to a number of factors, such as short running processes within the operating system that are not logged to the accounting file, or long-running processes that have not been terminated within the period under consideration. These 'overheads' should be checked to see if they can be neglected, or if present, to be allocated in an appropriate manner across the workloads. If it is not catered for and is present to say some 10%, then it may well be the 10% that causes response times to degrade beyond user acceptability.

4.2.3 Tuning

Tuning is designed to make optimum use of hardware resources and eliminate any extreme bottlenecks. Bottlenecks are inevitable when there is a complex of servers or devices linked to provide a service. Each device will have its own service time and algorithms for handling requests and that in turn will lead to contention and delays. The analysis described above will lead to a focus on particular issues or devices where problems are beginning to occur. Sometimes an imbalance in a system can be addressed by techniques such as priorities, extra channels, more devices, increased cache, increased block sizes or many other system and device tuning parameters. However, there is a danger of 'chasing the bottleneck' and reaching the 'law of diminishing returns' so it is worthwhile assessing the potential benefits of any tuning recommendation before recommending a change.

---

24   Fourier analysis is a standard mathematical technique used to analyse wave forms and other frequency or time-based
      series and derives underlying patterns such as those that musicians know as fundamental harmonics. It can help iden-
      tify daily, weekly, monthly and other seasonal patterns.

Imagine a juggler is repeatedly launching a ball representing a CPU request and catching it a second later. He then launches a different ball representing an I/O request. Assuming the performance is that of a recent laptop (but without a solid state drive), how long will the I/O ball take, given the CPU one takes a second? The answer is over three months. (Consider a 2 GHz CPU which has a cycle time of 0.5 nsec or $5x10^{-10}$ sec versus a drive with a service time of 5 msecs or $5x10^{-3}$ sec. Their ratio is 10^7 and 10^7 seconds is over 115 days.) So there is a major mismatch which has to be addressed by having multiple I/O channels and devices and using levels of data caching. The real life situation becomes more complex as multiple users, multiple threads and multiple services become involved.

4.2.4 Implementation of proposed tuning changes

Change management is described as a separate process in ITIL, but implementation of proposed tuning changes are described as an activity in the iterative loop of monitor, analyze, tune and implement changes. It essentially describes the introduction of recommendations for change, which then go through the change management process.

Before tuning a component you need to be sure this component is the real bottleneck in the service chain. This is the essence of the TOC approach. Also, this raises the difficult issue of root cause analysis where there are many reported issues and it is necessary to identify the root cause before considering actions.

Tuning recommendations are requests for change (RFC's) and as such will be submitted to a change advisory board (CAB) for scrutiny and approval and will only be exercised after due process. The range of tuning activities runs from changing operating system parameters (such as cache or virtual memory page sizes) to RDBMS parameters to application options or enhancements or hardware changes. Although there are many solutions which endeavor to 'self-optimize' it is often beneficial to the efficient use of resources to check that unnecessary major bottlenecks are avoided.

Of course there is a limit to triggering the full formal rigor of a change management process, as that is a very resource-intense process only to be used for activities that require careful processing. Most sites will triage changes and have different procedures for low risk changes (such as a new version of a look-up file with just a few new entries). When the tuning activity doesn't have enough impact (risk) to require handling through change management, it might typically result in a service request (standardized change) or other locally defined procedure. Some sites refer to 'authorized remedial actions' with known actions and pre-defined outcomes which have less external control.

The whole question of emergency changes is addressed differently in practice in different sites. Some initiate retrospective authorization where approval and administration of the emergency change is actioned after the change is executed and the emergency change itself goes through a smaller emergency change committee (sometimes ad hoc).

Any changes implemented under the capacity management practice will be tracked to ensure that the impact is as expected. Given that the CAB meetings are usually daily or weekly, any changes are properly considered with less reemphasis on dynamic real time tuning and 'parameter tweaking'. Most of the justification for change process control and the CAB lies in the significant numbers of problems otherwise caused.

Sadly, although change management is a recognized ITIL process, it is not always effective and can yield major issues for capacity management such as unadvertised changes to 'sysadmin' logons or other 'trivial' changes that can impact on data capture and collection from target servers.

4.2.5 Demand management

Demand management is described in ITIL as "the control of resources and requests to meet specific levels of demand that the business is willing to support". For example, user demand might have to be limited for a period if additional capacity cannot be purchased immediately. Or if there are known configuration problems, it may be possible to pre-define the services that can be sacrificed for short (or longer) periods.

If there is a chargeback mechanism in place where real money is involved, customers can be encouraged to move workloads away from peak periods by preferential rates. This applied traditionally to batch work on mainframes but can also be applied to any workload that is under customer control, such as management reports, backups or archiving. If the operating system concerned supports workload identification and priorities, then in conjunction with chargeback even finer control by demand management is feasible. Demand management in that situation can be underpinned by modeling, which can show what level of demand can be supported for a given level of resources. This is essential in disaster recovery planning, showing what demand can be supported if a given component in the infrastructure fails.

An important activity in demand management is to define quotas/limits on the use of services e.g. a limit on the personal data for filing purposes, maximum size of mailboxes. These limits are then managed by sending warnings to the end-user or blocking use of the service when second level thresholds are breached.

Demand management is "an IT governance process that enables IT and the business to optimize the investment in IT through fact-based decisions". It captures, evaluates, and prioritizes all of the demands or requests placed on IT, from high-volume routine service requests to deploying changes across core applications.

Demand management deals with the influx of requests for IT services, maintenance, and operational support – each varying in its level of importance to the organization. These requests typically fall into four key categories:
- **strategic demand** – requests for new projects that have major strategic impact on the company, such as implementation of a new ERP solution
- **tactical demand** – routine, day-to-day requests such as upgrading users to a new version of their software, etc.
- **operational demand** – management of key IT assets that impact the company's ability to conduct its core operations: improving network security and identity management capabilities, patch management etc.
- **application enhancements** – requests for upgrades or revisions to existing applications and business processes

The overarching objective of demand management is to create and control a front door to IT so that all incoming requests are collected, prioritized, scheduled, and fulfilled based on objective, consistent criteria according to business priority. Essentially the goal is to create a complete picture of all the requests made to IT – past, present, and future; tactical, operational, and strategic – so that IT can make better decisions and identify trends. Sadly, in practice, demand management is often more of an order taking and service provisioning activity than a management process. It should identify relative needs for special support such as the degree of availability, continuity, integrity, security and performance rather than accept a blanket requirement across all demands.

4.2.6 Modeling

Forecasting is not new.
"Study the past if you would divine the future."
Confucius, 551-479 BC – The Analects

"Declare the past, diagnose the present, foretell the future."
Hippocrates 460-357 BC Epidemics

"Forecasting is very difficult – especially if it is about the future."
Anon.

Modeling and prediction are at the heart of proactive capacity management. It enables you to know what service can be provided for a planned workload or what workload can be supported on a given set of resources. Modeling is the term that ITIL uses to cover all the techniques of workload forecasting and performance modeling. Modeling covers a wide variety of approaches to forecasting and forecasting has been a technique used to try to avoid problems for a long time.

Forecasting
Forecasting has two main areas of application in capacity management: assessing the pattern of change of behavior of the business demand and service workload, and assessing the impact of that change on the physical resources available to support it. The former lends itself to simple linear trending in most environments. There are, of course, step functions to be allowed for such as mergers and acquisitions. But, for example, if a marketing department suggests a dramatic growth in traffic in the face of a long term linear growth, the experienced capacity planner is able to review options and present a sensitivity analysis for a proposed solution. This review lends itself to linear trends only if utilizations of key components are at issue. However, if there is a service level agreement imposing performance requirements in terms of response times or throughputs, then a more advanced analysis is probably required. This will have to take account of queuing and contention and is usually addressed by either discrete event simulation (DES) or queuing network models (QNM) although some solutions use a combination of the two.

The approach to forecasting depends on the accuracy required and the costs involved in achieving it. It may also depend on the amount of time required to get approval to action changes, and how long the changes themselves may take. Consider the situation when the CMT proposes a significant change in the IT budget for next year. This will have to take its place in the annual budget round which often takes a significant amount of time.

There is a wide range of forecasting options and many sites will adopt a mix of them. Figure 4.3 shows a simple summary of these options and suggests their positioning. It is only indicative and assumes that in each case the technique has been applied by an experienced practitioner so that the pitfalls of bad exploitation are excluded.

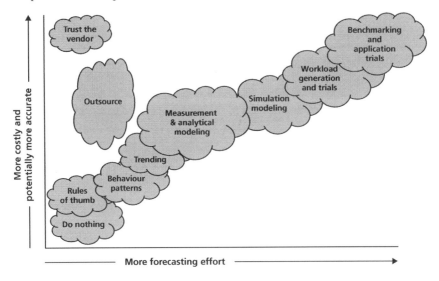

Figure 4.3 Cost and potential accuracy versus forecasting effort – showing the spectrum of options which are not mutually incompatible and most sites adopt a range of techniques to match the range of applications and their stages in their lifecycles.

The low cost option of doing nothing takes no effort but yields no benefit. Rules of thumb can be relevant for stable services running for a long time under stable operating systems where a pool of experience can be built over time. Looking at patterns of behavior or trends of a simple metric can yield a useful basic indicator. For any service where there are devices capable of supporting queues and there is contention, either of two approaches can be used (and in some cases, a combination of the two). Analytical modeling using queuing network theory to generate queuing network models (QNM) or simulation modeling using discrete event simulation (DES) will account for traffic variations and thus be much more accurate. Trials using either a real application or a scripted subset and a load generator will yield potentially even more accurate results but will require more expertise, time, effort and resources. Trusting the hardware supplier will probably yield the most costly solution with a top rate service, which may have been accurately sized. In the case of outsourcing, the level of capacity management adopted will largely depend on the detail of the contract.

The most popular of these approaches in many commercial and financial data centers is that of analytical modeling. The activities involved in performance forecasting are expanded in figure 4.4.

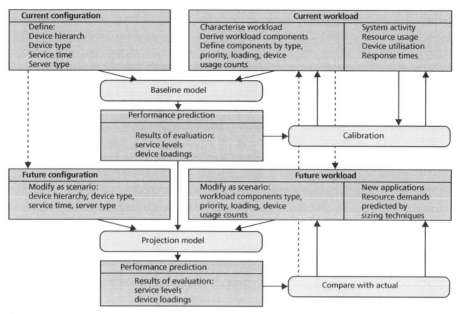

Figure 4.4 Performance forecasting

Trending

Simple linear trending provides adequate analysis for those things that behave in straight lines. In practice there are some where this is a viable approach and some where it is not. There are two key factors which can negate the approach. The first is the presence of unknown discontinuities. Consider the automatic reporting of the disk space available. If this is being reported on a large number of machines and a particular database administrator (DBA) exercises a major pruning exercise on his data, then any trending will be badly skewed by taking all the available figures into account rather than restarting the trend after such a discontinuity.

> The standard (perhaps apocryphal) story on the issue of discontinuities impacting on previous trends is the warning in the late 1890's that, given the increase in horse-drawn carriages, the trend in the height of manure in London by 1930 would submerge all the buildings. However, as we now know, there was an un-anticipated four-wheeled discontinuity in the actual event.

The other major factor when linear trends fail is when the underlying attributes of a system is not linear. The main examples of this in capacity management are throughput and response time. Although the workload may increase in a linear fashion and the device utilizations likewise, the effective throughput is dependent on contention for resources. This has been shown to be suitable for analysis by DES and QNM, not by straight lines. Fitting straight lines to a scatter of points on a graph is a good technique for variables that behave in a linear fashion. The issues lie in the choice of period to analyze so as to ensure that it is a consistent set of data without discontinuities (known or unknown). Linear regression is the formal name for drawing a straight line through a scatter of points such that the sum of the squares of perpendiculars from the points to the line is minimized.

Linear regression was first proposed by a cousin of Charles Darwin (of the Origin of Species and 'survival of the fittest' fame). He was Francis Galton (of eugenics fame). He measured populations and found that tall fathers had tall sons and small fathers had small sons, but that there was a 'regression to the norm' in that the differences in height between the sons was less than that between the fathers. He was also a friend of Florence Nightingale (of Crimean war hospital fame) and helped her present her business case for soap to improve health care outcomes in the field. She found compelling statistics but was amongst the first to suggest using graphics such as a pie-chart to present them in a form suitable for hospital administrators. Though she used the radius of the circle to reflect the variable, rather than the arc.

Analytical and simulation modeling

The essential difference between simulation modeling and analytical modeling is that the former uses a form of model where the traffic is defined and run against a simulation of the configuration until it converges to a solution whereas in the latter the traffic and configuration are defined in equations and algorithms used to solve the equations to provide the required answers.

The underlying approaches have both been well proven over the years. DES has tended to be the approach of preference for network analysis and application development analysis in domains where there is local expertise and detailed knowledge of the environment and a requirement for as much accuracy as practical in the solution. QNM has tended to be the approach of preference for server analysis in business domains where there is a requirement for a reasonably accurate solution in a short period with minimal input from the user.

An element of a computer system, such as a processor or a disk, can be considered as the provider of some kind of service (such as a CPU second or an I/O transfer). A job or a transaction joins the end of the queue for service by the device, and remains in the queue until all prior arrivals have been dealt with. The transaction then receives its unit of service and departs, to look for its next unit of service from wherever it requires it. The total service time at the device is the sum of the service time and the queuing time. The former is dependent on architecture and the latter on queue length (and service time).

Grumlin #4: No matter what the chipset or architecture, all computers wait at the same speed (zero).

There is an exact analogy with a queue of customers being served by a single counter assistant in a shop. Over a reasonable length of time, such as from opening to closing with nobody in the queue at the start of the day and everyone out at the end, the total number of customers joining the start of the queue will be equal to the total number of customers that get served. This means that the Arrival Rate is the same as the Leaving Rate over a reasonable period of time. (If it is greater, then the service is over-loaded, the queue will grow and the system will soon saturate; if it is less, then customers have materialized from nowhere.)

The higher the rate of arrivals, the greater the average queuing time. In fact, in a simple situation, you can assume that if the server is n% utilized, you will spend around n% of the total time queuing.

DES:
- simulates the arrival, service and dispatch of individual workloads
- workloads are defined as a transaction, database query, batch job et cetera
- uses statistical methods (Monte Carlo) to randomize the:
  - individual times of arrival
  - service requirements on CPU, I/O et cetera
  - flow routings through the system (visit counts per arrival et cetera)
- outputs trace/log of dynamic state of system through 'time'
- analyses results of simulation to derive:
  - queue lengths, busy or idle, arrivals or leavers, utilizations et cetera

QNM:
- makes assumptions about the statistical characteristics of workload arrival rates, service requirement distributions, I/O device visit ratios, workload populations
- solves analytical equations based on these assumptions plus:
  - information about a queuing network
  - server configuration
  - how many servers for each queue
  - queue management algorithms
- outputs utilization levels, queue lengths, throughputs and response times by device and at system level

An understanding of contention and queuing is key to appreciating computer performance as perceived by the end-user. The underlying mathematics and statistics used in the discipline is the subject of many text books, but a simple introductory overview of key results and related laws is presented here.

Introduction to statistics

A lot of statistical techniques are used within capacity management. This section attempts to provide a simple introduction to the topic. In 'Sources' at the end of the book are some more references to more formal introductions to statistics. Although the examples used in this book are all somewhat light-hearted, they are valid analogies. The arrival of transactions waiting for service from a CPU or a disk is analogous to waiting in a queue at a post office for a book of stamps. Equally, similar considerations apply to trouble tickets arriving at a service desk or other aspects of ITSM. However, most of the examples are based on papers given at CMG where issues to do with wine and beer prove to be better analogies.

Example: Wine estimates

In order to introduce some of the relevant statistics for a distribution, consider a simple set of seven numbers, perhaps estimates of the amount of wine in centiliters left in a glass at the end of a meal with seven diners. The samples are 12, 15, 20, 25, 22, 17 and 15. Thus there are 7 samples, with a maximum value of 25 and a minimum of 12. The sum of the values is 126 so the mean is 127/7 = 18. The mode, the most frequently occurring value, is 15. The median, the value which splits the samples in half, is 17. The geometric mean (used in economic evaluation, being the Nth root of the product of N values) is 17.51. The harmonic mean (used when values are in units such as speed, being the number of samples over the sum of the reciprocals of values) is 17.03.

There are thus five separate values which can be used as an indication of 'central tendency', even with just a simple set of seven numbers.

Another measure often used in CMP is a 'percentile'. This is the value that includes a given percentage of the sample measured. In this simple series, 22 is the value which includes six of the seven samples and corresponds to an '85 percentile'. Depending on the environment and the degree of safety in the overhead defined, different sites will adopt different percentiles for a single measure to reflect a metric's distribution. Popular values are 75, 80 and 85 percentiles.

The measure selected for a given purpose needs to be selected carefully and consistently. The average or mean is the most popular, being simple to understand and calculate. A percentile is often used to avoid issues of the mean being skewed by outliers.

The spread of a series of numbers in a given distribution can also be assessed in a variety of ways. Given the same series, 12, 15, 20, 25, 22, 17 and 15 and comparing each value with the mean of 18, yields a set of deviations of 6, 3, 2, 7, 4, 1 and 3. The average deviation is 3.7. However, if the deviations are squared and summed and then divided by the number of samples, this yields an attribute called the variance with a value of 17.7 in this case. The square root of the variance, defined as the 'standard deviation' is 4.2. Further, if you choose the standard deviation on many calculators and apply it, it will produce the figure of 4.5 as that is based on a slightly different equation to deal with the fact that the selected values are only a sample from a larger population. So, once again, we have a variety of indicators for the spread of a distribution and the one used should be selected carefully and consistently. The standard deviation is the most popular as it has useful relationships between the sum of the mean and standard deviations related to percentiles. This is discussed in section 4.5.2.

The same series can be plotted as a trend if the numbers are presented as a time series with increasing values such as 12, 15, 15, 17, 20, 22, and 25. The line drawn through the points yielding the best fit is $y = 2x + 10$. This line can then be extrapolated to indicate future values by using the equation and predicting 26, 28, 30, 32 et cetera. This is known as linear regression. Note that linear regression is essentially a method for fitting a line to a series of points. It needs to take account of issues such as potential discontinuities and 'outlier' points which may be erroneous or may be included as valid extremes. The line drawn is not necessarily a valid forecast, but is often a reasonable approximation if the variable is linear and there are no significant discontinuities and minimal 'noise' on the observations causing outliers.

If the original sample values had been estimates of the amount of, say, wine in centiliters in a glass and a separate set of estimates of the amount of, say, port in a glass was generated, the two could be compared. Consider the first set of values as 12, 15, 20, 25, 22, 17 and 15. Imagine that the same people who produced these estimates, produced a corresponding set for port of 4, 7, 12, 12, 11, 8 and 7. These two series could be plotted on an x:y scattergram and again a line fitted to derive a potential relationship between the two variables. This is an example of a multiple regression analysis (with 2 variables) and the correlation coefficients would indicate the strength of the derived relationship. In this case, the equation would be port = (wine * 0.6) -2.6. The correlation is high, with a correlation coefficient of 0.97 and a correlation (the square of the coefficient) of 0.94.

Correlation can be described informally as 'how much of the variation in one quantity is accounted for by the variation in some other quantity'. It is not a measure of direct cause and effect but rather an indication of some synchronization in behavior that may be an indication of some relationship between the two quantities.

There is a lot more to understand about correlation, significance, hypothesis testing, probability, statistical process control, multivariate adaptive statistical filtering and analysis of variance as well as population parameters, random sub-set samples and their statistics and using that to estimate the population parameter values. These are covered in a variety of statistical and capacity management text books and some are listed in section 2 of Appendix D.

It is fitting that a lot of the annual conferences of CMG are held in Las Vegas and Reno. A lot of the underlying mathematical probability theory arose from considerations of the chances of events occurring with selections of 1 from 6 (a die) and 7 from 52 (card hands). It has been said that the theory of probability arose essentially from a simple gambling game played by Antoine Gambaud, the Chevalier de Mare. He would throw a single die and win a bet if he got a six within four throws. He assessed (correctly) the chance of getting a six in a single throw is 1 in 6. He assumed (incorrectly) the chance of getting a six in four rolls is 4 in 6; i.e. 2 in 3.

As most people reckoned the break-even point as three throws (incorrectly) and the chances of him winning were four out of six (incorrectly), he got few takers after a while, especially as he did indeed win on average. So instead he offered 24 throws of two dice to get a double six. He assessed (correctly) the chance of getting a double six in one roll is 1 in 36. He assumed (incorrectly) the chances of getting a double six in 24 rolls is 24 in 36; i.e. 2 in 3. Again most people would initially (and erroneously) estimate his chances as 24/36 and so not a good bet for them, but it turned out in practice that Chevalier lost on average. He asked his friend Blaise Pascal to work it out (around 1654). He did in conjunction with Pierre de Fermat, as follows:
- single die – possible outcomes in four throws = 6 x 6 x 6 x 6 = 1296
- bad outcomes (no six) = 5 x 5 x 5 x 5 = 625
- good outcomes = 1296 – 625 = 671, more than the bad, 52% of the total, good news.
- two dice – possible outcomes in 24 throws = 36^{24} = 22.4 x 10^{36}
- bad outcomes (no double six) = 35^{24} = 11.4 x 10^{36}
- good outcomes = 11.0 x 10^{36}, less than the bad and 49% of the total, bad news.

Apparently Chevalier offered the bet with 25, 26 or even 27 throws but presumably had even less takers. However, Pascal and others became involved in discussions arising from generalizing the case and the derivation of relevant equations. So Blaise Pascal, Pierre de Fermat, Jacques Bernoulli, Abraham de Moivre and others began to develop the mathematical theory of probability.

Introduction to queues
Queuing theory has evolved over the decades, starting from early telecommunication and operational science work. It has been applied to computer systems for some decades and has been modified to address new architectures and approaches to queue handling. Again, rather than

jumping straight into the underlying mathematical algorithms for 'queuing network models' or discrete event simulation which are the two main techniques adopted, a simple example is used to introduce some of the concepts involved. The laws introduced and their application to CMP is fundamental when mixed workloads are running on a given server and there is a need to evaluate performance in relation to workload.

Example: post office

Consider a new case. You are sitting in a coffee house outside a post office. You take ten minutes over your coffee. During that time you are able to monitor the activity in the post office. You observe that during the period of 10 minutes (time T), 8 people arrive (arrivals A) and 8 people leave (leavers L). This situation obeys the 'flow balance assumption' of A = L. The throughput is defined as X = A/T = L/T = 8/10 = 0.8 per minute.

You begin to consider the overall picture as in figure 4.5.

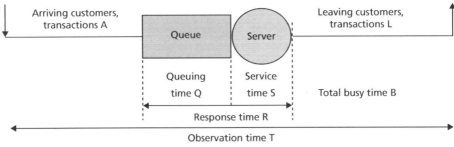

Flow assumption: A = L & Throughput λ = A/T = X = L/T
Utilization Law: Utilization U = B/T = B/L * L/T = S * X

Figure 4.5 Mathematical queuing servers – showing the representation of a queue and its service

You also make a series of observations of the queue length (Q_L) of people waiting for attention (including the one at the single hatch as one of the queue). Say the values were 6, 7, 6, 5, 4, 3, 2, 1, 0, 0, 6 average = 4. (Note that this simple example has significant problems in that the sample size is so small and the observations so few, that the 'end-effects' are high and the arrival pattern is forced to be eccentric). Thus the observed average Q_L = 4.

Assuming your observations are representative, what do you estimate is your likely time to be spent at the post office if you go to get a stamp? On the basis of seeing 8 leave in 10 minutes and an average queue length of 4, you are likely to estimate half the time or 5 minutes. Thus response time R = 5. This assumed the simple relationship R = N/X (i.e. 5 = 4/0.8). This is known as Little's law[25].

---

25   This was first published in 1961 by John Little. The long-term average number of customers in a stable system N, is equal to the long-term average arrival rate λ, multiplied by the response/residence/long-term average time a customer spends in the system R N = λR or R = N/λ or R=N/X in a stable system. Although this seems entirely reasonable, it's a remarkable result, as it proves that this behaviour is entirely independent of any of detailed probability distributions involved in the inter-arrival gaps or services times.

What is likely to be the time actually at the hatch (service time S) and how much queuing (Q_T)?

The time at the hatch for a person is the service time S. Utilization of the service is defined as total busy time B/total time T. U = B/T. But if L is inserted to show U = B/L * L/T then U = S * X. This is the utilization law.

Busy time in this case was observed to be 8 out of 10 (i.e. the hatch was empty just twice in 10 samples). So B=8. B = S * L and both B and L = 8 so S = 1. The average time spent at the hatch getting a service is 1 minute.

The response time is the sum of the queuing time and the service time R = Q_T + S. In this case, we have derived that R = 5 and S = 1 so that Q_T = 4. Also utilization U = B/T = 8/10 = 0.8 or 80%.

Other relationships can be derived.
Q_L = U/(1-U) = .8/.2 = 4
Q_T = S * QL = 1 * 4 = 4

Response time law

Another important relationship, in certain conditions (known as 'M/M/1'), is that the response time is a function of the service time and utilization R = S/ (1-U). This is the response time law. As utilization of a system increases, the response time increases. Consider the two extremes of U = 0 and U = 1. If U = 0 then R = S and the response time is the same as the service time. If U=1 then R is indeterminate/infinity and the system is saturated. A few other examples show the nature of the curve. If U= ½ then R = 2S and the response time is doubled when utilization is 50%. If U=3/4 then R = 4S. If U= 0.8 then R = 5S. If U=0.9 then R=10S. This is shown in figure 4.6.

The M/M/1 notation is discussed below, but it is worth noting at this point that for M/M/N the response time law is modified to be R = S/ (1-U^N)

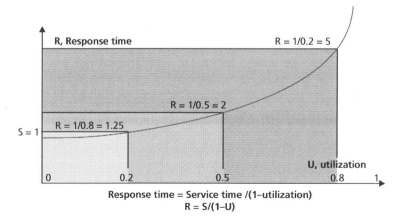

Figure 4.6 Utilization and response time

This shows the nature of the curve in that it starts to increase gradually and then accelerates after a distinct bend like an elbow. The curve is plotted more accurately in following figures, this is just an indication of the shape.

All of this only applies under certain conditions:

1. The distribution of service times has to be exponential. In the case of the post office, some services will be fast (buying stamps) and some slow (getting a new license) and the distribution will tend to be exponential with a given minimum value and a peak of short transactions and a tail of longer ones.
2. The distribution of inter-arrival gaps is exponential. Think of a single transaction occurring at a hatch. Say it takes 1 minute. The time it takes if there are two such transactions within a given period depends on whether they collide or not. In the best case there is no collision and both transactions take a minute each. But if they both arrived at the same moment then one would take 1 minute and the other 2 (1 minute queuing and 1 minute being service) so that the average response time would have degraded from 1 to 1.5. In the general case, the pattern of the gaps between arrivals determines the queuing behavior.
3. There is a large population of people or transactions. The mathematics becomes more reliable once the number is greater than 100 although it is acceptably accurate for values of over 20.
4. There is no priority system or work class mix. In the case of a post office, the queue jumper would invalidate the equations. In the case of a computer, an operating system that supports batch or timesharing or resource sharing will require more refined algorithms.
5. There is a single server. In the case of the post office, this is a single hatch rather than a row of hatches. In the case of a computer, it is a single processor rather than a multi-core, multi-processor or cluster.
6. The queue capacity is assumed to be infinite; that is, every arriving customer is allowed to wait for the service to be provided and never be turned away.

The model described above is known as an 'M/M/1 model' and for this type of model $R=S/(1-U)$.

The operational laws used in CMP can be summarized as:

Response time: $R = Q_T + S$

Flow balance assumption: $A = L$

Utilization law: $U = S * X$

Little's law: $R = N/X$

For M/M/1 models the following is true:

Response time law: $R = S/(1-U)$

$Q_L = U/(1-U)$

$Q_T = S * QL$

For M/M/N models the following is true:

$R = S/(1-U^N)$

The M/M/1 notation was derived by Kendall and is a simple case of the general expression A/B/s/q/c/p where:
- A is the arrival pattern (distribution of intervals).
- B is the service pattern (distribution of service duration).
- S is the number of servers.
- Q is the queuing logic (FIFO, LIFO, RR…) omitted for FIFO.
- C is the system capacity, omitted for unlimited Q (open).
- P is the population size, omitted for open systems.

Some sample values for arrival and service distribution characteristics:
- M is Poisson (Markovian) process – exponential distribution. This is 'memory-less' where for example the inter-arrival time does not depend on previous inter-arrival times.
- E_m is Erlang distribution of intervals or service duration.
- E_k is Erlang k-distribution of intervals or service duration
- H_k is k-stage hyperexponential distribution of intervals or service duration
- D is deterministic arrivals & constant service duration.
- G is general (any) distribution.
- GI is G with independent random values.

Do not worry if you are beginning to think there is too much mathematical detail here. The CMT just needs to comprehend the options and be able to use appropriate tools selectively. It does not need to be able to derive the equations or program the algorithms.

Introduction to distributions

Figure 4.7 shows two distributions. The left hand curve shows the probability distribution function for a 'normal' distribution. The right hand curve is the same equation but presented as a cumulative distribution function, where the values on the Y axis are aggregated. The first distribution is also known as a Gaussian[26] distribution (or 'bell-shaped') with a mean of zero and a standard deviation of one. The well known result for such distributions is that the mean plus or minus one sigma covers 68% of the values, plus or minus two sigma covers 95% and three sigma 99.7%. However few natural observations obey normal distributions and for computers a more relevant distribution is exponential.

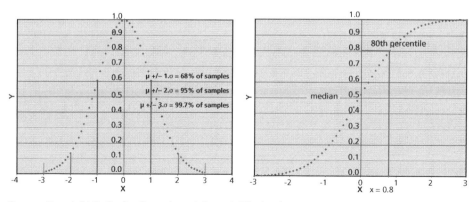

Figure 4.7 Normal distribution function and cumulative probability function

---

26   The equation for this curve is $y = (1/\sqrt{2P}) * e^{x^2/2}$ & m = 0 and s = 1

The left curve is the usual representation of a normal (Gaussian) distribution. The right is the cumulative probability function and is useful for identifying percentiles.

Nature avoids normal distributions, where they are rare. Computers abhor normal distributions where they are very rare if ever present. Most computer distributions are more exponential in shape, with a minimum value for the majority of observations and then a decaying number of observations with lesser values and typically a long tail, such as in figure 4.8.

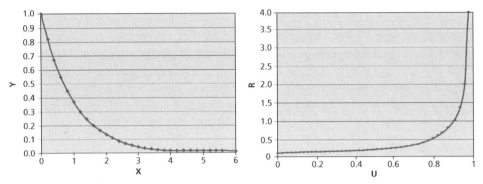

Figure 4.8 Exponential distribution and response time law

The exponential function[27] is shown on the left. The response time law function[28] is shown on the right.

The first curve is an exponential distribution with a minimum of zero and a long tail to the right. This reflects most computing performance results for metrics like throughput or response time where there is a minimum service time with a large proportion of the samples close to it but with a long-tailed distribution of degraded values. This leads to many adopting measures of percentiles rather than means or using standard deviations.

For most computer observations, the exponential function will be shifted by a value corresponding to the service time.

Under certain assumptions, certain mathematical techniques apply and the response time can be estimated by a simple equation. The assumptions are listed under figure 4.5. The response time taken as representing the average will then decay as contention for the service causes queuing delays. The second curve shows the response time law for a single server with a service time of 1.

Figure 4.9 shows that equation again for a single server on the left and a multiple server on the right. The curve in the middle is the same as the one on the left, but plotted over a wider range.

Note that the apparent shape of the curve for the response time law, depends on the axes scales selected. This can be demonstrated by showing the plots for U from 1 to 0.9 and 1 to 0.98 as below. The first rounded curve is for U up to 0.9 and the second is up to 0.98. The perception

---

27    $Y = e^x$
28    $R = S/(1-U)$

of where the 'knee' or 'elbow' of this curve lies can thus be affected[29]. The third plot shows a set of curves with U from 0 to 0.98 dealing with the M/M/N cases where N = 1, 2, 4, 8 and 16. Note that the more the servers (typically CPUs) the better the response times at higher levels of utilization.

This improvement is the key to the answer to an apparently simple question. If an upgrade to a CPU can be done by adding another of the same power or swapping for a new one with twice the power, which is likely to be better, assuming the cost the same? The one with twice the power will roughly halve the basic service time (under certain assumptions) but will not handle much more traffic. The two CPUs will not impact the basic service time (under certain assumptions) but will significantly increase the amount of traffic supported before service levels degrade.

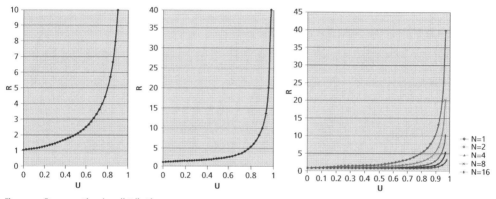

Figure 4.9 Response time law distributions

It should be noted that the above simple introduction is based on very simple configurations. Various approaches have been developed to develop modeling concepts to deal with the real-world practical issues such as multi-threading services, multi-core/multi-processor CPUs, parallelism and latterly virtualization.

Introduction to modeling concepts

This section is designed to explore the concepts of modeling in a little bit more detail. However, it is not a mathematical treatise nor is it intended to be taken too seriously. It is presented in the light of the previous drinking examples, extended to cover a few more considerations.

COCS model

Modeling concepts can be introduced formally as in various learned texts or via a simple introductory evolving model, as follows. The model described is defined as the COCS model – computer optimization client-server model. Or maybe it applies at computer conferences such as UKCMG, where it might stand for 'Conference organizing committee services'.

---

29   It is a long standing challenge within UKCMG, first coined by Mike Ley, to define an absolute derivation for the location of the knee or elbow. Many assume it is where the slope of the tangent to the curve is at 45 degrees, or where the response time is so many times worse than the service time.

Let's start with a simple outline and a key question at such events such as – 'How long will it take on average to get a drink at the bar tonight?' The answer is provided by Little's Law:

Little's law states that:
"If a number of customers N are observed in a queue in a stable system and served in a period of time T and there are an equal number of arrivals A and leavers L, then:
Throughput is defined as $X = A/T = L/T$
Response time, the long-term average time spent resident in the queue and being served is R
Then $R = N / X$"

This requires just two performance metrics, the number in the queue and the throughput to derive a performance time. This is important for situations when response times are not available from the instrumentation.

But a more basic question is 'How long will it take me to get a drink tonight?'. The answer depends on both the queuing time and also the service time (the time spent negotiating the response from the service point for the particular drink required). Little's Law again will give an average time, but my question needs a particular answer, based on my own selection of drink and the time it takes to serve it. Response time = queuing time + service time

Open and closed systems
In an open system, the customers are allowed to enter or leave the network. These are also called infinite population models since there is no limit to who may come in the door, and the actual number of people present is unknown. The requests over the network on a remote client-server system may be modeled as open systems. In a closed network, the number of customers is constant in the network at all times, hence they are also known as finite population models. In practical terms, batch and interactive systems are often modeled as closed systems.

One of the frustrations waiting in the queue is the apparent inactivity of the barman. His utilization is readily defined:

In a period of time T, the barman is seen to be busy for a total time B.
There are L leavers in the period and throughput is defined as $X = L/T$
Utilization is defined as $U = B/T$
Mean service time at the bar is defined as $S = B/L$ and the rate of service = $1/S$ and the barman is busy for X.S of the total time
But $U = B/T$ and B/T is the same as $(B/L) . (L/T)$ thus $U = S. X$
That is the utilization law: server utilization, $U = S.X$

Multiple server model
The model discussed so far is based on a simple single server, but modern techniques apply in some hotels, where a separate server is used to take the money at the till. Or even to have two separate tables with pre-poured wine and beer with a front man taking the request, providing the result and collecting a token on completion. So the model has to show the network of these multiple devices, each with their separate queues.

The flows of customers between different servers in a network are governed by the Forced Flow Law. Assume that in an observed interval, 10 customers are served and there are 30 less bottles on the beer table and 20 less on the wine. The system throughput is 10 and the individual servers have throughputs of 30 and 20.

Each transaction has a visit count of 3 beers and 2 wines and each throughput can be expressed as the visit count times the system throughput.

> Forced flow law: The throughput for any device is found by multiplying the throughput for the system by the number of requests at that device.

Another case of multiple servers is where there is a single queue but multiple servers, called for example M/M/4, as in many post offices or quad-processor machines. Forced flow is not relevant here – but then this model is not used in many bars (perhaps sadly, for the smaller of us).

The main factor not considered so far, is the most enjoyable. The 'drink time' or 'think' time is independent of any contention and is determined only by the residence time at the particular consumer. This can be represented in a model by a 'delay server' where each customer has their own server and so there is no competition for service.

Multi-class model
The model, so far, assumes the barman makes no distinction between the customers, but life isn't like that. There is a need for a multi-class model to introduce priorities: committee members have special rights to submit priority interrupts and get better treatment. First-time delegates don't know the rules of the game and are second class citizens by definition, getting serviced on a time-sharing basis. The main body of experienced delegates works through the normal interactive systems. Bulk deliveries of replenishment stock tend to be actioned in batch well in advance of the busy time (hopefully).

So multi-class modeling is necessary for the different levels of service and the scheduling algorithm used by the particular barman. The scheduling algorithms used can vary, with the main ones being:
- **'First come first served (or First in first out – FIFO)'** is the most democratic (and applies to disks).
- **'Round Robin'** is the methodical service at each service delivery point in turn for a given interval [and applies to Unix processing] and can be extended to cater for processor sharing by reducing the service interval to a very short time so that each customer is processed effectively at once and gets a fraction of the server.
- **'Shortest services first'** (such house wines already poured), or 'shortest remaining time to completion first' (such as those proffering exact change).
- **'Last come first served'**, with pre-emptive resume (where the previous customer already being serviced is abandoned) only seems to apply when I'm already in the queue.

Computer modeling also caters for the high profile demand that always gets its request in first – (especially when I'm in the queue) – for a genuine emergency (system interrupt).

Model solution methods

These problems can be solved using convolution, mean value analysis, decomposition and aggregation, and other mathematical techniques and are 'exact and efficient' when applied to the models which can be reduced to a 'solvable form' (that is, product form models). These terms are all within the mathematical vocabulary and typically well described within Wikipedia. But in real life there are detailed practical variables that impact on the situation, such that pursuing extensive mathematical solutions can be counter-acted by more simple approaches.

Consider the barman and his stock of immediately available services (such as beer and house wine) but with more specialized drinks in the cellars – with maybe different cellars for different wines and vintages. So when there are requests for a specific fortified wine such as Madeira then the barman has to decide which cellar may have it, and the service time taken depends on the level of his expert knowledge and the efficiency of the path length taken to find the bottle.

Some people like to model the service time in great detail – the time taken to lift the glass from the rack, to pull the lever or open the bottle, to fill the glass, to push back the lever or recork the bottle, to wipe off any spillage or froth and the time to push the glass across the hatch – followed by all the detail of the end of transaction negotiation, with passing of tokens and updating of registers.

However, all this detail is often unnecessary, since the mean time to serve a glass of wine or pint of beer is not so variable and is dominated by the pouring time and final negotiations. So the model could simply reflect these two functions and remain within say 10% (or better) tolerance accuracy.

Workload components

Resource demands and arrival rates tend to be highly variable – but can readily be grouped based on type, for example. The arrival rate is related to the percentage of the population concerned and also to their drinking time (also known as 'think-type time'). The number of visits to each server is also a significant variable. Beer drinkers have a high arrival rate, high visit count and a short service time. Wine and spirit drinkers have a lower arrival rate, lower visit count and a longer service time.

If think-type/drinking time = TTT and response time = R and number of delegates = N then the throughput is the number of delegates divided by the response time plus the think-type/drinking time.

$$X = N/(R + TTT)$$

Returning to the question of the manning of the bar, different bars use different systems to try to add value to their services. Some just stick to one very efficient and friendly processor of requests. Some add a second, who may work beside the first in an equal way sharing the load, or one may take the requests and feed some on to the other. Some add a second, but it is only loosely coupled to the first by, say, a fast hatch between two adjacent bars. Some have a whole row working side by side, with all requests at the bar decomposed into single drink requests to enable parallel working – and some massively parallel processing where 64 or even 128 barmen work side by side. That's what we call a bar – and perhaps the way to the future.

Client-server and n-tier systems

But nowadays, more exotic techniques have evolved, known as client-server and n-tier systems. The local network of a group of friends at a single table, with a crude but effective communications mechanism (talking), can make their requests to a single point (which should be the largest client to ensure the best service at the hatch, but tends to be the smallest because nobody wants to waste time on overheads like going to the bar). This end-terminal server can then make of requests at the bar. If there is a single hatch, he has to wait for each request to be serviced. But if there is more than one server at the bar, and he can communicate with them, he can multi-program his demands. The bar has only a certain amount it can provide locally, and has to send off requests to the cellar for other functions. Fino sherry requests, for example, may require a request to a remote server in a central wine cellar.

The problem comes with the detail of networking to be modeled. The communications between the drinkers on the table, and the time it takes them to allocate the drinks once centrally received are negligible in the overall picture. But the communications between the end terminal server and the main processing server and the time between the main server and necessary accesses to its master cellar (or different cellars with wines, spirits, fortified wines et cetera) are a significant part of the total service time.

So the answer to the question is now: response time = time in network to joining queue + time in queue + service time + time in network to close.

However, the service time is now more complex too, since it incorporates the server's own processing time and also the time of further server demands' responses. The further server demands are those where access is made to remote cellar(s) whose response time also consists of network delay, queue delay and processing time. These more complex situations can be modeled using combinations of established mathematical techniques such as convolution[30] and Laplace transforms[31].

Various mathematical approaches have been developed to address the issues concerned with parallel processing and with virtual machines. Equally, given the complexity of end-to-end architectures, many solutions are now based on simpler approaches to give less accurate analyses which are, nonetheless, more than adequate for business decision support. These are mostly aimed at providing rapid answers on an automatic basis that can be readily applied to a large number of servers. One of the factors in adding more processors to a server is governed by the parallelism of the processes being run and is defined by Amdahl's law.

---

30   *Convolution* is a mathematical operation on two functions, producing a third function that is typically viewed as a modified version of one of the original functions. Convolution is similar to cross-correlation. It has applications that include statistics, signal processing, electrical engineering, and differential equations.

31   The *Laplace transform* is one of the best known and most widely used integral transforms, perhaps second only to the Fourier transform in its utility in solving physical problems. It is commonly used to produce an easily solvable algebraic equation from an linear ordinary differential equation. It has applications that include mathematics, physics, electrical engineering and probability theory.

Amdahl's law is used when you are considering the benefits of adding more processors to a machine. If only a portion P of the process to be run can be made parallel, then the limit of throughput improvement is $1/(1-P)$. If the impact of using parallelism is to make the parallel portion run faster by a factor of S (the speedup), then the overall improvement is $1/((1-P)+P/S)$

This demonstrates an example of the law of diminishing returns as each new processor added to the system will add less usable power than the previous one and the speedup ratio will eventually limit as above.

However, this is not the place to extend the discussion of underlying laws and techniques in greater detail, or to identify the boundary conditions for applicability or other mathematical considerations.

4.2.7 Application sizing

Application sizing is the forecasting of application resource requirements before the service has been developed or fully tested. This activity relates primarily to the introduction of major new services, although major application revision releases should also be addressed. It requires significant cooperation between development, testing and capacity management. It is also related to the main activities under what is often used as an umbrella title of performance assurance: Software performance engineering[32] (SPE, or sometimes just referred to as 'performance engineering'), performance testing and trials.

This topic is best introduced by an extract from the ITIL V2 book, quality management for IT services: "Quality must be built in. Some aspects of service quality can be improved after implementation. Others, particularly aspects such as reliability and maintainability of applications software, rely on quality being 'built in', since an attempt to add it at a later stage is in effect redesign and redevelopment, normally at a much higher cost than the original development."

This applies equally to performance aspects. Although application sizing is a well recognized discipline, there are factors affecting its adoption. Application development is less often in-house and increasingly bought-in via a package or outsourced to others (maybe off-shore) to specify, code, test and implement. There is thus less local expertise or awareness of the detail of the development and domain knowledge required to action application sizing.

The primary objective of application sizing is to estimate the resource requirements to support a new or changed application, to ensure that it meets its required service levels. To achieve this, application sizing has to be an integral part of the applications life cycle, preferably incorporated within a development practice such as SSADM[33] or documented requirements exploiting use case scenarios[34].

---

32   This phrase was coined and described in the authoritative books on the subject written by Dr Connie Smith.
33   SSADM Structured Systems Analysis and Design Method (SSADM) is a rigorous document-based waterfall systems approach to the analysis and design of information systems produced for the CCTA; now somewhat superseded by more contemporary rapid application development methods such as the scrum and sprint approach in the agile Dynamic Systems Development Method (DSDM).
34   Use case and use case scenarios were first introduced in 1986 to specify functional software requirements by Ivar Jacobson, who also was a major contributor in the development of the Universal Modeling Language (UML) and Rational Unified Process (RUP).

This is more difficult when the application is not developed in-house. There is an increasing use of packages from major suppliers, on which a single site has limited influence or access. Also, other factors decrease the local knowledge and control of the application itself. As well as the major packages, a lot of software is bought-in from software houses where again there is limited access.

No matter which application development route is adopted, there is a high failure rate in systems implementation with many applications having a life of less than two years. By pursuing good practice in this area some performance disasters can be avoided.

Performance assurance for applications is the technique for avoiding performance disasters when a new or greatly changed application is launched into production.
During the initial systems analysis and design the required service levels should be specified. It is much easier and less expensive if the application design considers the required service levels as early as possible in the development project. Similarly, the resilience aspects that may be necessary should be built into the design of a new application.

The sizing of the application should be refined as the development project progresses. The use of modeling can be used within the application sizing activity.
When purchasing packages from external suppliers it is just as important to understand the resource requirements needed to support the application. As this may be difficult to obtain form the supplier, it is beneficial to gain an understanding from other customers of the product or to undertake performance benchmarks or application trials.

Performance engineering is a technique to size the anticipated application resource requirements from the logical specification. It is a difficult practice requiring a significant amount of expertise. It is often embodied within a knowledge based information system (KBIS) solution, with specific knowledge for the target domain operating system and RDBMS such as likely IO cache hit ratios, file handling overheads, disk index navigation and so on. It is written about by Dr Connie Smith and others. It is most relevant where the application is in-house, critical to the business and has a long development timescale for a major new implementation.

It is usually recognized that the earlier performance can be considered in the design phase, the less likely there will be performance problems. However, the exact point in the development lifecycle where performance is addressed varies significantly between sites. In a few mature sites, the interface is such that performance metrics are estimated in the earliest stages and refined as the service moves through the steps from design through to testing. The early estimates can be derived by comparison with existing applications, or at the least, assessments of the likely number of users, degree of computation involved, levels of traffic, sizes of databases and so on. In many sites, the first practical point to collect information is in advanced testing such as quality assurance or a test lab prior to production roll-out. In the worst cases, it is left until the first pilot site with all the associated risks of poor performance. In the best cases, some assessment of a new architecture may be derived from observations at other sites of the workload or settings used to control the main parameters available. Such professional sharing of technical information is at the core of CMG and its networking.

SPE has evolved with a good set of different approaches to support systems that are complicated to model (such as n-tier) as well as approaches to front-end solutions, virtual machines and application server/database performance testing. Some tools have been developed using simulation techniques and some using knowledge based approaches (with a rule base and inference engine). Both techniques benefit from a stable environment where experience and rules of thumb can be developed to a reasonable degree. This applies in particular to the mainframe which has a longer and more stable, consistent experience than most distributed systems.

A major risk with implementing a new application or making significant changes to existing services is that they no longer perform to required service level targets. Many development teams use load testing and analysis techniques to allay some of the fears.

Application performance assurance is outlined in figure 4.10.

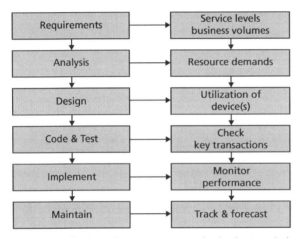

Figure 4.10 Application performance assurance – showing the stages in the development lifecycle and the potential performance issues

There are various typical generic steps in the development which need to be taken: statement of requirements, systems analysis, functional specification, system design, software performance engineering, program specification, module coding, module testing, application performance assurance, system testing, benchmarking, alpha testing, application trials, beta testing, pilot/ reference site production trials, managed availability, general availability. This is a huge topic area and not part of this book. The key issue is the link between development and capacity management.

In most cases, the main link is forged as trials begin. The more performance information that can be derived the earlier the better. This will ensure that performance is always kept in mind. Trials can be adopted at different points in the lifecycle as indicated in figure 4.11 with links to capacity management incorporated.

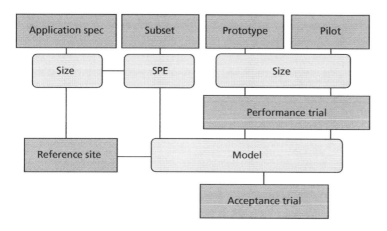

Figure 4.11 Trials – showing the options for trials at different stages in the lifecycle of a service

The level of trials and performance tests undertaken should be related to the significance of the application and its role in business services. Often these tests can only be implemented on a small system with a sample scripted traffic, but in conjunction with modeling techniques, the results of such trials can prove very useful in both assessing likely capacity demands and also in highlighting potential performance problems early.

ITIL service transition describes a range of tests, from 'deployment readiness test' to 'deployment verification test'. From a performance point of view, the range of tests that often need to be added to a quality assurance or test lab procedure are those for load testing, soak testing and saturation testing. These can all yield useful numbers for capacity management and help to avoid performance disasters if addressed as early as practical. It is well established that building performance, like quality, into the design project is much more effective than attempts to retrofit to resolve problems.

Only a good analyst can do software performance engineering (SPE) but only a bad one needs to. That is, it takes a lot of experience of systems and their behavior under a particular solution of hardware, operating system and relational database to relate logical requirements to physical resources. Those who have this knowledge will incorporate it automatically in their design. Those who don't have this knowledge, will not be able to relate logical to physical or do the related SPE either.

4.2.8 Storage of capacity management data in the CDB/CMIS

The capacity management database is likely to be provided by a tool of some sort, be it essentially based on spreadsheets, simple databases, relational databases or proprietary tools. It inevitably contains a huge amount of information for each target machine in the installation and will require its own controls for integrity and security et cetera. An extra requirement on top of the usual list of requirements for a database is a method of aggregation and archiving to ensure that historic data is kept but only at an appropriate level of summary. Thus if data is collected based on say 15-minute snapshots, this may be retained in detail for a month or two. It is likely then to be aggregated to hourly figures and that maintained for a longer period of say up to a year. After that figures may well be aggregated into a daily summary.

The detailed range of data required to carry out the activities described above has to be defined. This definition is unique to each site and is contained in a data model, including a data dictionary and process dictionary.
The general categories within which it resides are:
• business planning data for workload growth prediction
• operating system and technical design features for configuration and architecture
• IT infrastructure details such as network and terminal population
• existing and future workload characteristics and volumes

The range of data includes:
• business volumes from planners, reports
• workload volumes from users, logs, trails
• platform and middleware statistics
• virtualization statistics
• hardware and relational database management system (RDBMS) statistics
• detailed transaction statistics (possibly from the application response measurement standard, ARM which has been somewhat more successful than the previous universal measurement architecture standard UMA).)
• web/intranet/network traffic
• ERP/user application statistics
• service level agreements (SLAs), users, operations, monitors, logs
• new systems – developers, testers, users

The methods for obtaining capacity management data are varied. Some details may be extracted automatically from existing computer held data (e.g. operating system measurement data); whereas others need to be collected manually (e.g. transaction rates for existing and proposed systems). This workload information has to be combined with data relating to the IT infrastructure on which applications are to run.

Figure 4.12 shows a generalized data model which provides the basis for developing the detailed capacity management data requirements.

All of this data has to be gathered and maintained to provide the bedrock for the capacity management practice. The detail for each entity and the elements of data to be collected will vary from site to site. The essential activity is to ensure a well structured information base with as much normalization as is practical. The danger lies in having a formal repository for some of this data and then to have alternative unofficial sources emerge locally which are reputed to contain the 'real' position.

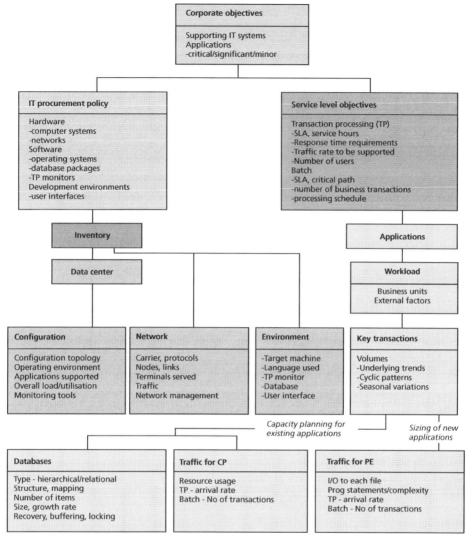

Figure 4.12 Data model of capacity management data

The volumes of data involved are such that tools are required. In the case of some of the data, standard office systems on a PC may suffice. However, once the capacity planning and sizing information for existing and new applications are being addressed, comprehensive capacity management packages are essential.

4.2.9 Capacity planning

Likewise, the activities involved in capacity planning are outlined in figure 4.13.

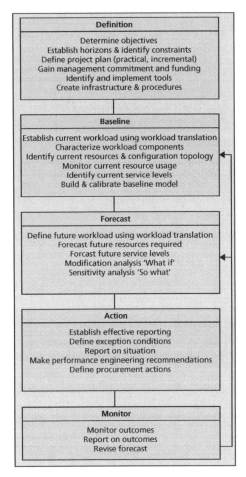

Figure 4.13 Capacity planning

Characterizing workload components is a key step in capacity planning. The activity is essentially one of translation. The objective is to convert the business planners' estimates of future growth in terms of 'number of products sold' to the resultant demands on the computer in terms of 'CPU, IO, RAM, network and other resource demands'.

There may be many steps in capacity planning, as the business planner talks in what are called 'natural business units' to the end-user manager. He in turn may talk in terms of say 'lorries or trucks' to the end-user who may think in terms of 'number of delivery notes or dispatch sheets'. To translate this to a transaction, the capacity planner may talk to the designer who talks in terms of typical paths for specific application transactions. The programmer on the other hand may talk about the detailed level of program interaction at process level. This finally has to be related to the network traffic and services demanded from each device in terms of CPU instructions or IO accesses.

This demonstrates the way raw data must be translated in order to obtain meaningful input to performance assurance.

4.2.10 Reporting on performance and capacity

A key requirement is to produce regular, exception and ad hoc reports on performance in the past, currently and in the future. These need to:

- Describe typical demand profiles – the diurnal demand curve of a typical day for each point in the plan.
- Show a clear and simple picture of demand and how it is to be satisfied.
- Reveal potential bottlenecks and how to resolve them.
- Forecast demand curves having selected the preferred statistic from each diurnal profile and catering for business requirements for each planning point.

This is supported by a range of reporting activities to provide:

- analysis by service, workload, server, resource
- summary and exception reports (all to defined standards)
- comparison of actual and target (requires defined targets and measures/trends of workload volume, resource consumption, and maybe service level achievement and costs)
- ideally (or maybe not) complete coverage of all platforms, resources, workloads, services, costs
- resource accounting to define who is using what and how efficiently
- identification of areas needing attention, focusing attention to where it is needed, bottlenecks, trends, alerts, exception management
- reassurance that targets are being met

4.2.11 Production of the capacity plan

The capacity plan for a service or for a datacenter may be viewed as one of the prime deliverables from the capacity management practice. A typical template for a standard capacity plan is shown in section 1 of Appendix D, with a simple example in section 2. Each site tends to develop its own approach to the scope and format of the plan. Given that the production of a formal capacity plan for any service is likely to take a few weeks (often 10-15 days man-effort), it is usual to restrict it to a given service or set of services and issue it periodically depending on circumstances. A full enterprise or datacenter capacity plan is likely to be a much more significant document and typically be produced as part of an annual budgeting cycle. It has the risk of developing a life of its own as a large document, especially if it is subjected to rigorous procedures such as Fagan review[35].

The list of contents is fairly easy to outline, but the business and technical detail involved will vary from service to service. It is the skill of the capacity manager to provide a meaningful report in the minimum of pages with the optimum level of detail. The assumptions have to be clearly stated and the alternatives objectively considered prior to committing to a recommended proposal.

---

35   In 1986 Michael Fagan introduced a formal procedure for assessing documents to identify defects such as a functional requirements or other development documentation.

4.3 Capacity management control

The control of the CMP is a challenging issue. Governance of ITSM is discussed within Control OBjectives for Information and related Technology (COBIT, documented by the IT Governance Institute) with capacity management controls identified. Experience of Enron and the related SOX[36] controls has led to greater focus on this issue, but it is difficult to achieve more than a veneer of control.

Unlike a process, the function that CMP is doesn't have clear controls like an incident management process has. And controls in terms of the processes used in the CMP are already covered in these specific processes. Controls for the CMP, related to the function, will be found in the achievements of agreed capacity parameters: how well has the CMP realized the targets that were set in agreements and policies. How well has the CMP improved in its performance, according to the service improvement plan (SIP)?

The tools of project management are well established and described within ITIL and PRINCE2 and elsewhere. Clearly defined projects with targets and deliverables, formalized activities, documented roles and responsibilities all help to set up the regime. Establishment of KPIs for the activities itself as well as identification of gaps and risks enable improvement. These are discussed in chapter 8. Calendars, schedules, time-sheets and other mechanisms can be used to monitor and improve progress.

And yet in practice the CMT is often left to its own devices. Historically the job was done at many sites by technicians on a part time basis as an enthusiastic hobby. It has more recently been encouraged to develop as a bona-fide group activity, often under the auspices of an enterprise management umbrella or part of an ITIL initiative promoted by management consultants. If it remains a 'techie' job then obtaining enough 'clout' to insist on business input or getting exposure to decision makers is challenging.

4.4 Inputs, outputs and deliverables

4.4.1 Inputs

There are numerous inputs to the CMP. These vary, ranging from the 'difficult to obtain' business information about predicted workload growth to the 'difficult to contain' voluminous data spewed out from the operating system and database tables.

The sorts of other data that may be available and may be required for analysis are:
- business strategies, plans and volumes – planners, reports
- IT hardware and software strategies, plans, projects and requests
- service information from the service catalogue/portfolio
- new technology information
- provisioning and deployments; changes and operational changes

---

36   Sarbanes Oxley, the act passed by the US congress in 2002 to improve company governance after the accounting scandals at Enron (which led to bankruptcy) and other financial institutions.

- workload volumes – users, logs, trails
- platform or middleware statistics
- hardware and RDBMS statistics
- detailed transaction statistics/ARM
- web/ intranet/ network traffic
- ERP/user application statistics
- other related statistics e.g. telephone statistics for the service desk
- service level agreements (SLAs), operational level agreements (OLAs)
- metrics and statistics from users, ops, monitors, logs
- resource usage – monitors, accounting
- operations, incidents, problems, events, alarms and alerts
- new systems – developers, testing, users
- finance and budgets

See a detailed checklist of metrics to collect in section 4 of Appendix C.

The key inputs can be grouped as:
- resource utilization data (defined metrics at an agreed level of granularity)
- SLA information (availability, DR requirements, response times, batch deadlines, business volumes et cetera – all of which requires involvement in service management)
- application related information such as resource requirements for new applications (gathered from (conformance/load/soak/stress) testing) or technical changes to application or software environment and using application design for modeling to evaluate feasibility
- infrastructure design information with detailed configurations for all resources within scope

The available application workload information is enterprise-dependent but should enable:
- workload classification by business priority, platform and maybe mode of operation (online/ batch, normal/ contingency)
- workload characterization quantifying resource consumption demands
- Business forecast unit (BFU) values (the bridge between business needs and IT resources)

For existing workloads there needs to be a way of grouping users as appropriate and possibly also a tracking of application maturity which may affect resource demands. For new workloads, estimating techniques will be required.

4.4.2 Outputs

The main deliverable outputs from capacity management practice are the performance reports, tuning recommendations and capacity plans. But there are many others and checklists are given in sections 7 and 8 of Appendix C.

The reports required cover a wide range, all related to performance and capacity:
- performance reports
- capacity plans
- workload forecasts
- service baselines and profiles
- bottlenecks and abnormal patterns

- SLA guidelines and violations
- thresholds, alarms and events
- new application sizing
- audit, costs and charges

The types of report required can be categorized:
- internal interactive/review, external intranet/published
- nature of report
  - descriptive, trend, resource accounting
  - evaluative, actual versus plan
- workload volumes
  - actual vs. plan in terms of business units
- resource usage
  - actual vs. plan in terms of who is using what
  - how much the resource is being used
- costing reports
- performance reports, both regular, ad hoc and exception
  - hardware/software
  - service level objectives (SLOs) achievement and violations
- capacity plan (format template as in Appendix D)

Standards need to be established for the reports:
- external report formats based on actual versus plan to give:
  - control and feedback
  - improved accuracy of estimates
  - highlighted abnormal situations
  - an objective yardstick
- actual and plan data must be compatible:
  - same units over same time periods e.g. transactions in peak hour
  - standard look and feel, standard use of colors
  - avoid 3D for 2D, fix scales to 100%, show 0/0
  - standards for report identification and axis labeling
  - using defined granularity
- resources covered:
  - processor, disk, memory, RDBMS, LAN, et cetera

The standards need to be set in the light of thresholds and SLAs:
- scope SLAs and SLOs
  - service quality, utilizations, workload volumes, availability, response, et cetera
  - resource usage – by service
  - utilization thresholds – by device type
  - budgets/costs
- technical: utilization thresholds (comparatively easy to develop)
- service quality: response and availability (comparatively hard to develop)
- standards for output reports
  - pre-defined, objective, quantified

- meaningful, realistic, measurable, relevant
- consistent across platforms, services and servers
- metrics objective and subjective:
  - operational perception of response time and availability of service
  - operational view of service, application, workload, transaction
  - user perception of response time and availability of service
  - user view of service, application, workload, transaction
- instrumentation available for platform and application
- timescales for performance alarms and capacity reports
  - real time, near-real time, regular, exception, post-hoc

For any given reporting framework there are many issues to define. The opportunities for poor reporting and creative statistics abound, with bad practices ranging from unlabelled and unscaled axes to axes without the origin. These have been discussed and many recommendations for improvements have been put forth, such as the consistent use of color in CMG papers by Ron Kaminski[37].

4.4.3 Deliverables

The actual deliverables[38] from capacity management are all of the reports above, but also a number of other outcomes from the work:

- resource usage monitor reports, bottleneck analysis, trends and advice
  - showing actual usage (against plan) to provide management control
  - regular, ad hoc and exception reporting or publishing regimes
  - baselines and profiles
- thresholds and patterns for alarms and alerts for event management
- demand management criteria for new projects, priorities and charging
- workload forecast scenarios (WFS) based on business forecast units (BFUs)
  - statements of requirements for capacity and category
- resource plans by domain/equipment class to meet service demands
  - showing forecast capacity and usage over time derived from WFS
- capacity plans and acquisition plans
  - predicted impacts of changes to be applied at service and business levels
- SLA targets with service level management
  - performance, throughput, response times, continuity and availability requirements
- application design assessments in liaison with SPE/lab testing
  - performance predictions, impact analyses, SLO evaluations
- resource inventory or asset register aspects of CMDB in conjunction with configuration management
  - list of equipment, topology, software and environmental information
  - configuration diagrams complete and up to date

---

37 Again, see CMG proceedings on web www.cmg.org/proceedings. In this case, select, for example, 2003 and Kaminski.
38 Note that the ITIL V3 glossary states that 'deliverables' are only those things that must be produced to meet a commitment in a SLA or other contract but the word 'deliverables' is also used (more informally and more popularly, as in this case) to mean any planned, useful output from any practice.

- designed and assured performance
  - risks minimized as appropriate to the business requirements of the services
- optimum supply/demand and capacity/cost balances
  - all to ensure the best business outcome.

4.5   Relations with other practices

4.5.1   Relations with ITSM processes

The main interdependencies with other ITSM practices are tabled in Appendix C, section 2. This lists all the relationships involved. For example, tuning actions require integration with change management or operations management; capacity related incidents link with incident management; capacity related problems may require capacity changes; financial constraints impact on capacity decisions; testing and development provide information for application sizing; demand management requirements should be reflected in capacity allocations; event management alerts should be triggered by capacity management traps. Appendix C section 2 shows in the checklist the typical considerations for what should happen in all the main relationships and in each direction (to and from capacity management across the interface to the other ITSM practice).

The dominant relationships are with the CMDB/CIS and service level management. The CMDB/CIS and the CDB/CMIS essentially share the same common index and focus on different aspects and attributes of a shared repository. Service level management ideally establishes the targets for the CMP.

Service level management

The ITIL/ITSM goal of service level management (SLM) is described as:

> *"to maintain and continuously improve business aligned IT service quality, through a constant cycle of agreeing, monitoring, reporting and reviewing IT service achievements and through instigating actions to eradicate unacceptable levels of service".*

A service level agreement (SLA) is a written agreement between an IT service provider and customer(s). The agreement covers at least two main areas: the functions that the service will provide, and the periods within which the availability and service level requirements will be satisfied. SLAs are becoming more important financially as more computer services are provided in some form of external charging arrangement, even if it is within the same organization. All the SLAs are maintained in a service portfolio or catalogue, on paper or on a database as appropriate.

Some organizations prefer to call internal or facilities management SLAs operational level agreements, or OLAs; and also define underpinning contracts, or UCs, as those between an external supplier and the IT service provider. Often the payments for service, either in budget terms or real money, are greatly affected by the negotiations around the achievement (or, more typically, failure) of performance indicators.

SLAs perform three main functions in that they provide a:
- formal method of defining service requirements
- repository for performance targets
- contract between the provider and the consumer of services

The performance targets defined in many SLAs are minimal. Often they are quoted from other documents such as requests for proposals (RFPs) where response times may be quoted out of context, in that there are no associated traffic volumes or application path definitions.

SLA verifiability

It is not enough just to state in an SLA, for example, 'provided that no more than 200 sales orders per hour are input by the sales department between 8am and 4pm, the system will give a 'desirable' response time at the user's terminal of less than 1 second on average and 'mandatory' of less than 3 seconds on average and also less than 5 seconds desirable and 8 seconds mandatory for 95%ile of the order transactions'. A wide range of related issues and necessary infrastructure must be in place for such a statement to have any meaning in reality or **any means of verification**. Basically, any contract element should be SMART: Specific, Measureable, Achievable, Realistic, and Time-bound.

The problems with this sort of SLA begin when the application has no relevant instrumentation, as is often the case. Stopwatch measurements are unlikely to be of any use as most transactions will be a complex set of interactions in an end-to-end path of multiple calls to different devices. Assessment of the application in testing is unlikely to be able to replicate genuine workloads to the level of detail where individual transactions reflecting real user profiles can be generated. What is needed is some form of practical measure. The workload arising from the application has to be assessed in some way from the aggregation of the resources consumed by the commands invoked by the relevant group of users.

The need for a yardstick is clear. Some sites pursue the approach of predefined benchmarks or other standard workload mixes for targets. These take a lot of effort to establish and control and do not provide the metrics that are of interest to the actual users of a particular system. They want a measure of the performance of their own production system. This can be achieved using periodic reports from monitoring and modeling techniques which can provide application views.

4.5.2 Relations with Six Sigma

The ITSM practices described within ITIL are just one set of a number of approaches defined within business. The relationship with ISO/IEC 20000 has been mentioned in section 1.8. Other areas such as Balanced Score Card (BSC), quality, audit have also been mentioned. This section will consider process improvement and just one of the approaches in a bit more detail, namely Six Sigma. This is because Six Sigma uses techniques like control charts that can be used to monitor capacity and utilization. There are structured principles on how variations within these control limits can be treated as a special case to be rectified or a normal case to be ignored.

Six Sigma is a well established approach to optimizing industrial and business processes. In industry, it typically assumes a critical measure applies to a mass-produced part and if the value for a particular part lies outside a given tolerance, it is spoilt and rejected. Therefore the objective is to minimize the number of spoilt parts. In business, it assumes the availability of a measurable metric to assess the quality of service (QoS) or key performance indicator (KPI). It looks at the spread of values of that metric. That is, the Six Sigma approach tries to minimize the spread of the distribution of a variable, such as tolerance or inaccuracy or spoilt parts or delays in responses in business processes. This spread is shown by the value of a mathematical expression called 'kurtosis', or the 'peakiness' of the distribution showing the spread of that variable.

The peakiness of a distribution has to be considered in the light of a standard shape treated as the norm. The 'normal' or 'bell-shaped' or 'Gaussian' random distribution was first derived by De Moivre in 1733 and is referred to in figure 4.7. It has a mean of zero, a standard deviation of one and a kurtosis or peakiness of three. The results below the curve consider the defects per million as expressed in six sigma.

The probability distribution function and cumulative distribution function for a normal distribution are shown earlier in figure 4.7. The well known results for a normal distribution is that the mean, μ is 0, the standard deviation σ is 1 and there is a relationship between the sum of these and the percentage of the sample included within it:

μ +/- σ = 68.3%

μ +/- 2σ = 95.4%

μ +/- 3 σ = 99.7% or 0.3% outliers

For Six Sigma, there are levels of 'six sigma' which indicate the number of 'defects' per million of the sample as follows:

6 σ level = 3.4

5.76 σ level = 10

5 σ level = 230

4 σ level = 2,610

3 σ level = 66,800 or 6.7% defects per million

The objective of Six Sigma is to increase the peakiness to higher values with more samples nearer the mean (and hence less spoilt parts or threshold violations). So Six Sigma perhaps could be termed more accurately as 'lepto-kurtosis' as that is the mathematical name for the preferred 'skinny' shape of the distribution of a metric.

Rather than define values for peakiness, process engineering is based on the number of defects for a given population. For a normal distribution the well known result is that about 95% of all samples fall within the mean plus or minus two standard deviations or two sigma (μ +/- 2σ). So for that distribution, around 5% or one in 20 lies outside two sigma. Further, for the same normal distribution, around 99.7% of values fall within three sigma, so 3 in 1000 (0.3%) lie outside three sigma.

The 'six sigma level' is defined as having 3.4 defects per million, the five sigma level 230, four sigma level 6210 and three sigma level 66,800 per million (or 6.7%). A distribution with one part failure in a million has a sigma level of 6.25. One in 100,000 is a sigma level of 5.76 and so on. One in 100 is closer to the rate of exceptions aspired to in the commercial world's processes. So maybe a three sigma level is a more relevant business parameter, but less alliterative.

There is an apparent contradiction between the mathematical definition of having 0.3% samples outside three sigma and the 'six sigma' definition having 6.7% defects outside the three sigma level. This is because the 'six sigma' definition assumes an 'intrinsic drift' of +/- 1.5 sigma in the mean for any practical long-running engineering process. So the value quoted as 'three sigma level' is the same as that given mathematically for 1.5 sigma and so on.

These specific values can often apply to industrial machining processes, but rarely to IT or business processes as in the natural world, normal distributions are rare and in IT 'computers abhor normal distributions.' Essentially, most IT measures have an absolute minimum value and a spread with a long tail, known as an 'exponential distribution' with a 'positive skewness' (i.e. a long tail to the right).

The framework Six Sigma and IT function CMP are often used in conjunction to establish and improve ITSM, despite of, or maybe thanks to, the fundamental differences in character and approach. Six Sigma deals with refining quality against a consistent process background where the deliverable itself is constant. It arose from a traditional view of linear industrial processes and can be used to optimize some capacity management techniques
Capacity management is not linear, is useful for interdependent practices and deals with optimizing performance under change: new or changed services/ applications/ servers; responding to alterations in markets, customer, populations, experience and industry expectations; and taking account of new technologies, architectures and economic environments.

5 Who: Roles and perspectives on capacity management

Peoples' roles in capacity management determine their perspectives of CMP. The main roles are that of the customer (who is paying for the IT service), the end-user of the IT service (in the customer organization), the manager and provider of the capacity management service, the employee member of the CMT and general management within the organization.

5.1 Customer perspective

The customer has a role and responsibility in demand management. Typically, as the manager of the end-users, the customer is able to steer activity and focus requirements to meet business needs. The customer needs to understand the service drivers and how they can be influenced. The customer knows the business drivers and has some awareness of the links from business to service to resources. The customer appreciates the business impact of running out of capacity.

The customer expects to see a clear definition of the service levels to be achieved and at what cost under varying circumstances based around defined SLAs. These are defined and discussed under service level management in section 4.5.1. This currently only applies in reality at the leading edge sites. Most SLAs give little priority to performance and contain little or no realistic detail on performance targets, being focused on availability and continuity. Also, the precise costs and related customer charging and budget allocation varies in practice from 'notional' to 'internal charging' to real 'financial chargeback' in outsourced environments.

The customer needs to understand the implications of user demands in terms of the SLA requirements. In essence, it is a binding contract that provides a given service under agreed constraints for the business traffic. This usually takes a significant amount of mutual understanding before such an agreement can be achieved.

In practice many customers do not have a clear definition of their workloads and the capacity manager has to work from a basis of assuming the current performance is acceptable and it will degrade by no more than an agreed percentage before an upgrade is triggered.

Some customers will request a certain amount of information in regular or exception reports. In order to help them understand these, typically some form of interpretation has to be added manually or automatically to production reports to the intranet.

The major report for customers is the formal capacity plan that summarizes the technical understanding of the current service and the required changes if the assumed scenario for growth in workload occurs. The main requirement is that this report is clear and unambiguous (and preferably short) and not designed to lose the customer in an avalanche of spurious technical detail. Often there is too much information about the forecasting model used or the data model involved so that the customer despairs and refers to it all as 'model twaddle'. There is a danger that the whole practice can become tarnished and branded as 'bogus hocus pocus'.

> The CMT has to avoid modeling in too much detail and reporting in too much technical detail. The KISS principle states 'Keep it simple, stupid'. This becomes more important as less time is available for analysis or reporting. There is no need to drill down into exceptional detail or complexity.

This principle has been identified long ago. There is always a danger of over-analysis and too many entities and attributes being added to a data model and hence reports, especially if some structured methods are used blindly by novices.

> "Entities should not be multiplied unnecessarily. No more things should be presumed to exist than are absolutely necessary."
> Okhams Razor, William of Okham 1280-1349

Equally, the importance of keeping a message simple is well established.

> "The ability to simplify means to eliminate the unnecessary so that the necessary may speak."
> Hans Hoffmann 1880 - 1966

5.2   End-user perspective

The end-user hopes not to be involved with any of the service delivery practices. That is the business of the provider. The most likely area of interface is in the definition of workloads and business drivers, where the end-user may be required to log their understanding of workload achievements on a regular basis. In the absence of application statistics, the user may be asked to record such things as a manual count of the number of particular forms actioned per day. In better sites, application statistics are incorporated in the application instrumentation.

The end-user has a role to play in determining acceptable system performance and what are the extreme limits on doing a transaction. Especially in e-business, where the true end-user is outside the enterprise, pilot tests are required. The saying that "the competition is only a click away" is vital in this area, where long processing times lead the end-users to leave the web site.

5.3   Provider perspective

The provider of capacity management is typically the capacity and performance manager (or someone with a similar title) who is responsible for both day-to-day performance issues as well as longer-term capacity planning. Ideally this person is essentially a project leader who understands the detail, as it is intrinsically a very technical activity. Administration of such activity can be related to administering any process that varies from service to service and cannot be undertaken by rote from a pre-defined worksheet.

The provider will be working from the SLA specifications on capacity aspects of agreed services, or from internal policies that are set to enable the delivery of standard services. This means that the provider will be involved in contracting (SLAs), in delivering (planning, execution, and monitoring), in repairing (recovering from incidents), in changing, in administering (CMDB, CMS, capacity database), and in planning and preventing.

The effectiveness of the team is a very difficult issue to assess objectively. KPIs for the capacity management practice can be introduced but tend only to look at deliverables rather than quality. A suggested template is available in section 1, Appendix D.

It is important before introducing such measures to look at the likely impact. For example, if it is stated that a KPI will be based on producing capacity plans on time for all services, then either the team will probably have to increase, or the quality of the plans will be reduced. A better measure might be on producing capacity plans on time for all key services (with some control mechanism to assess when the outliers should be brought into the key area). This still does not address the quality of those plans.

The initial parameter for the quality of the plans might be the number of service desk incidents and problems that are capacity or performance related. But these measures are dependent on a large range of factors. If the number of incidents is small it may be that the application is lightly used or the users have given up on the service desk. If the number is large, it may be that the application has been poorly implemented or the users are not using it correctly or the traffic is more than predicted. The only way to assess which is the case is to use the skill of a member of the CMT to assess the available data. The service desk itself is unlikely to be able to identify that capacity is a root cause of an incident. This is more typically raised as a possibility by a second line of support, calling on the CMT to support it.

There is often a problem in the management of a capacity management team. They are often highly technical staff with specific domain expertise that is in high demand. Thus they are often allocated to resolve urgent performance problems on particular machines or particular projects. This raises issues in their management and it is usually necessary to separate daily administration and optimization tasks away from the capacity management team.

Technical expertise is always highly in demand and the problem is there is 'always time for fire-fighting, never for fire prevention'. Reporting and analyzing without an immediate problem needs good management to ensure the benefit of proactive capacity management is understood by all involved.

End-to-end management of the services is actioned by a multi-disciplined team, with effective communications required between network, application, database and server support teams.

Another related problem is that the expertise of the CMT can be such that a manager has little awareness of the detail of their techniques and can be easily misled. It is best for the CMT manager to be a practitioner. Then the chances are diminished of being mal-advised by a grey-haired capacity management guru saying that some practices are impractical or some domains un-measurable.

Arthur C. Clarke recognized this danger and explained it in his three laws, which are introduced as they can be related to ITSM, CMP and the CMT and the difficulty of gaining the right perspective on technical issues.

Arthur C. Clarke's three laws were coined with due acknowledgements to previous sets of three laws from Isaac Newton and Isaac Asimov:

1. "When a distinguished but elderly scientist states that something is possible he is almost certainly right. When he states that something is impossible, he is very probably wrong." So beware when an aging ITSM guru says you can't manage the capacity of some new architecture, he may well be wrong. Note that Clarke defined old (in the days before political correctness raised issues such as ageism) in this context as "In physics, mathematics and astronautics it means over thirty; in other disciplines, senile decay is sometimes postponed to the forties. There are of course, glorious exceptions; but as every researcher just out of college knows, scientists of over fifty are good for nothing but board meetings, and should at all costs be kept out of the laboratory". This possibly applies to the CMT as well.

2. "The only way of discovering the limits of the possible is to venture a little way past them into the impossible." In ITSM sometimes it is necessary to make assumptions about the limits of a solution in forecasting scenarios just to identify the true limiting factors.

3. "Any sufficiently advanced technology is indistinguishable from magic." In ITSM this is important in that as new architectures emerge, they initially appear to be as magic (consider hypervisors and virtualization) until they become part of the landscape and their true issues, such as overhead, integrity and fiduciary become known.

Arthur C. Clarke was born in the seaside town of Minehead, Somerset, England in 1917. He wrote many technical articles, including the proposition of geo-stationary satellites in 1945, in Wireless World. He also proposed photon power and so paved the way for warp factors in Star Trek. He claims that he did not name the disturbed computer HAL to belittle IBM who had been less than cooperative in some aspects of making '2001'. Maybe he called it HAL 9000 in honor of HP. Note that the HAL-IBM 'one-letter-shift' relationship was carried on by Microsoft when naming Windows NT (WNT) as developed largely by a team of Digital/DEC VMS engineers.

5.4   Employee perspective

A CMT may well comprise a technical team leader and a team of experts who support specific projects or domains. In many cases, there is also an element of a virtual team in that there are few/none with a CMT defined role but many experts in each technical discipline called upon to act as a CMT in some manner. In some sites there may be others associated with the team in supporting roles such as coordinator or administrator, but in most sites the core team is fairly small and led by a single team leader per major domain (mainframe, networks, distributed, x86 etc.).

The roles involved create some challenges for the Human Resources department. It would seem logical to call anyone who undertakes the practice of capacity management, a capacity manager. But the title of manager usually carries other implications in many organizations. So although the members of the CMT are all called capacity managers in some sites, in most sites other terms apply. These were traditionally often performance engineers and capacity planners, some now refer to capacity engineers. However, whatever title is used for the members of the team, there is then the challenge of naming their manager. This is simplest as capacity management team leader. Capacity management manager sounds tautologous. ITIL uses the term capacity manager. Other phrases used to describe job titles involve combinations of selected words from the list of performance, capacity, engineer, administrator, manager, coordinator or other words with local interpretations. The other terms for those involved in some of the related activities also vary but typically include domain experts, systems architects, service architects, network planners, database administrators and so on.

In most cases, as well working within the core members of the CMT, there will be a need to work together with other parts of the business such as development, testing, end-users, customers, service and business managers.

The team will tend to have a myriad of views on their role and effectiveness. The key directive is to address the objectives of the CMP and this can be extended into three laws of CMP, as coined by Mike Ley (UKCMG) with slight modification of Isaac Asimov's 'Three laws of Robotics'.

Isaac Asimov coined three laws of Robotics:
- The first law states that a robot may not injure a human being, or, through inaction, allow a human being to come to harm.
- The second law states that a robot must obey orders given it by human beings, except where such orders would conflict with the first law.
- The third law states that a robot must protect its own existence as long as such protection does not conflict with the first or second law.

These can be redrafted in a minor way to address the capacity management practice (CMP) in the three laws of CMP:
- First law of CMP: make sure you have enough capacity for today, but not too much.
- Second law of CMP: make sure you have enough capacity for tomorrow, but not too much and only after satisfying the first law.
- Third law of CMP: by all means optimize the cost of your infrastructure, but only to the degree the business requires and only after satisfying the first two laws.

5.5   Management perspective

Many CIOs today view IT governance as an iterative cycle of planning and execution with three core goals:
- better visibility and control over IT costs, risks, and resources
- improved ability to meet compliance requirements, harnessing IT to automate processes and controls and managing compliance projects from concept through production
- better alignment between IT priorities and business objectives to maximize the business value delivered by IT

While demand management and capacity management are not new disciplines, their importance is growing in relation to the above goals. An increasing number of businesses insist that IT maximize existing assets, support year-on-year increases in business volume, accommodate the increasing reliance of business processes on IT, and enable shorter time to market for new initiatives.

Four specific factors are driving the move to more effective demand management and capacity management:
1. threat to revenues
2. rapidly rising power and cooling costs
3. low utilization rates
4. declining service levels

5.5.1 Threat to revenues
If IT is unable to accommodate new business initiatives because a data center or other IT resource is already at 100 percent capacity, the results can be hugely damaging to the business. Being unable to provision new equipment can have direct consequences, ranging from loss of revenue to a delayed new product launch. Obviously, these will negatively impact the bottom line.

5.5.2 Rapidly rising power and cooling costs
Modern servers demand substantially more power than previous generations using equivalent floor or rack space. And for every kilowatt-hour you use to power the IT infrastructure, similar energy will be required to power the air conditioning that will cool it and a similar amount will be lost in energy conversion inefficiency. (This is an approximate but valid rule of thumb: power requirements are used roughly one third each to useful power, required cooling and conversion inefficiency).

As a result, many data centers are rapidly approaching full capacity in terms of power. In addition, power costs have risen dramatically. The result is that power may soon be the single largest item on an IT budget and there is an abundance of green legislation on the horizon. The move towards 'sustainable' IT is growing.

5.5.3 Low utilization rates
With an increasing proportion of the business budget being spent on IT, it is no longer acceptable to have assets running well below capacity. Yet experience shows that many businesses typically run many servers with under 20 percent utilization—a situation that has too often been caused by fragmented IT provisioning.

To address this issue, CIOs are increasingly turning to virtualization, consolidation, and the need to use existing assets more efficiently. However, effective demand and capacity management is an absolute prerequisite to successful virtualization.

Not only would effective demand and capacity management have prevented many of the problems that have led to the opportunity for virtualization, it also underpins any attempt to implement virtualization on a significant scale.

Business activities drive demand for IT services. The demand management practice should include workflow and define approvals required to handle variances or unplanned needs. Business relationship managers should be intimately involved as their knowledge of customer strategic plans will factor into future resource needs. Plus, the relationships managers will leverage measures and metrics to publicize service delivery performance or look for improvement opportunities. The demand management practice should reveal priorities for required services and also identify when demand for services diminishes or when services should be retired.

5.6 Project management perspective

Enlightened project leaders seek out capacity management to provide performance and capacity planning information as a tool critical to their success. Others may view the information as potentially disturbing to their timescale estimates and thus threatening. The earlier the CMT can engage with project managers for new applications, the better for the enterprise. If an organization follows change management principles as described in ITIL, infrastructure projects will be subject to the change regime. However, in many cases projects are started in the customer domain, involving the service provider too late to get an optimized result. It is in the direct interest of both the provider and this project manager to discuss service characteristics in terms of capacity as soon as possible.

6 Get there: Planning and implementing capacity management

Capacity management is often assessed as being one of the lower priority practices within ITSM and the implementation of a regime such as ITIL. However, it should be clear that it is an essential ingredient in successful ITSM. It is at the hub of the other practices in that it provides the instrumentation, metrics and understanding to feed key information to them. It does require a fair degree of implementation of some other processes and functions to be most effective, but it does not need to wait for them all to be introduced. For example, configuration management can provide an essential index to the CDB, but any form of asset register will suffice to start with. Likewise, service level management can provide the vital SLAs and targets for capacity and performance. But in their absence, relative degradation can be used as a sensible starting point.

The plan is to move from chaos to ITSM. This might be done for any one of the ITIL practices in six stages:
- self-audit and review current practices to identify points of pain and gap analysis
- define practice statements suitable for local requirements
- identify clarifications, amplifications, qualifications and exceptions to suit local needs
- define practice
- implement practice
- maintain and enhance practice

6.1 Plan for capacity management

Establishing a plan for capacity management requires the adoption of some of the previous points. There has to be senior management commitment, not merely lip service. The CMT needs to have the influence to be able to affect others in the organization. There have to be individuals in the CMT with the understanding, drive and enthusiasm to undertake the technical aspects. The practice, if not already established, has to be introduced in a step-by-step approach with an early focus on valuable findings on a key service.

As part of this exercise, a cost justification may well be needed, with typical cost savings like increased use of hardware or better discounts for planned procurements. Building this case and initiating the practice of effective capacity management is one of the major challenges and is discussed in section 3.6.

There are numerous options for ITIL self-audit available on the web. The next step is to review the current practice objectively, usually by reference to a set of recommended good practice guides. Section 1 of Appendix C shows a set of statements (with sub-clauses) for capacity management based essentially on that ITIL ITSM chapter. Each site should consider these statements and modify them to suit their own needs and then identify the shortcomings and exceptions. This will then help to focus the definition of the required business process to address the gaps and weak points. It will also be qualified by the practical considerations of price, politics, priority and so on so that the level to be attained will be a compromise between all these.

The last three stages above are common to any engineering. First define it (boundaries, interfaces, data flows, and process diagrams). Then implement it. Finally maintain and enhance it.
In practical terms this often amounts to deciding which services may be omitted from the regime (if any) and which services are significant or critical to the business.

Once again six degrees of potential evolution are typically involved in terms of the capacity management activities involved (each organization has to determine at what level their objectives are satisfied):
- Nil (nothing)
- Monitor current behavior and track recent behavior
- Analyze recent behavior and measure pilot implementations
- R/CCM as described in ITIL (the IT asset-base)
- SCM as described in ITIL (the service provision)
- BCM as described in ITIL (the business requirements)

Most sites with any interest in performance at all will implement OS tools for monitoring resource utilization and maybe track some key metrics. Typically this will be applied on all significant servers. The level of use made of that data and the degree of analysis of it varies. But for priority services the results will typically be reviewed periodically. The progression presented in this series of levels is not necessarily a natural progression of maturity over time. It is more a question of assessing current levels of activity with a view to determining how much further some the locally key activities need enhancement as part of a unified approach to CMP as a whole.

6.2   Design CMP

The CMP has to be embedded in the overall ITSM approach. Appropriate procedures, instructions and documents have to be generated to make the practice effective. The organizational structure and individual responsibilities have to be clearly defined.

6.2.1   Six key steps
Six key steps can be suggested for the design of a practical adoption of capacity management practice:
1. Select a practice owner, budget champion and discipline evangelist.
2. Identify core services, servers and resources; capture and collect metrics.
3. Analyze results, review and report on utilizations and performance.
4. Assess workloads and track service levels.
5. Define workload forecast scenarios and model corresponding resource scenarios.
6. Produce capacity plans.

Step 1: Select a practice owner
The first step in developing a robust CMP is to select an appropriately qualified individual to serve as the practice owner (who may in turn delegate capacity management for specific services

to others). This person will be responsible for designing, implementing, and maintaining the practice and will be empowered to negotiate and delegate with developers and other support groups.

First and foremost, this individual must be able to communicate effectively with developers and business planners because much of the success and credibility of a capacity plan depends on accurate input and constructive feedback. He/she also needs to be knowledgeable on systems and network software and components, as well as software and hardware configurations. Ideally he/she will also act as an evangelist for the practice. The role also needs a powerful champion with the financial and management influence to take forward the project.

Step 2: Identify core services, servers and resources to be measured and identify and collect available key performance metrics

One of the first tasks is to identify the infrastructure resources that are to be measured. Which services are important, which servers are key and which devices and which metrics are most significant. This determination is made based on current knowledge about which resources are most critical to meeting future capacity needs. In many shops these resources will revolve around network bandwidth, the number and speed of server processors, the size and speed of memory and the number and speed of disk volumes providing storage. There are thousands of performance metrics available from a typical operating system or relational database management system. The practical approach is to collect many but to focus on the key ones for that application. During normal operation, the collection of data may be constrained to an essential core, with the ability to turn on more detail when performance issues are raised. This is part of a data collection strategy which must be defined with its own overhead in mind. However, most systems collect data and the overhead is mostly concerned with cutting records to disc and retaining larger amounts of data, which is why another part of the same strategy determines the aggregation and archiving policies.

The resources should be measured as to their current performance. These measurements provide two key pieces of information. The first is a baseline from which future trends can be predicted and analyzed. The second is an indication of the capacity available and potential bottlenecks. These figures can be averaged daily for a selected service window and plotted on a weekly and monthly basis to enable trending analysis. They will need to be visited more formally for modeling as appropriate. Modeling is necessary to allow for the assessment of traffic changes causing increased contention and queuing, leading to the identification of potential saturation.

Step 3: Analyze and publish results

The CDB/CMIS can be used to analyze results, assess utilization, review resource demand profiles, identify rogue users or applications or processes (memory leaks or program loops) and determine peak users, sessions or resource bottlenecks. The utilization or performance of each component measured should be compared to the maximum. Note that the maximum usable is usually less than the maximum possible. The maximum usable server processor capacity, for example, may be only 70–80% depending on the operating system, application and the mix of transactions. By extrapolating the utilization trending reports and comparing them to the maximum usable, the practice owner should now be able to estimate at what point in time a given resource is likely to exhaust its spare capacity.

There is a need to publish reports and alerts to intranet or email as required. With the numbers of nodes involved, most sites work with an automatic reporting system to an internal intranet which can be accessed by relevant staff.

Step 4: Collect workload forecasts from users and assess performance in terms of defined KPIs and QoS – relating business drivers to workload components

This is one of the most critical and difficult steps in the entire capacity planning activity. Developers are often asked to help users complete IT workload forecasts. The capacity planning output is only as good as the workload forecasting input. Working with developers and some selected pilot users in designing a simple yet effective traffic worksheet can go a long way to easing this step. Ideally, as part of performance engineering, such numbers have been estimated and refined throughout the development and testing lifecycle.

Testing of new applications in the test lab should address not only conformance with the specification, security and other issues such as not crashing the system. It should include an array of tests in the area of load testing and performance testing. Tools are available for exercising such matters by scripts and the like without incurring the need to generate multiple transaction paths and related traffic. But in practice this is not always done. Equally, application statistics produced by the application itself (if any are present at all) are not often meaningful to the user or the planner. Further, in the ideal case, the user has business drivers that can be reflected in the definitions of the planner's workload components and also the customer has defined KPIs and QoS metrics that can be collected and reported on. After the workload forecasts are collected, the projected changes need to be transformed into resource requirements (typically by changes in the transaction arrival rate for the workload). This can then be used to assess any performance degradation.

Step 5: Model requirements onto existing utilizations, assess spare capacity and consider potential scenarios and their impact on performance

The projected resource requirements derived from the workload projections of the users are now modeled to show the quantity of new capacity that will be needed by each component to meet expected demand and when and how best to map to alternative configurations. Issues of consolidation, virtualization, et cetera need to be taken into account. Also sensitivity analysis and risk analysis considering the validity and accuracy of the source data (i.e. the estimates of workload growth may well not be too accurate).

The results of the modeling exercise need to be summarized and made available in accessible reports. Section 1 of Appendix D shows typical displays that might be incorporated in a formal capacity plan.

Capacity management is not a one-shot event or a product but rather an ongoing practice. Once implemented, its maximum benefit is derived from continually updating the plan and keeping it current. The plan should be updated at least once per year. Shops typically update key plans every quarter or two. The release management practice also uses a form of interim capacity planning when determining resource requirements for new applications.

Step 6. Produce capacity plan, and reporting regime to monitor plan and checkpoints

ITIL describes a generic format for a capacity plan. The emphasis might vary somewhat depending on the readership. Clearly a manager wants a straightforward business case for any recommendations and is not interested in the technical detail that a system administrator wants. For most sites, the outline structure works. Although the scope and detail of that is debatable, it is generally used as a guideline and most planners will produce reports containing a management summary of their study and a recommended action plan. If it is a complex study of a multi-tier application, they may well make use of meta-models to show the end-to-end breakdown of response times. Appendix D, section 1 shows a sample template and section 2 shows a simple example.

There is then clearly the need to establish a tracking regime, usually based on redefining alarms and alert levels in the automated reporting system to reflect metrics of interest and thresholds of concern as highlighted in the capacity plan. These alarms can be used to trigger when that particular service capacity plan needs to be revisited.

The effort involved in these activities clearly varies from site to site and service to service. Assuming a trained CMT is in place with a defined CMP and an appropriate toolset, some approximate timescales can be suggested. Establishing data collection for some core services and servers and creating a capacity database will take a few weeks or months, depending on the level of detail required and the numbers of services and servers involved. Creating a new capacity plan for a previously unplanned service can take typically a few weeks per major service. Setting up a new reporting regime can take so many days or weeks for a new suite of reports, depending on the suitability of available reports and the level of customization required.

A number of stages are necessary to analyze the requirements in detail and to identify the solution such that formalized procedures can be specified. Pilot implementations will finally evolve into the operational adoption of capacity management activities. For the project to be successful, it is essential that a practical, step-by-step approach is adopted. The standard approach is first to scope, then prototype, then implement and finally to review. Capacity management activities need to be developed in four main functional areas:

Function	Activity
System development	Performance prediction
Quality assurance	Performance testing
Service delivery	Performance assurance
Service review	Capacity management audit

The capacity management strategy must be designed as a whole, although there will be different emphases at different sites. There are five inter-dependent stages:
1. Scope project and develop relevant capacity management framework.
2. Develop performance prediction for systems development.
3. Develop performance testing within QA conformance testing.

4. Develop performance assurance for service delivery.
5. Introduce capacity management audit within service review using outputs from stages 2-4.

IT infrastructure is established in a variety of manners in different businesses. There are various descriptions of the roles and responsibilities involved, including within ITIL and also a complete suite of job descriptions right across IT within the British Computer Society (BCS). The BCS also encourages the adoption of good practice and a code of ethics and various levels of membership. BCS and CMG offer extensive training and education options for those in the CMT.

The various functions involved range from application development and testing through to computer operations and network management. These can be viewed from a number of different angles, via the management view, the operations view, the developer view, the QA view, the help desk view.

Figure 6.1 indicates the total IT infrastructure and position of capacity management and its activities within it.

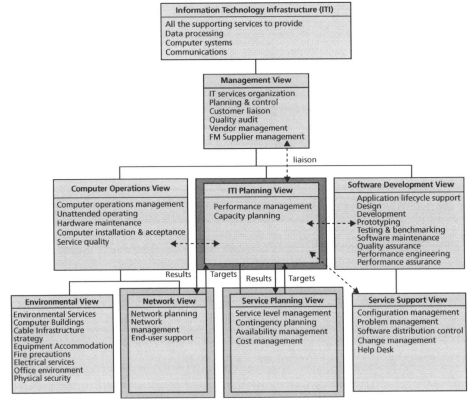

Figure 6.1 Outline of IT infrastructure and different functional views

6.3   Deploy capacity management

The deployment of a new practice such as capacity management will fall into the local standards for project management and then, after sign-off, handing over to regular management.

Once a capacity management regime is instituted, it typically starts at the resource level for significant services with a capacity database established and trends assessed. As the resource demands are aggregated to reflect the demands of groups of transactions, or applications, or services, so it starts to reflect the service level of capacity management. As those services are in turn aggregated and weighted to reflect the business implications, so the need for liaison with the business is increased. Agreement on business drivers and the parameters for demand management should be collected with resultant reporting requirements back to the business. This will increase IT visibility by clarifying how capacity management together with service level management helps the business itself, with reports on key services and dashboards emerge to show the business critical issues.

Ideally these definitions would be top down with business KPIs, workload QoS metrics and service level agreements with performance targets. In practice, they tend to be defined bottom up, taking the current status as the baseline and assessing potential degradation. In reality there few organizations with such performance dashboards, some more with formal performance targets in SLAs but a great number doing resource level capacity management.

The activities incorporated in capacity management vary from performance monitoring and analysis, through to workload trending and capacity planning.

ITIL defines a formal capacity plan contents and scope, but in reality with hundreds of services and hundreds/thousands of servers, most sites now perform multiple 'mini-capacity plans'. There are also more complex issues arising in today's IT systems with the need to relate network and server performance to assess the real end-user experience via 'end-to-end' multi-tier meta-modeling.

Performance assurance will require the adoption of major relevant activities:
- performance management
  - performance measurement, monitoring and analysis
  - resource accounting and management
  - tuning and optimization
- capacity planning
  - workload characterization and prediction
  - trend analysis
  - hardware planning
- performance forecasting
  - future performance prediction
- liaison with service planning
  - service level management
  - contingency planning

- availability management
- cost management
- Liaison with other resource management
  - for example, network capacity planning

Also there will be links as required with other parts of systems management such as for management of incidents, problems, changes, releases and configuration.

Thus there are many activities potentially involved with capacity management. The key activities and their relationships are shown in figure 6.2.

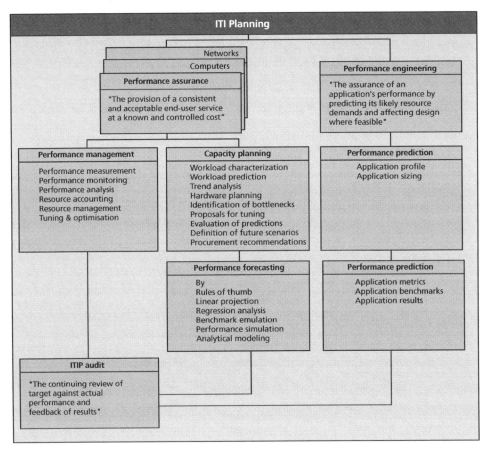

Figure 6.2 Outline of capacity management

6.3.1 System functions

A typical project to assess the CMP will cover the main activities laid out in section 4. These individual activities will be reviewed within four overall functional areas:

- **Development** – Application systems that are being developed may be carried out by in-house development or an external software house using bespoke code or standard packages.

- **QA and Testing** – Appropriate quality assurance procedures for new releases are carried out in conformance testing. The overall requirement is to provide an early indication of likely sizing needs for operational sites. This is best achieved by generation of standard application performance metrics. In order to refine figures produced from the development stages, carry out more realistic sizing at the stage when the total system is available for initial testing or piloting.
- **Service delivery** – At operational sites it is necessary to manage all aspects of the IT service so that current business needs are adequately met, future developments are accommodated and hardware upgrades are adequately planned. This activity is traditional performance assurance or capacity management.
- **Service review** – To provide some measure as to the effectiveness of this entire practice it is necessary for details of operational experience to be fed back. This activity is defined as capacity management audit.

The actual reports selected and project deliverables necessary are a function of the requirements and objectives at each site. However, a typical framework can be based around the functions and processes of capacity management. Then it can be addressed using selected applications from within the selected solution. Table 6.1 shows an extract from a typical set of project objectives, with details that are largely dependent on the size of the company and the frequency of application changes.

Objective	Deliverable	Milestone
Effective and timely performance assurance		
Alerting of performance problems across all nodes	Reports	Exceptions
Effective reporting of the status of all target machines	Report	Daily
Effective advice for all target machines	Report	Weekly
Web presence for performance metrics for management	Web site	Hourly
System-level and workload component level models	Projections	Quarterly
Formal and effective liaison with other teams to provide CMP input		
Product and architectural design	Projections	Monthly
QA and test lab	Projections	Monthly
Network planning	Projections	Monthly
SLA	Projections	Monthly
DBA	Projections	Monthly
Configuration matched to workloads		
Money not wasted on redundant hardware	Projections	Quarterly
Users able to meet business demands	Projections	Quarterly
Financial leverage on delaying purchases		
Reliable hardware plans and timely procurement planning	Projections	Quarterly
Impact of upgrade properly sized	Projections	Quarterly

Maintenance of service levels		
Predict impact of workload growth	Projections	Quarterly
Size new applications	Projections	Quarterly
Improvements in performance		
Identify potential bottlenecks	Projections	Quarterly
Detect and report on process pathology anomalies	Report	Regularly
Evaluate tuning strategies	Projections	Quarterly

Table 6.1 Sample extract from typical objectives for capacity management

Table 6.2 indicates some of the related capacity management functions and their status as of now and as targeted for a typical project. This will require detailed consideration of all the constituent processes and how the organization can most readily change to accommodate them and thus move towards the defined objectives.

Performance Assurance	❶❷❸❹❺⑥⑦⑧	Monitoring done OK – needs planning
Performance management	❶❷❸❹❺⑥⑦⑧	Done against sample – *needs 100% for alerting*
Performance measurement	❶❷❸❹❺⑥⑦⑧	System level – *needs user/command accounting*
Performance monitoring	❶❷❸❹❺⑥⑦⑧	System level – *needs user/command accounting*
Performance analysis	❶❷❸❹❺⑥⑦⑧	System level – *needs workload analysis*
Performance reporting	❶❷❸❹❺⑥⑦⑧	Dumb reporting – *needs exceptions defined*
Performance alerting	①②③④⑤⑥⑦⑧	Not done – *Needs thresholds set*
Capacity planning	❶❷③④⑤⑥⑦	Little done – *required*
Workload prediction	❶❷③④⑤⑥⑦	Some thresholding
Trend analysis	❶❷③④⑤⑥⑦	Some linear assumptions
Identification of bottlenecks	①②③④⑤	
Performance forecasting	①②③④⑤⑥⑦	Not done – *required*
Service level planning		Little done *(only availability – add performance)*
Network planning		Little done (autonomous) – *outside scope*
PERFORMANCE ENGINEERING		
Performance prediction		Not done – *outside scope until much later*
Performance testing	❶②③④⑤	Some done – *needs liaison*
SERVICE REVIEW		Some done – *add more later*
Process engineering	❶❷③	Some done – *improve with new processes*
Capacity management audit		Not done – *much later (once rest established)*

Table 6.2 Extract from list of related capacity management functions

Note ❶❷❸ indicates level of implementation as of now;   ④⑤ target for a typical project. Note also that in this case the scores have been on a scale of 0 to 10. Some sites prefer to use CMMI scores from 1 to 5.

6.4   Compliance issues

The need for compliance and proven governance and control has been a major driver in the growth of process definitions for ITSM. SOX in the USA and Basel II in Europe have been major catalysts for change. Other examples include record retention laws where different countries have different durations for regulatory archiving (typically five or seven years) which impacts storage requirements.

In the case of capacity management most compliance reviews focus on the coverage of data collection, the range of performance reports and frequency of capacity plans.

A growing number sites have successfully undertaken ISO/IEC 20000 certification, with 355 at the time of writing, with 52 in the UK, 50 in Japan, 42 in India, 35 in both China and S Korea, 20 in Germany, 18 in the USA and less than 10 each in 30 other countries. Many of these are outsourcers or others with an interest in promoting their services with as many badges ticked as possible, including quality standards and ITSM standards.

6.5   Organizational change

Implementing capacity management requires organizational change. Often, people tend to resist change, from all kinds of reasoning. Nevertheless, improvement mostly requires a change of the way things are handled in the organization. In this respect, capacity management is no different from any other practice.

6.5.1   Main enablers

The following summarizes the main enablers for successful implementation of capacity management:

- Capacity management should be introduced on an integrated basis with existing functions and other business and service planning activities.
- All application and infrastructure development should include an explicit prediction of the performance and resource requirements at pre-defined stages during the development cycle (typically 'non-functional' requirements such as performance and capacity are elicited in the requirements gathering stage).
- Quality assurance (QA) conformance testing should include specific performance tests to confirm and refine the above predictions.
- Performance management of existing configurations should be extended to provide a clear picture of the resource utilization and performance of business applications, and to provide a historical picture of trends.
- Service delivery should develop capacity planning activities to incorporate Performance Forecasting by using current performance data to predict future performance based on observed trends and predicted developments.
- Service level targets should be established to reflect the requirements of individual business units, and should be used as an input to application functional specifications, as well as providing a yardstick for day-to-day performance management.

- The total performance cycle needs to be closed to form an iterative loop by introducing a review process to compare actual and predicted behavior and action accordingly.

Failure to recognize these enablers will lead to problems.

6.5.2 Six guidelines towards successful implementation

1. Start small

If a site has no previous experience in this area, it is wise to start with just a few of the most critical services and key metrics for core resources – e.g. processor utilization or network bandwidth – and to expand the program as more experience is gained. Define the scope of the program in small, easily incremented steps.

2. Aim for 80/20

Always aim for the 80/20 rule in terms of benefit vs. effort. Select 'low hanging fruit'. That is, identify key services for easiest analysis and maximum return and likewise with key servers, resources and metrics. The greater the demonstrable benefit from the earliest work, the better is the overall perception. Avoid an extended definition stage leading to process paralysis by activity analysis and resulting loss of credibility.

3. Speak the language(s) of customer(s)

When requesting workload forecasts from developers, business planners and end-users, discuss these in terms that they understand. For example, rather than asking for estimated increases in processor utilization, ask how many additional concurrent users are expected to be using the application. Or ask how many of a specific type of business transaction is likely to be executed during peak periods. However, the word transaction means many things to different people and it is necessary to try to find the business driver and 'natural forecast unit' that make sense to the user. This has to be related to application sessions, named users, process commands or whatever to aggregate resource demands to reflect that business driver. Similarly, the business may be able to define KPIs that make sense to it, or QoS measures that they understand. These in turn have to be translated into available metrics.

4. Consider current and future platforms

When evaluating CMP tools, keep in mind existing architectures as well as new architectures that your shop may be considering and select packages that can be used on both current and future platforms. Tools that have a long heterogeneous history with an open data dictionary and generalized import/export are more likely to meet all the likely requirements. Also bear in mind possible changes in corporate directions and their potential impact.

5. Anticipate nonlinear upgrade cost ratios

The costs of capacity upgrades are often non-linear. Some upgrades will be linear in the sense that doubling the amount of a planned increase in processors, memory, channels, or disk volumes will double the cost of the upgrade. But if the upgrade approaches the maximum number of cards, chips, or slots that a device can hold, a relatively modest increase in capacity may end up costing an immodest amount for additional hardware. Also remember that most upgrades to infrastructure hardware resources will have many costs associated with them, such as software licensing increases in proportion to capacity. Sometimes the costs are hidden or difficult to quantify (like the upset to user processes caused by changes to application software).

6. Strive continually to improve the practice

One of the best ways to improve capacity planning continually is to set a goal to expand and improve at least one part of it with each new version of a plan. A new version of a plan should be created at least once a year and preferably every six months. Over time all organizations will experience some degree of personnel turnover so that a single point of failure in expertise is a potential risk. To minimize the effects of this on capacity planning efforts, ensure that at least two people are familiar with the methodology and that the practice is fully documented. Further, check with your customers and users that they view the regime as effective by discussion, survey and measures such as the number of hits on any intranet web reporting system.

6.6   Pitfalls and problems

Organizational change often runs into all kinds of resistance. If a change project isn't taking the right approach, it will run into many pitfalls and problems. This paragraph summarizes some problems a project can run into, and then presents a long list of myths that can also stand in the way of a successful implementation of capacity management.

6.6.1   Six excuses for inactivity

Understanding and avoiding these six common reasons for why capacity management is not always done well can help build a firmer foundation from which to develop a successful capacity management program.

1. **Capacity management is not part of the infrastructure culture nowadays in a dynamic modern distributed IT environment where there are hundreds or thousands of servers and they are cheap.**
   The key fact is that although the incremental costs of hardware have dropped, the total IT expenditure is typically increasing or level, such that the financial leverage gained from efficient use of the resources is as justified as ever. Furthermore, although hardware is getting cheaper, exploitation is becoming more expensive due to higher energy prices and cooling/accommodation requirements. Over-capacity has to be managed as much as under capacity, especially in areas where local autonomy has previously been the rule such as for x86 systems. Also, with so many extra services and hue numbers of servers there is often still the same number of staff (or less) to capacity manage them. It may be that these factors often mean that the nature of the job has moved from in depth analysis of architectures and code towards more practical and automated assessment of performance.

   Many IT infrastructures were created solely to manage the day-to-day tactical operations of an IT production environment. What little planning is done is sometimes at a low priority and often focused mainly on budget planning. Many today still have little formal planning activities chartered within their groups, leaving all technical planning to other areas inside IT. This is slowly changing with world-class infrastructures realizing the necessity and benefits of

ITIL and sound capacity management. This inherent interaction with other ITSM practices enables capacity management to be implemented at its best, but it can be effective in reducing chaos on its own.

2. **Analysts are too busy with day-to-day project activities.**
   The four groups of people outside the CMT who need to be most involved with an effective CMP are systems analysts from the infrastructure area, programmer analysts from the application development area, load testers from the QA area and business planners. But these groups are typically heavily involved with their own core activities with little time set aside for planning. The best way to combat this focus on the tactical is to assign a group within the infrastructure to be responsible for the entire CMP.

3. **Corporate politics or IT directions may change from year to year beyond capacity planning control.**
   One of the most frequent reasons expressed for the lack of comprehensive capacity plans is that strategic directions within a corporation and even within an IT organization change so rapidly that any attempt at strategic capacity planning becomes futile. While it is true that corporate mergers, acquisitions, and redirections may dramatically alter a capacity plan, the fact is that the actual activity of developing the plan has inherent benefits. The main one lies in the establishment of a reasonable baseline reflecting the current position. This yields a greater understanding of the potential impact of changes. Furthermore, the ability to respond quickly in a measured way to changing circumstances is an objective for any 'agile' company.

4. **Users are not interested in predicting future workloads accurately.**
   Predicting accurate estimates of future workloads is one of the cornerstones of a worthwhile capacity plan. But just as many IT professionals tend to focus on their own tactical issues, so also do end-users. Their emphasis is usually on the here and now, not on future growth in workloads. Developers and capacity planners can mitigate this tendency in three ways. First, explain to end-users how accurate workload forecasts will assist in justifying additional computer capacity to ensure acceptable system performance in the future. Secondly, simplify a future workload worksheet to make it easier for users to complete. Thirdly consult with users to show them how to do it.

5. **Capacity planners may be reluctant to use effective measuring tools.**
   Newly appointed capacity planners are sometimes reluctant to use new or complex measurement tools that they may have just inherited. Cross-training, documentation, consultation with the vendor, and turnover from prior users of the tool can help overcome this reluctance. Equally, long-established capacity planners may feel that they can do the job better on a bespoke basis (but maybe not as a reproducible activity). Or they may think that their experience alone is enough, or that as experts they just 'do it' (using whatever freeware tools they can find and spending whatever time they think is justified on bespoke coding) and make decisions that others won't understand anyway. Sadly, such planners tend to forget the importance of both effectiveness and the perception of effectiveness.

6. **Managers sometimes mistake resource management for capacity planning.**
   Resource management involves optimizing the utilization or performance of infrastructure resources. Managing disk space to ensure that maximum use is occurring is a common example, but this is not capacity planning. Resource management is a tactical activity that focuses on the present. Capacity planning is a strategic activity that focuses on the future. Capacity management embraces both. Resource and performance management is sometimes viewed as difficult enough to implement. But the cost justification lies in the leverage on financial savings and efficiency in the use of existing resources. So the best solution is often to do performance management on most services and capacity planning for key services.

6.6.2 Twenty myths on capacity management

The status of the CMP is often reflected by the attitude of the organization to the CMT and how well or otherwise they have communicated the benefits of capacity management. This can be assessed by the prevalence of some common myths.

These 'top twenty' myths are intended to be thought provoking rather than being presented as major obstacles to the adoption or improvement of the CMP. However, it is often some of these negative perceptions that have to be overcome at new or failing sites in order to establish the need for improved CMP. Only then can a formal cost-benefit model be used to confirm the value of a CMP project.

Myth 1: I don't need to do capacity management until there is a crisis.

Reality: It's better and cheaper to predict an issue and implement a solution before it occurs, rather than merely react to events.

The basic goal of performance management is to anticipate resource requirements, to identify difficulties while they are still potential problems and to implement the appropriate solution before a failure occurs. It is a reasonable assumption that the cost of doing the prediction, and actioning it, is less than the cost of fixing the problem after the event.

Myth 2: Hardware is so cheap that performance management and capacity planning is unnecessary.

Reality: Total IT expenditure for most organizations is still rising and still needs to match the business requirement so that there is increased cost justification leverage – and lack of control of procurement obscures the TCO whereas capacity management exposes it.

Furthermore, although unit hardware costs are dropping, the costs of facilities to house, power, cool and operate the hardware are rising exponentially. Estimates indicate that hardware costs represent only some 20% of the total cost of ownership of IT systems during their life cycle. Also, capacity planning can help avoiding incidents such as disk space shortages. Hardware price performance is typically estimated as improving at around 40% per annum. The demand for IT resources is reported as increasing in most enterprises at around 60% per annum. Furthermore although each component may have a lower unit price IT systems are increasing in complexity and size to the point where informal, ad hoc, planning methods are totally inadequate.

Myth 3: Performance management and capacity planning is a purely technical exercise which is all about using the right tools.

Reality: Maintenance of service levels is now business critical to many sites, especially in e-commerce and requires the best of CMP.

Performance management and capacity planning is all about delivering the quality of service that your organization requires. The objectives must be set by management. Investment decisions must be made by managers based on the results of studies. Thus the direction, content and goals of capacity management must be key concerns of management and must also be communicated to the technical specialists. Tools are of course core components of capacity management, but without appropriate definition of local best practices and an effective CMT with other resources to implement , manage, support and improve the use of tools, the real benefits may not be achieved.

Myth 4: Capacity management only needs to be done once a year.

Reality: It is best done as a continual practice of measuring, analyzing, predicting and tracking.

Performance management and capacity planning is a continual practice in which the projection of future requirements is based on monitoring and analyses that take place regularly during development and production. (It is a *continual* practice rather than *continuous*, as it happens on a frequent but not un-interrupted basis.) If you don't understand both the current situation and how it developed you will not be able to forecast your future requirements. Without continuity, performance becomes event driven – the antithesis of planning. Also, special events (such as Christmas) or seasonal impacts are often such that specific planning is required to cater for peak traffic.

Myth 5: Performance management is just looking at results from a monitor.

Reality: There is a need to understand the numbers, identify the implications and report on current and future performance to assure service levels.

Performance management is concerned with the efficient utilization of existing resources as well as predicting future requirements. The activity includes:
- performance measurement and service level management
- forecasting the resource requirements and performance of new applications
- predicting the total resources required to achieve the organization's objectives

All of these activities require an appreciation of the business, service and resource level techniques of capacity management, not just performance observation.

Myth 6: Real time monitoring and tuning/optimization is all you need.

Reality: In order to do effective CMP, you need a combination of detailed monitoring for analysis and aggregated results for planning – real time monitoring is an indication of panic measures which can be avoided by proactive capacity management.

The level of real time that is applicable to systems depends on their timeframe. Many commercial systems can be managed on five minute snapshots so long as the system can be seen as of five minutes ago at any time on a browser. Finer granularity for the purposes of cockpit style displays are not effective for solving capacity/performance problems where patterns of behavior of large populations of users are involved and where changes have to be submitted to a CAB or similar procedure.

Myth 7: I can't do capacity management until I have tuned my system first.

Reality: The two practices work best together.

There is no such thing as a fully tuned system. Fortunately CMP highlights system bottlenecks and simplifies the choice of remedial actions. A good CMP model will allow you to identify the benefits to be obtained from particular tuning actions. Clearly, the CMP model is more reliable once the worst excesses of poor tuning are removed, but such a model will nonetheless highlight the unnecessary bottlenecks.

Myth 8: I can leave capacity management to the system supplier.

Reality: Only if your budget is of no concern.

This approach is only valid if you are prepared to allow a supplier to make your investment decisions for you. Many application package vendors have little or no idea about the capacity management implications of their products.

The explosive growth of information technology and its exploitation, coupled with the problems of expressing corporate and functional growth in physical resource usage terms, often make forecasting and budgeting a nightmare for IT management.

As a result, the activity of capacity management is carried on by a mixture of intuition, observation and measurement. But the need to be seen to be a critical resource in the organization, can lead to a self-fulfilling role as 'supervisor over panics'.

Myth 9: Well performing systems need no supervision or capacity management.

Reality: Good resource managers and domain experts are needed for such systems (and are scarce).

Well performing systems have the correct balance between the applications and hardware. The solution lies in providing effective tools for the resource manager and domain experts to do their job efficiently and to free them to concentrate on improving the service. This calls for good communication between the CMT, resource managers, developers et al. Silo mentality and the protection of territory or guarding 'turf' all need to be eschewed. Information needs to be shared and all sides need to be receptive to each others observations.

Myth 10: Management reporting to the web on a regular basis takes up too much time.

Reality: With the right tools this activity can be entirely automated.

The need to provide regular management update reports is increased with the higher profile and business criticality of systems. Rather than issue piles of paper, or stick colored plots on the wall, most sites now want automated dynamic reports on the web showing the status of any node as of five minutes ago, using a browser. This empowers the CMT and other technical staff to make better informed decisions and assist in diagnostic firefighting, leading to a reduction in overall effort.

Myth 11: Analysis and interpretation of monitor reports is too complex and takes up too much resource and time to be worthwhile.

Reality: Automatic advice and exception reporting makes the data easy to understand.

The growth of distributed systems with large numbers of nodes requires that management reports are exception based and can also incorporate some intelligent interpretation automatically.

Myth 12: Statistical analysis is not relevant, lies, damned lies et cetera.

Reality: The right user with the right tool can readily produce reliable interpretations.

It is very easy to generate meaningless statistical confusions, but with tools tuned to select the appropriate techniques for correlations or regression and trends or seasonality, piles of performance data can be readily converted into real information. Any tool, as with statistics, can be misused. Given the volume and complexity of the data involved, if statistical methods are not used, the choices will be based on perceptions. The best approach is to define a hypothesis and then validate it with common sense and statistical analysis as appropriate.

Myth 13: The volume of CMP data is too much to organize and its overhead is too high so that it just contributes to performance problems.

Reality: It can be controlled with effective data collection strategy parameters and effective filtering and aggregation options.

The key concern for any CMP is not to incur any unnecessary overhead on the target machine and not to impose undue workloads on the network or other servers to manipulate the data. Parameters to select the level and granularity of the collected data, with facilities for dynamic updates are key. Likewise, the control of any data transfers to suit the strategy is important, such as downloading outside prime shift. Once the data is on a CDB/CMIS it is vital to be able to 'slice and dice' at will across nodes, operating systems and measurement periods.

Myth 14: Only a good analyst can do performance engineering.

Reality: Only a bad one needs to.

By the very act of undertaking performance engineering the worst problems are avoided. Thus it is good practice, but it is difficult to find a 'before and after' since this is tantamount to asking a designer to admit to being ineffective prior to doing PE. The solution lies in importing expertise to help a bad analyst learn from the experience of the good, and the good to learn from his peers and so become better.

Myth 15: Money is not wasted on redundant or irrelevant equipment.

Reality: Excessive spend remains undetected until measured by capacity planning.

Redundant equipment not only costs money for the hardware, but also related software, accommodation, power, cooling and operation. The solution lies in establishing and maintaining a well controlled and timely procurement plan to the benefit of the enterprise. The alternative is the problem of trying to resolve performance panics and shorten procurement cycles.

Myth 16: A capacity planning regime is not cost effective.

Reality: This is only readily countered by stopping doing it.

Capacity planning is a business function, currently requiring a level of expertise such that it is undertaken by technicians. The danger is that the technical interest overrides the business objectives: modeling purists waste time on irrelevant detail. There is the desire to try the latest hardware/software available as opposed to staying with what works adequately now.

Myth 17: Capacity plans are too technically demanding to generate and take so long they are irrelevant to the business.

Reality: Capacity planners enjoy technical detail but also have to address the business significance.

There is also a primary communication problem, in that the technician may well use terms and approaches alien to those he is trying to inform. This is compounded by the management view of the role of the technician in that he is seen as just providing a highly detailed service to the operations department. The solution lies in using tools that reduce the level of technical expertise required.

Myth 18: Multi-tier multi-pool, multi-operating system solutions are too complex to manage.

Reality: If control over each node is managed, then end-to-end management is possible.

As client-server systems proliferate, there is an increasing need to measure end-to-end response times and model throughput degradation with increasing workload. It is possible with meta-modeling techniques to address this complex area, given a controlled workload and the ability to associate network traffic with server application workloads.

Myth 19: Network capacity plans need too much time to define traffic and workloads.

Reality: Networks are readily incremented and utilization can be assessed by bandwidth calculations.

The optimal solution lies in automatic collection of a set of performance data by network manager systems for input to tools for effective planning of networks.

Myth 20: Service level agreements need too much effort to establish and track.

Reality: SLAs are often only agreed when the service provider knows he's safely covered.

Traditionally IT managers have concentrated on functionality, usability and reliability and have assumed that performance is something that the technicians will put right once they have made the system work. The results of this approach are readily apparent from a quick scan of the computer press. It is manifest that applications have been delayed or abandoned because they couldn't be made to perform. The service portfolio is intended to identify applications which are not used any more, so that they can be retired. Otherwise, there is the likelihood of many servers which should have been decommissioned not being so. This situation has been highlighted in the x86 world where virtualization projects have often revealed many VMs that are effectively unused.

Many computers and networks have had to have unscheduled upgrades to handle their work. Whilst this policy may have sufficed when IT systems were relatively simple it is fraught with danger as systems have grown in size, complexity and criticality. The importance of defining and managing service levels effectively is now widely recognized, especially in terms of e-commerce.

7 Be there: Managing the capacity management practice (CMP)

Once capacity management has been installed as a function in the provider's organization, it needs to be managed. This involves maintaining awareness and acceptance, operational embedding in the procedures and policies of the organization, setting up internal structures required to get the capacity management work done, and performing or managing all required activities that are incorporated in the CMP.

Capacity management, as a function, uses the basic processes any IT service provider should have in place: contracting, delivering, recovering, changing, administering, and preventing. Being focused at capacity issues, the CMT sees these processes through 'capacity glasses', applying them to their primary interest: ensuring optimized use and delivery of capacity according to external agreements and internal policies. In practice, a CMT follows procedures and work instructions, and processes are just the 'underlayment' of their work. CMT staff will discuss activities in terms of procedures, instructions, and internal standards thereof in terms of policies. Being a function, i.e. a mix of people, process and technology, the CMT works in 'the applied mode'.

7.1 Operational management

The factors involved with operational management of the CMP are essentially those of applying the basic processes and gaining agreements with line management of related areas, setting up communication and meeting structures and then maintaining awareness and acceptance. It is also important to show clearly the added value of outcomes from regular action of capacity management to operational management. Sometimes it only seems to be appreciated in the mind of the operational manager and others after there has been a major capacity incident. Effective capacity management reveals itself only by the absence of capacity and performance incidents and problems and as such can be low in the pecking order for operational management focus.

There is a need to establish regular, formal and informal, contact between all the teams involved with the CMP, both directly and indirectly. The contents of workload forecasts and business demands and related SLAs and priorities need discussion and formal documentation to agreed parties. The circulation of performance reports, exception reports, capacity plans all need to be agreed. The CMT leader has to ensure compliance within the CMT of all the practices agreed to be part of the local solution for CMP.

This can be made all the easier if the CMT has the right balance of people able to do the technical work and also to communicate effectively with business, development and testing areas. So start with the right manager and the right team. Then make sure that they all appreciate the objectives and benefits of the CMP. If the local definition of CMP is wholly adopted it becomes part of the soul of the CMT and mates it with all its related ITSM practices. It is easier if some of the CMT are already well versed in capacity management and feel comfortable with it and the underlying knowledge and techniques involved.

When asked the status of a glass that looks to be around 50% filled, the answers can usually be classified thus – 'the glass is':
–   Half full? Optimists or IT service providers.
–   Half empty? Pessimists or IT services customers or users.
–   Both? Pedants or management consultants.
–   Neither because you can't tell from the evidence presented? Lawyers or engineers.
–   In need of filling? Party maker or lush.

But it is only the natural capacity manager who says the glass is twice as big as needed.

7.2   Positioning the CMP in processes

Being a function, the CMP will potentially use all (relevant) processes in the IT organization.

This means that the CMT will be involved in each new or updated agreement, to cover the aspect of capacity. The service level manager will involve the expertise and knowledge of the CMT to translate functional requirements into technical specifications, and determine quality and costs to be offered to the contract partner. The CMT will also report to the service manager, to provide capacity achievements on behalf of the service reports.

The CMT will make sure that all (internally and externally) agreed capacity will be planned and delivered, and it will see to it that capacity requirements are monitored and reported, and that action is taken if anything irregular is happening.

In case of incidents that relate to capacity, the CMT will have ensured that incident management will deliver recovery as agreed in service agreements. The level of detail required for an effective reporting can be supported by classifying incidents as capacity incidents, or by focusing on the status, history and performance of capacity-related CI's.

Registration of capacity information can be supported by configuration management. The CMT is one of the stakeholders that determine the scope of the CMDB/CIS, and they can query the CMDB/CIS for any information required for reporting or planning issues.
The CMT will be a regular participant in the CAB, in the change management process. Capacity will be a default checklist item in all changes, involving the CMT when necessary.

Most of what the CMT will be busy with, will be capacity planning. This is meant to make sure that agreed capacity is delivered as agreed, and also to optimize the use of capacity infrastructure. Based on information from other processes, like monitoring information from the operations management process, or demand management information that reaches the CMT through either monitoring or service level management, the CMT will seek for risks that threaten agreed service levels, or for opportunities to optimize the use of available resources(which can be perceived as a risk towards the effective use of financial means). As a result of these capacity planning activities a number of actions can be triggered:
•   The CMT can forward an RFC to change the configurations used to deliver the agreed services. This will result in a regular change according to change management, with the CMT

as the change initiator. These changes often will also involve the service manager, who will have to check whether the involved cost is covered by external agreements or internal policies and budgets.

- The CMT can request to adapt the agreement or policy, when the organization is not able to deliver the required capacity.
- The CMT can trigger the operations management process to adjust or tune a system to influence capacity aspects, in cases where this is out-of-scope of change management and configuration management. This often involves capacity-related performance issues of the infrastructure.

This way, the CMT can reuse all basic processes that (hopefully) are in place, without creating duplicate processes. The CMT won't need to teach involved staff new processes, they will only have to discuss the application of existing processes to their primary interest: the capacity of the services, systems, and components.

The CMP is a 'back office' function. It doesn't interface directly with the customer. Interfaces always run through customer-facing functions like the Service Desk, the service manager, the account manager. This simplifies the position of the CMT as an internal force, aimed at managing and improving a specific aspect of the provider's capabilities.

7.3   Measurement and reporting

The measurement of the CMP and reporting on its performance is achieved via a range of controls. The main measures and metrics involved are discussed in section 8. The relevant information about management, employees and customers will need to be used for administrative purposes and will typically be established as part of company-wide procedures. All of this information is likely to fall within company standards for repositories as regards security and confidentiality. Further, most enterprises have a set of handbooks to address these issues and so they are unlikely to be defined specifically for the CMT or within the CMP.

Most enterprises have a combination of controls for different situations. Many use project initiation documents (PIDs) for new projects requiring specific project control. These impact mostly on the requirements for implementation of new projects, but also help define the thresholds for many performance and capacity issues. Many also use a defined amount of time allocated to 'business-as-usual' activities. Then there is the unidentified time that is usually ascribed to urgent panic situations or other investigative or support work. The control of the time of the CMT is usually exercised with timesheets with codes related back to these different projects and procedures. The control of the entries and whether time is recorded in hours or more precisely varies hugely, as does the use made of such time recording systems.

The whole issue of project control is discussed in PRINCE2 and this book is not designed to summarize that. However, some well known lessons that have been published in the past apply to the CMP as much as to any other practice.

Grumlin #5 – borrowed from Parkinson's law: 'work expands to fill the space available (in time or resource)'

In a particular large, public sector site, the time for a project may be estimated by a practitioner (accurately as regards their own contribution) as X and then the requirement is documented and formalized as 2X by his manager and then becomes 4X in the enterprise plan with time for formal project management and QA built in. In the event it finally takes 4X and everyone is happy.

In another (small, private sector) site it may be estimated by the practitioner (again accurately as regards their own contribution) as X which is then redefined as X/2 by his manager. It takes X but is done under pressure and is wrong so it has to be repeated to allow for all the missing features and takes 3X the second time. In the event it finally thus takes 4X and everyone is unhappy.

Grumlin #6 – borrowed from Hofstadter's law: 'Everything takes longer than you plan, even when the plan takes Hofstadter's law into account'.

However, no matter how complete the requirements analysis and detailed the project specification, the project may well take longer than planned. This has been the experience in IT for many decades, even with all the improved techniques in development, testing and service delivery.

Grumlin #7 – all projects are reported as 90% complete for 90% of the time.

Project control systems will usually combine the time spent on given activities with some indication of the status of that activity and its % completion.

Grumlin #8 – borrowed from the 80/20 rule – 80% of the detail/benefit/resource can be gleaned/gained/consumed by the top 20% of time/effort/workload.

When any project or process is being defined, it is always important to assess the priorities of the objectives and the contributions of the different facets under review. Focusing on the key issues in all cases can often yield highly satisfactory results without becoming embroiled in unnecessary detail.

7.3.1 Customer information – service reporting system

Designing and building a reporting system to meet the unique communication needs of an organization requires careful consideration. Most vendor tools offer a vast library of standard reports and facilities to customize them. This will represent a large superset of a firm's needs and generating them all will lead to few of them being read or used. There is also a danger of significant 'parameter bashing' effort to establish all the tuning of graphics and web pages and other local preferences for minimal return.

The CMT needs to apply its own disciplines to its own reporting regime. The information to be used in service reporting will be based on the data logged in the six basic processes. The more the CMT wants to report on, the more this will have to be agreed with the relevant process managers.

E.g., if the CMT needs to report on all capacity incidents, the incident management process will have to make sure that all capacity incidents are identified as such.

Most of what the CMT will be interested in, is monitoring data. This will enable them to plan for any extension, reduction or other change in the infrastructure, or support the request a change in agreement or policies.

Capacity reporting will either be input to and support service reporting towards the customer, or it will be management information for the IT organization. The latter will enable managers to take decisions, in terms of planning their resources , analyzing trends, re-adjusting supplier or platform strategies, adjusting policies, et cetera.

8 Improve: Optimizing the capacity management practice (CMP)

Capacity management is not the first practice to be implemented in an IT service organization. It often follows after the organization has taken on the challenge to implement practices in terms of incident and change management, configuration or service level management. This means that an explicit CMP often will be a new phenomenon in the organization. As with all organizational change, new policies and procedures need to be rooted into the organization's practices, and this takes time and effort, and continuous attention.

8.1 Critical success factors

Critical success factors are entirely site specific, as the selection of which metrics (or combination of metrics) are to be used, is dependent on local factors. In practice, they may well be a subset of the available KPIs, being chosen as they impact on key local factors, be they business results or service desk activity. Critical success factors define the objectives for the outcome of the service, such as optimal performance or a certain reduction in energy usage. In essence, the objectives are reflected by the critical success factors and the KPIs indicate a measure of those success factors. In the case of the CMP carried out by the CMT, there is usually a need to try to determine the key objectives and success factors in the overall light of the company culture as regards IT. For many sites these days it is essentially to do more with less, but for many others, the provision of a highly reliable service is still the dominant requirement.

8.2 Key performance indicators

Key performance indicators are used to quantify and report on the degree the critical success factors are being realized.

The list below shows sixteen typical measures used for the CMP, with key attributes shown in brackets. This is not a definitive list. As with any KPI, each of these can be debated as to its significance, openness to abuse, objectivity, value, quality, et cetera. The danger of using ill-advised KPIs which lead to bad practice merely to meet those targets is well known and has to be guarded against. Likewise, KPIs which do not have a readily measurable, defined, absolute, objective metric are difficult to control. Some practitioners may choose to use, for example, attitude surveys of customer aspects. Others may choose to use ones with complex, relative measures, such as the accuracy of business demand forecast estimates, service traffic estimates or resource performance.

Some discussion of the selected metrics is given after the list. The same list of indicators is given in Appendix C, section 10, with extra notes on possible measures to be used:
- % of agreed target services with business capacity management (BCM) in place (KPI)
- % of agreed target services with service capacity management (SCM) in place (SLA)

- % of agreed target servers with resource/component capacity management (R/CCM) in place (monitor)
- % of agreed service capacity plans are on time (plans)
- % of agreed regular reports in place (intranet)
- % of agreed exception reports and number of apt threshold alarms raised (ticket severities, emails, pager)
- % of purchases not defined in relevant plans (unforeseen)
- % of agreed target CMP activities at risk (assurance matrix)
- % cover of agreed target services with resource monitoring
- % cover of agreed target services with service monitoring
- % cover of agreed target services with business monitoring
- number of capacity related incidents
- number of capacity related problems
- number of capacity related SLA breaches
- number of 'must-have' workloads that have gone missing with no resource usage for long periods (examples include backups, virus scans, defrags and other admin tasks)
- overall system utilization (no excess, with a target defined such as 50%)
- peak system utilization (spare capacity, with a target defined such as 90%)

Clearly coverage is a useful indicator of the level of implementation of a practice, but is it necessarily good to apply it to all services? For example, how well are the caveats defined for the 'agreed target services' and how are ones outside the target range assessed for changes requiring them to move inside?

Reporting to the intranet is good, but counts of the numbers of hits, by whom and for what purpose are necessary to identify some of its actual worth. Reports geared to specific sub-groups or interested parties can greatly increase patronage. For example, while a large retail chain may have many systems, reports concentrating on individual stores or districts enables local management to home in on the subsets that affect them, yielding additional advocates for positive change.

Numbers of alarms are particularly difficult to assess. Clearly, out-of-the box alerts for any system may either generate none or a lot. There is a tuning activity necessary to identify the normal pattern and then an acceptable level of alerting defined.
Deliverables being on time is also a long-standing criterion for some enterprises, although the date of a report, its format or the number of pages is not often a guide to its quality or value.

Utilization is often used as a top level indicator for top level management that they have not invested in idle equipment and yet have enough spare capacity to address likely peaks in demand.

Considering these issues a bit more, let's consider the two issues of using the number of capacity related incidents as a KPI and also utilization:
- The number of incidents that are categorized as capacity related is a regular choice of KPI. It requires that the CMT educate the service desk and second line support to identify such a category. But the causes of such incidents are as likely to be related to other factors such as poor development, incorrect implementation, bad tuning, poor user education, training or ability.

- Utilization is a poor indicator of spare capacity. It depends on the operating system and the application workload just how the utilization relates to performance and spare capacity. Also the key measure is usually related to a pattern of behavior, time of day, seasonality and other factors. The required levels of duplex, hot standby, recovery and related architectural decisions impact on the required utilization levels. Nonetheless, it is a readily available measure that is readily interpreted to say for example that the servers should all be at least 50% busy but not more than 90% busy. Of course, if the operating system allows for workload priorities and uses batch to soak up spare capacity, then 99% busy or even higher is a 'good thing' for IT infrastructure planning, if not for management reporting.

8.3   Risks and countermeasures

The service assurance matrix (SAM) is a table describing the status of target services with respect to agreed criteria.

It is as long as the number of services addressed and as wide as the number of criteria concerned. This tends to make it rather a large report, but it is aimed at providing the detailed information necessary for the technical management of the CMP for all the important services.

The danger here is that there are so many potential metrics being collected that there is a temptation to report on too many. Also, there is a danger of placing too much weight on questionnaires with subjective scores allocated by a non-representative statistical sample population. Or of monitoring readily available metrics without a clear understanding of their true significance.

Complicating factors lie in the typical history of previous IT standards imposed in the past leading to a variety of standard builds for different platforms being used for different waves of applications. Each of these will tend to have its own culture as regards data capture, collection and interpretation and they all need to be 'normalized' across the enterprise to yield a meaningful SAM.

A typical set of risk measures (and their weighting) for a SAM is:
- **indicators (20%)** – business, service and resource level; thresholds set for warning and alert
- **incidents/problems (20%)** – incidence of incidents or frequency of regular problems
- **confidence (10%)** – infrastructure spare capacity for known workload changes
- **reporting (10%)** – Coverage of automatic, regular, ad hoc and exception reports
- **capacity forecast (10%)** – existing capacity models and tests
- **demand history (10%)** – existing CDB history for trend and seasonal analysis
- **instrumentation (10%)** – availability of tools to measure application and impact
- **ownership (10%)** – application owner defined and involved

The presence and use of KPIs and their mapping to business drivers for service workloads and resultant resource demands is a typical top weighted factor (20% in this case), possibly incorporating an assessment of the presence and use of performance thresholds for alarms and alerts.

The numbers of incidents and problems that are capacity related is another popular and highly-weighted measure.

Confidence in the practice and the instrumentation and the history of workload understanding is a necessary indicator of tolerances in the estimates.

Reporting criteria usually include coverage and timeliness of reports and plans.

Forecasting criteria usually include the existence of formal models and performance tests on new applications in QA or pilot trials.

The CDB/CMIS coverage and history act as indicators for any trending.

The coverage and granularity of any data collection tools for target configuration items is another indicator.

The ownership, involvement and attitude survey of the customers and users is another popularly suggested measure but is difficult to define.

8.3.1   Special firm-specific risks

A firm, outsourcer, package or subcontractor may be prone to coding techniques that result in poor performance. Process pathology anomalies such as loops, ramps (memory leaks, disk space increases etc.), excessive java stacks, mammoth disk usage increases, can exhaust all available resources. Special checks can be instigated, possibly some them automatic, to isolate these, raise tickets and try to eliminate them.

IT malfeasance is also often an issue. If there is a complete backup standard defined for the organization, it may require checking, especially at remote sites. Checking for all the likely commands used by the approved backup routines can be built into the reporting regime to try to highlight offenders. This has been reported at some major sites, including retailers and entertainment chains, where some machines were thus discovered with no known backups ever.

8.4   Self assessment

A popular way to start addressing implementation of the CMP is to use a self-assessment or self-audit questionnaire from the web. The OGC have their own version and very many suppliers also offer templates based on ITIL. These can seem simplistic, especially if the form is only used by the CMT. However, as soon as users, customers, IT management and others respond, the views will begin to diverge. At this point many sites will call in an experienced independent practitioner to act as an objective referee.

Assessment of the maturity level of a practice in an enterprise is subjective. Self-audit is of limited use, unless it is applied across departments and different views are pulled together by an objective analyst. There is a large element of self-delusion otherwise. Most members of a CMT may well score themselves somewhere in the reactive/proactive area whereas they may be surprised to learn that others outside their team view the entire practice as ad hoc.

Sometimes this can lead to clever consultants' Kiviat diagrams. These are also known as radar charts or star charts or even spider's web charts. The Kiviat diagram is a chart that consists of a sequence of equi-angular spokes, called radii, with each spoke representing one of the variables under consideration. The data length of a spoke is proportional to the magnitude of the variable. A line is then drawn connecting the data values on each spoke. This gives the plot a star-like appearance. It is used in this case to show the spread of answers from different respondents for various aspects of a survey of their perceptions on the status of 16 quoted deliverables, based on the list in section 4.4.3.

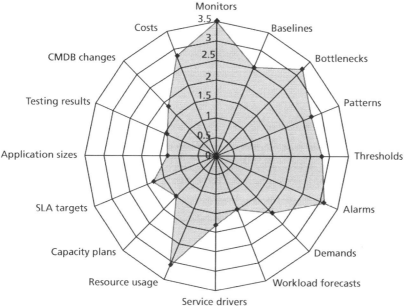

Figure 8.1 A sample Kiviat diagram

In this case, it shows a definite bias towards the resource/component level and current levels of activity (event management as opposed to capacity planning).

However, a survey based on asking people to score from 1 to 5 and then averaging the numbers out to, say, 3.47 is spurious statistical accuracy. Given that the selection of a level to ascribe is somewhat arbitrary, then averaging them out over a random population of estimates is even more arbitrary and might possibly justify one decimal place in the result[39]. A more relevant presentation is a simple frequency distribution plot of the five given values. Nonetheless, using these subjective estimates of levels as a gauge and an indicator for points of pain and targets for improvement within practices or projects may be beneficial and is often appreciated by management.

---

39   The OGC method of assessment only allows average scores to be presented to one decimal place.

8.5   Gap analysis

The analysis of a combination of self-assessments should lead to a gap analysis. Some consultancies will offer full process audit and compare the assessments with peer companies.

The whole approach of KPIs and SAMs for the CMP is an emerging discipline. The sample KPI dashboard and SAM tables outlined above are based on a mixture of experience in this area at different sites. Taking five major studies at particular sites, they can be reviewed at a high level to demonstrate the variety of approaches and expertise:

- A short study at a successful ecommerce site demonstrated the difficulty of establishing business processes when the business growth was such that capacity planning amounted to deciding how many new machines should be added to each pool of the multi-tier solution every day.
- A long study at a telecoms provider showed the situation where a CMT was doing CMP well and ensuring good use of existing capacity and planning well for the future, but without reporting it widely or well.
- A short review of a public sector site showed that it had understood the requirement for ITSM practices and documented proposed ITIL practices in some detail but had little resource to actually do it.
- A short study at a finance house showed that there was the experience and expertise within the data center for effective and efficient capacity management, but less coverage outside their local domain.
- A short study at a retailer showed that there was a wealth of capacity management experience and expertise but with difficult times and various mergers and acquisitions, less staff were trying to do more work on more machines with less money.

Each of these five sites finished up with five very different levels of CMP. Some did very little whilst others were on the leading edge. Reporting on their own activities varied from nil to extensive. But for different reasons, all five required good CMP to provide the measurement numbers they needed and should have the associated CMP control in place. The culture of each site and its attitude to capacity is indicative of the level of process management and control likely to be considered worthwhile.

The ecommerce site felt that non-optimal upgrades were fine so long as the growth continued. A short review of the capacity would remove the panics for performance.

The telecoms provider had the practice in place but had no demonstrable deliverables or external measures of performance.

The public sector site had limited resources that were absorbed into daily performance issues and project work rather than establishing the framework to avoid such issues. A reporting regime would have highlighted this for management.

The finance house had previously worked to a protocol of triplexing everything and making sure that there were always three levels of support for every key component (such as power supply by grid, generators and solar panels with triplexing of each). However, as times change, so the move was towards duplexing and 50% spare capacity based on peak of peak predictions.

The retailer had a wide variety of separate domains which largely behaved as separate silos. Event management and availability were widely recognized, but performance and capacity less so. There was a large development team and the culture was one based on the software development life cycle (SDLC) and project management. The infrastructure was not highly regarded and there were few processes in place to maintain an effective capacity management regime so that upgrades were not particularly optimized.

9 Leverage: Tools

ITIL has developed into a world-wide certification scheme for individual practitioners. It does not purport to reflect experience or expertise but rather the attendance at short courses and passing examinations that are largely multi-choice (especially at foundation level). For products and tools it was felt that there was no such thing as ITIL compliance, since the books are merely descriptive. However, many tools marketed under such phrases erroneously (or implied it with words like 'alignment').

The area was muddied by the fact that companies can become ISO/IEC certified for some of their practices and as this is indeed a pass/fail certification, it can be associated with the in house development practices for a product.

Further, Pink Elephant developed a scheme to 'recognize' software tools (but not to certify them as ITIL compliant, rather to certify the software as supporting the definitions and workflow requirements of specific ITSM practices). A lot of tools very quickly adopted this certification as it became a 'tick-it' item on a tool selection list. Gartner and other providers also set up similar schemes. Recently (March 2009) various press leaks indicate that the OGC has officially endorsed a compliance scheme to audit vendor products, documentation and processes against the published best practices of ITIL (versions 2 and 3), to be launched in 2009.

9.1 Requirements for a capacity management tool

There is a wide range of requirements for tools across ITSM and they are discussed in generic terms in ITIL. This chapter looks at the requirement for tools that address capacity management in particular, though some solutions claim to cater for all the ITSM requirements. Most of the tools are proprietary, but there is a growing number of open source solutions such as osf/dce-dme being adopted. The proprietary solutions can be split into frameworks and point solutions. The comprehensive 'framework' solutions contain a large portfolio of packages, typically from major hardware and software suppliers such as BMC, CA, HP and IBM. A large number of different packages have been generated or acquired and integrated into the family of tools within a framework. Other software suppliers provide 'point solutions' that address capacity management specifically, such as Bez, ISM-Perfmon, Metron, Opnet and Teamquest. A further option is to use packages that enable the creation of local 'do-it-yourself' solutions using open source tools, generalized statistics packages (such as SAS), spreadsheets (such as Excel) or general SQL database offerings. There is thus a wide range of tools that impact on the CMT and are typically seen at a CMG conference.

Systems administration framework with event management and other ITSM coverage
Network monitors, hardware and software sniffers such as the frameworks and various point products
Real time monitors for diagnostic tracing
Performance monitors for analysis and reporting on selected domains, such as networks, web performance, operating system, application, database
Performance data collection & maintenance of a CDB

System faults and diagnostics
Generation of SNMP traps for alarms and alerts
Event management: SNMP alarms, alerts and automated responses
Analysis of performance, pathology and alerts advice guidance
Performance assurance (SPE)
Performance analysis
Performance trend analysis etc.
Performance prediction-capacity planning
End-to end performance measurement tools
Virtualization monitoring tools
Management information system and reporting
Benchmarking, workload simulation, emulation scripts and load generation
Chargeback
Software distribution
Security management
File system management
Account management
Console management (centralized)
Automated operations
Archive/backup/recovery
Configuration management, reconfiguration
Service desk: incident and problem management
Print spooler and batch scheduler
Corporate performance management
Activity auditing

Table 9.1 Range of some of the areas for software tools related to CMP

The features expected of a capacity management tool vary according to the area and level of implementation of CMP anticipated. The range is indicated in figure 9.1.

Most sites will find a use for each of these approaches to deal with a spectrum of requirements. Spreadsheets are often used to assess local workloads and workload forecasts and workload scenarios. Point solutions are usually used by the CMT itself. Frameworks are generally introduced potentially to support the entire ITSM practice.

The timeframes also vary. For long term planning, spreadsheets are often used for workloads and models for capacity plans. For short term prediction, models are used for bottleneck analysis, resource utilization and platform performance. Resource measurement is also used to monitor usage and raise alarms. Reporting mechanisms are required both in near-real time and post hoc

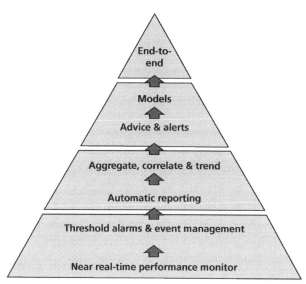

Figure 9.1 Capacity management pyramid of tools

situations. Near-real time performance monitors can be used to resolve diagnostic issues but may generate too much data for a longer term analysis.

The selection criteria vary from site to site but will include the cost/ease of use and scope of coverage of required analysis and reporting functions. Other criteria may include aspects such as ease of use, reliability of support, fitting in with existing architectures, current OS and database and data collection standards.

9.1.1   Data mining

The analysis of data and reporting from it is critical to the CMP. They should incur minimum overhead on the target machines and the CDB needs to have effective indexing such that maintaining an automatic reporting system as well as supporting general management information system enquiries is well within requirements. Batch reports need to fit into the reporting window (typically out of service window). In order to look at a longer time frame, first a series of data has to be mined – that is selected from the database in terms of days/hours/peaks or whatever criteria can be used to select the data that interests you. In order to allow useful data mining, a capacity management toolkit needs the following facilities, so that it is possible to:

- select data across platforms, across nodes and across time
- import self-defining sets of data from other time series
- filter out selected data by date, days of the week, hours of the day et cetera
- aggregate the data over required periods of time
- select the peak, average or 'top ten' or whatever
- select data by parameter – system or user et cetera
- select known peaks such as 'peak customers at lunchtimes' or known accounting pre-deadline bulges

9.1.2   Computational intelligence

Computational intelligence is a phrase representing the following kinds of analyses that are also required:

- trend analysis (linear regression)
- seasonal analysis (Fourier analysis)
- statistical analysis (correlations and significance)
- automatic analysis of patterns of behavior
- automatic analysis of peak or rogue users
- automatic analysis of anomalies e.g. memory leaks, rogue processes
- automatic advice and interpretation of metric values in context
- automatic identification of missing workloads

These tools and techniques allow the exploration of captured data, to identify trends and periodic variations. Other statistical functions should be available at the click of an icon for correlation, interpolation, de-trending, smoothing and so on. Also basic statistics like means (μ,mu) or standard deviations (σ,sigma) should be made available.

Ideally these techniques should be available both as a tool for the expert and as a packaged automatic service with explicit interpretation of the data, explaining the results for any given exception report.

9.1.3   Interactive use

The CMT will need a tool that provides an effective interface to the capacity management data base (CDB) and the data mined from it. This requires a large library of standard reports grouping all the predefined metrics likely to be involved with a particular issue (such as all the metrics to do with, say, disk activity). It also requires the ability for a user to define their own particular selection of metrics from the data dictionary for local purposes. This interactive use is typically required before a reporting regime can be applied effectively to a new range of machines or a new service. Although many sites establish a standard minimal reporting regime, it usually needs enhancing to address the issues raised by a new system. It is via this interactive use that the performance analyst can drill down into particular situations.

Another major aspect for interactive use lies in the need to characterize workloads, define thresholds and identify useful application views across a service or set of servers. These are necessary steps prior to establishing a modeling approach.

The modeling activity is essentially interactive, with the analyst applying his understanding of the configuration, workload and traffic to generate useful models for predicting service levels.

9.1.4   Reporting

Timely and appropriate reporting is a key discipline within capacity management. With the increased numbers of nodes in a typical corporation these days, the performance analyst has to cover more complexity with less time per node. This leads to the desire to have an automatic reporting regime where attention is drawn automatically to matters of concern. Also where the reporting can be made readily available to all interested parties, typically via the web or intranet.

Any tool for performance management, whether created in-house or acquired as a package, must be able to reproduce reports on a regular basis for management purposes. The following facilities have been found in practice to be the most useful:

- The ability to choose 'out-of-the-box' reports, for rapid and simple reporting on large numbers of nodes.
- Facilities to define local reports with user choice of metrics and formats, to complement the pre-defined set.
- The ability to schedule the production of reports, and to specify the time ranges that they are to cover.
- A mechanism whereby reports can be generated without any involvement by the performance analyst (or anyone else), and automatically distributed by a variety of means (but usually to a local intranet).

The reports above also need to be available on an exception basis, so that not just the latest state is available to view, but due attention is drawn to significant exceptions. This requires the ability to define specific multiple thresholds for metrics and also the patterns of behavior that are acceptable. Clearly the balance is site specific to ensure that useful alerts are raised rather than excessive blanket exceptions. The ideal is to avoid multitudes of reports which make root cause diagnosis complex.

Often firm-wide capacity management regimes provide too comprehensive a set of reports. It is helpful to have the report layouts structured to make it easy to go directly to the services and servers of local interest for easy control of matters of local interest.

Epilogue

This point just ahead of the appendices is the logical place for a summary and conclusion of what this book has discussed. However, in this case, the meat of the book may be only just starting. The appendices to this book are not the place where lesser material has been hidden for completeness. It is where a lot of key documents and checklists are presented. We hope that after considering a lot of the generalities in this book, the reader will find some real value in the appendices to help in pursuing their own capacity management practice.

Before the appendices are addressed, it seems apt to review the contents and purpose of this book. Bear in mind that appendices C (Checklists) and D (Capacity plan) probably provide the most 'meat' in this book and each checklist merits detailed consideration in its own right and the capacity plan template and example should help a new member of the CMT produce their first plan. Also, bear in mind that some of the information in the main body of the book should be reviewed and localized to reflect local practice in areas such as the data model and data flows used.

We also hope that the reader has found some of the observations useful and will use this book as a starting point for gleaning more information by experience.

Many of the authors we have referenced, explicitly or implicitly, share the feeling that practitioners of capacity management should share their ideas and experiences to try to improve the overall use of IT to achieve business objectives. Capacity management is an interesting, challenging area to work in and there is always a lot to learn for all of us. We hope that many readers will advise us of their thoughts on the contents, omissions and errors in this book so that it might be improved in any future versions.

We wish you joy and delight in the practice of capacity management and may we all continue to live in interesting times in capacity management, the most challenging aspect of IT service management.

Appendix A. Basic concepts for IT service management

A major aspect and benefit of ITIL is that it provides a common glossary and standard jargon that can be used across the IT service management industry. ITIL terminology is predominantly used in this book.

A.1 Good practice

Good practices such as ITIL, which have been adopted by many, can be used as a solid basis for organizations that want to improve their IT services. A good approach is to select widely available frameworks and/or standards, such as ITIL, COBIT, CMMI, PRINCE2 and ISO/IEC 20000. All of these can be applied to many different real-life environments and situations. Training is also widely available, making it much easier to develop staff with the required knowledge and skills.

Proprietary knowledge is often claimed to be good practice, however it is often customized for the context and needs of a specific organization. Therefore, it may be difficult to adopt or replicate, particularly where multiple suppliers are involved, and therefore it may not be as effective in use.

A.2 Service

A service creates value for the customer. ITIL describes a service as follows:

> A **service** is a means of delivering value to customers by facilitating outcomes the customers want to achieve without the ownership of specific costs or risks.

Outcomes (or outputs) are made possible by the performance of tasks. They are often limited in what they can achieve by a number of constraints. Services enhance performance and can reduce the pressure of constraints. This increases the chances of the desired outcomes being realized.

ITIL V3 has the concept of a service portfolio and the service catalogue. The service portfolio includes all services that are in development, in live use, or retired. The service catalogue represents the services that are available to the customers.

A.3 Value

Value is the core of the ITIL service concept.

*From the customer's perspective **value** consists of two core components: **utility** and **warranty**. Utility is what the customer receives, and warranty is how it is provided*[40].

Another way of looking at this is to consider the following:
- utility = fit for purpose. Does it meet the specification?
- warranty = fit for use. Will it perform, will it be available when required?

A.4   Service management

ITIL describes service management as follows:

Service management *is a set of specialized organizational capabilities for providing value to customers in the form of services.*

A.5   Systems

ITIL describes the organizational structure concepts which proceed from system theory. The service lifecycle in ITIL V3 is a system; however, a function, a process or an organization is a system as well. A definition of a system is the following.

*A **system** is a group of, interrelating, or interdependent components that form a unified whole, operating together for a common purpose.*

Feedback and *learning* are two key aspects in the performance of systems; they turn processes, functions and organizations into dynamic systems. Feedback can lead to learning and growth, not only within a process, but also within an organization in its entirety. Within a process, for instance, the feedback about the performance of one cycle is, in its turn, input for the next process cycle. Within organizations, there can be feedback between processes, functions and lifecycle phases. Behind this feedback is the common goal: attaining the customer's objectives.

A.6   Processes versus functions

The distinction between functions and processes is important in ITIL. So what exactly is a function?

*A **function** is a subdivision of an organization that is specialized in fulfilling a specified type of work, and is responsible for specific end results.*
Functions are independent subdivisions with capabilities and resources that are required for their performance and results. They have their own practices, and their own knowledge body.

---

40   The concepts utility and warranty are described in the ITIL V3 book 'Service Strategy'.

Functions are often recognized as teams or groups, with a specific set of practices and tools. Section A.12 offers various examples of familiar functions in IT organizations.

And what is a process?

*A **process** is a sequence of interrelated or interacting activities designed to accomplish a defined objective in a measurable and repeatable manner, transforming inputs into outputs.*

Processes convert inputs to outputs, and ultimately into outcomes. They use measures to assist control and as feedback for self-improvement. Processes have the following characteristics:
- They are **measurable** because they are performance-oriented.
- They have **specific results**.
- They provide results to **customers or stakeholders**.
- They **respond to a specific event** – a process is indeed continual and iterative, but is always originating from a certain event.

Changing to a process based structure in an organization often shows that certain activities in the organization are uncoordinated, duplicated, neglected or unnecessary.

When arranging activities into processes, you should not use the existing allocation of tasks into an organizational structure as a basis. Instead, start with the **objective** of the process and the **relationships** with other processes. As the definition states, a process is a series of activities carried out to convert input into an output, and ultimately into an outcome; see the ITOCO model (Input-Throughput-Output-Control-Outcome) in figure A.1.

The **input** to a process describes the resources that are used and changed or consumed by the process. The **output** describes the immediate results of the process, while the **outcome** describes the long-term results of the process in terms of meaningful effect. **Control** activities are used to ensure that the process achieves the desired output and outcomes, and complies with **policies and standards.** Controls also regulate the input and the **throughput**, ensuring that the throughput or output parameters are compliant with these standards and policies.

These individual processes are built together into process chains. These show what inputs goes into the organization, and what the outputs and outcomes are. They also provide suitable monitoring points to check the quality of the products and services provided by the organization.

The standards for the output of each process must be defined, so that the complete **chain of processes** in the **process model** meets the corporate objective. If the output of a process meets the defined requirements, then the process is **effective** in transforming its input into its output. To be really effective, the outcome should be taken into consideration rather than focusing on the output. If the activities in the process are also carried out with the minimum required effort and cost, then the process is **efficient**. It is the task of process management to use **planning and control** to ensure that processes are executed in an effective and efficient way.

Each process can be studied separately to optimize its quality. The **process owner** is responsible for the process results. The **process manager** is responsible for the realization and structure of the process, and reports to the process owner. The **process operatives** are responsible for defined activities, and these activities are reported to the process manager.

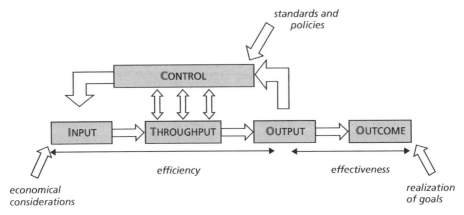

Figure A.1 Process diagram, based on the ITOCO-model[41]

Processes are composed of two kinds of activities: the activities to realize the goal (operational activities concerned with the throughput), and the activities to manage these (control activities). See Figure A.1. The control activities make sure the operational activities (the workflow) are performed to time, in the right order, etc. (For example, in the processing of changes it is always ensured that a test is performed *before* a release is taken into production and not *afterwards*.)

According to the ITOCO model:
- processes have inputs and outputs
- they can be adjusted by means of feedback and comparison against standards
- they can be rendered more specific by conversion to procedures and work instructions
- various roles are distinguished in relation to processes (e.g. owner, manager, executor).

A.7   Process models

The **process model** is at least as important as the **processes** because processes must be deployed in the right relationships to achieve the desired effect of a process-focused approach. There are many different process models available. A master process architecture should be defined before individual processes are designed.

*A **process architecture** identifies the processes and process clusters, their interdependencies and interactions, their relationship to the IT organization structure, and the IT process-supporting application architecture.*

Organizations should use standard methodologies for creating process diagrams. In-house developed methodologies are often difficult to interpret in an unambiguous manner.

---

41   Source: Foundations of IT Service management, based on ITIL V3. Van Haren Publishing for itSMF International, 2008.

The business process modeling world offers various methods to create process diagrams, such as the unified modeling language (UML), the business process modeling notation (BPMN), and the business process execution language for web services (BPEL-WS). Other systems design approaches can be used to create process diagrams such as the CCTA/OGC SSADM or the USA DOD IDEF methods. Figures A.2 and A.3 are examples of the BPMN method.

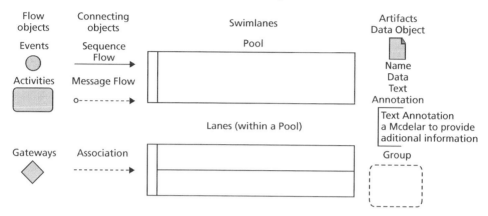

Figure A.2 BPMN elements

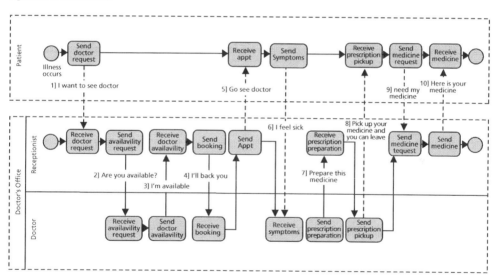

Figure A.3 Example of a BPMN process diagram

When described this way, it is easier to visualize and therefore manage a process. This is particularly true when processes are brought together in a process chain. Note that ITIL does not give much attention to creating these process chains.

An organization no longer stands out because of its unique IT management processes, but because of the extent to which these processes are truly controlled. It is therefore critical that organizations consider and build their own efficient process chains for IT service management, adopting and adapting the standard processes contained in available good practices.

In practice, there are many process models available in the form of supplier-based products. Unfortunately, the details of most of these models are not publicly available. This means that many organizations turn to developing their own based on the available non-proprietary schemas included in publicly available frameworks such as COBIT V4.1 and ITIL V3.

ISO/IEC 20000 clustering

ISO/IEC 20000 imposed clear clustering on its practices, see figure A.4. It is notable that the operations practices are out-of-scope in ISO/IEC 20000.

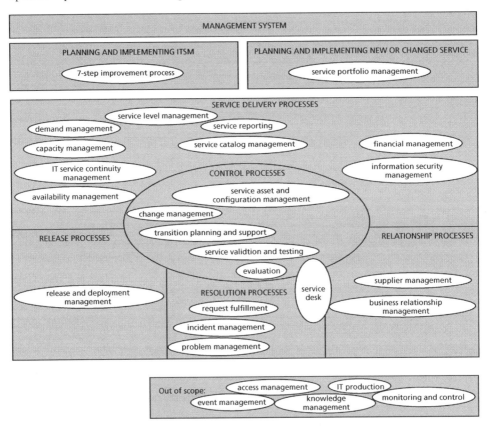

Figure A.4 Clustering of practices according to ISO/IEC 20000

ITIL V3 lifecycle clustering

The lifecycle concept of ITIL V3 consists of five phases in IT service management control. Each of these phases describes several practices ('processes'), functions and 'miscellaneous activities'. Many of these practices are applied across more than one lifecycle phase, see figure A.5.

A.8   Processes, procedures and work instructions

The management of the organization can provide control over the quality of each process using data from the results of each process. In most cases, the relevant **performance indicators** and

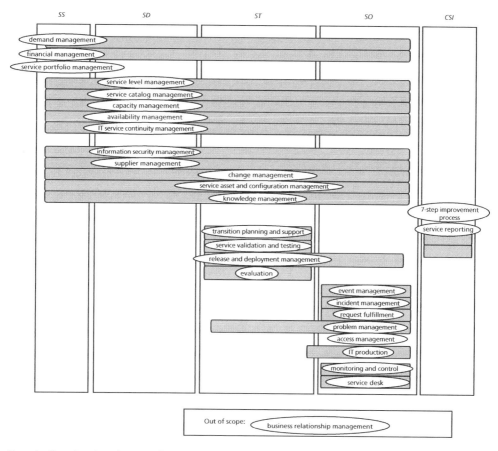

Figure A.5 Clustering of practices according to ITIL V3

standards will already be agreed. The day-to-day control of the process is then left to the process manager. The process owner will assess the results based on a **report** of performance indicators against the agreed standard. Clear indicators enable a process owner to determine if the process is under control, and if implemented improvements have been successful.

Processes are often described using **procedures** and **work instructions**, in accordance with the ISO 9001 quality management system model (figure A.6).

*A **procedure** is a specified way to carry out an activity or a process.*
A procedure describes the 'how', and can also describe 'who' carries the activities out. A procedure may include stages from different processes. A procedure can vary depending on the organization.
*A set of **work instructions** defines how one or more activities in a procedure should be carried out in detail, using technology or other resources.*

It can be difficult to determine whether something is a function or a process. A good example of a function is a service desk, a group of people executing the same set of processes, normally in the same department. A good example of a process is change management, where multiple people are involved who generally work for different departments. A practical guideline, based on ISO

9001, is to consider the contribution of people, process and technology to the subject. A process would only cover activities, a procedure would involve the people factor, and a work instruction would also involve the technology (see figure A.7).

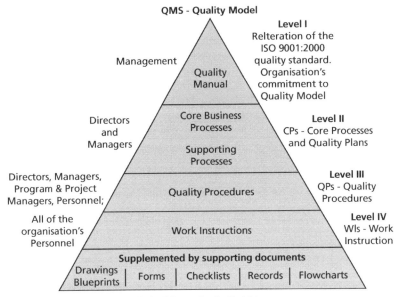

Figure A.6 Process documentation in the ISO 9001 Quality Model[42]

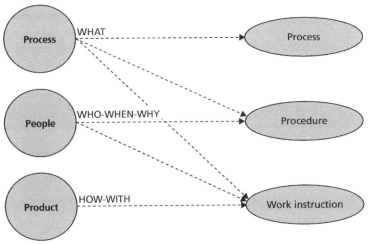

Figure A.7 Relations between the People-Process-Product paradigm and the ISO 9001 Quality Model[43]

In practice, it is not the process that instructs the people in an organization on a day-to-day basis, it is the procedure and the work instructions. Processes only show how the logic in a procedure is constructed, but they don't tell you who should do what/when/how. However, if you don't

---

42   Tricker, R., 2006. ISO 9001:2000 The Quality Management Process. Van Haren Publishing.
43   Source: Hoving, W. and J. van Bon, 2008. Functions and Processes in IT Management. In: J. van Bon (ed.), IT Service Management, global best practices, Volume 1, pp 363-384. Van Haren Publishing for itSMF International.

understand your processes and build your procedures from those processes, then procedures will often be inconsistent with related and interconnected procedures. Also, the reason for the design of a procedure will not be clear. This means that – before you can construct or improve a set of procedures that determine your effectiveness and efficiency – you must have your process system in place, and people must understand its basics.

A.9   Process and line management in a matrix organization

The hierarchical structure of functions can lead to the creation of 'silos' in which each function is very self-oriented. This does not benefit the success of the organization as a whole. Processes run through the hierarchical structure of functions; functions often share some processes. This is how processes suppress the rise of functional silos, and help to ensure an improved coordination in between functions.

Organizations manage their activities from two perspectives: **process management** and **line management**. An organization using process management structures its activities in a neat series of processes, so that 'floating' or 'un-attached' activities are eliminated. This way, the structure of the organization enforces the need to follow the processes. And since processes are generally accepted as the efficient and effective way to organize activities, this will support the organization's performance.

An organization using line management will also manage their activities in organizational structures: teams, departments, sections, business units. These structures are normally ordered along some kind of hierarchy. This way, the organization makes sure that it is clear how activities are allocated to organizational responsibilities.

If an activity is sufficiently important, it can be managed as part of one of the defined processes, or it can be managed from the organizational line. It is possible, and increasingly common, for activities to be managed using both of these perspectives, creating the **matrix organization**. It is important to establish to which extent an activity is managed from the process perspective and/or from the line perspective. Figure A.8 illustrates the Process Management Matrix, demonstrating how staff can be managed from different perspectives. Each individual organization can vary the extent to which it uses these two control mechanisms according to its own preferences.

According to the Process Management Matrix (PMM), the mix of the two 'pure' control models can be described in seven positions:
1. **The pure line organization** – often represented as the familiar rake or tree structure. All responsibilities are cascaded from the top down; interconnections between different lines are not recognized. The line manager is responsible for controlling their team, which consists of staff or other line managers. The performance of the organization is the sum of the performance of the departments. As such, the department's result is a direct responsibility of the department managers.
2. **The line organization recognizes some processes** – In terms of control, this organization is still a pure line organization. One characteristic of this variant is that it recognizes patterns in the activities of different departments that lead to positive results. By laying down these

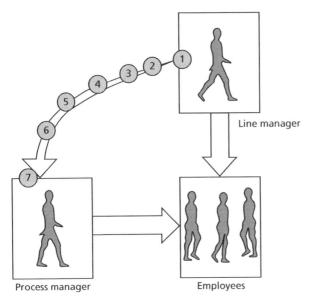

Figure A.8 The Process Management Matrix[44] (PMM)

patterns in a process description, it determines which activities must be executed, their order, and the quality criteria with which they must comply. The recognized processes are often cross-departmental. In this variant, the management of the department executing the activity and the staff involved bear exclusive responsibility for correct communication and collaboration.

3. **Tactical process management** – In this variant, the organization not only recognizes process-based relationships in the activities that it executes. In addition to variant two, it also decides to make someone responsible for the creation, maintenance, and reporting for the process. A key feature of this variant is that someone is appointed to this position of **process owner.** They own the process description and the manner in which the process is executed. As a result, the line management is no longer exclusively responsible for the control and results of the organization. The added value of the correct execution of well-structured processes and the negative consequences of their failure must be demonstrated not only by the process setup, but also – and especially – from the reports.

4. **Operational process control** – In this variant the process management, in addition to the responsibilities from variant three, is also tasked to monitor the correct execution of the defined process setup. In this case, 'correct' means that the process is executed according to the process description, and within the constraints of the agreement with the customer. 'Monitoring', however, does not mean correcting the execution, but detecting deviations and, if necessary, escalating this information. This means that the process management must be aware of the manner in which process activities are executed. It must also report (possible) deviations from the prescribed operating method or SLAs to the stakeholders, and inform them of the situation.

---

44   Source: IT Service Management – Global Best Practices, Volume 1, W. Hoving & J. van Bon, The Process Management
        Matrix, pp 309-323. Van Haren Publishing for itSMFI, 2008.

5. **Operational process direction** – Sometimes the organization may decide to strengthen process control by granting the process management a mandate of direction. The main characteristic of this variant is the transition in who decides and who escalates. In variant four, the staff or manager decides whether he will follow the suggestion of the process management. If the process management does not agree with the choice, it must decide whether it wishes to involve higher levels of the organization in the conflict or will accept the decision made.

6. **Operational and content direction** – While less obvious, it is possible to *also* authorize process management to decide which department – and which persons in that department – must execute activities. As a result, process management is allowed to influence content-related aspects. The process management selects the most suitable department and staff member in view of the situation. In this variant, the line management's role is virtually reduced to *resource management*. The line manager must ensure that the department has adequate resources with sufficient knowledge to execute the activities. In this variant, process management decides on deployment of the resources.

7. **Full process direction** – This is primarily a theoretical variant. It is the last step in allocating more responsibility to process management. This variant allocates the responsibility for resource management to process management. The result is 'process departments', meaning that all activities that must be executed for a process are executed by resources from those departments. In fact, it returns the organization to the start because it boils down to full management along one single dimension, just like the pure line management in the first variant.

For an employee, it is important to understand how these 'competing' management forces are balanced, to prevent conflicts in the prioritization of tasks. This problem grows even more severe if the same employee is also directed from a third perspective: **project management**. In PMM it is highly recommended that project management follows the balance of line and process management, running projects 'over these lines' instead of adding another competing perspective.

A.10 Process and maturity

There are two mainstream 'schools' of maturity thinking. They are based on different interpretations of the term 'maturity':

- **Capability maturity** – explaining how well certain activities are performed, in a technical sense. Examples are CMMI, SPICE, the Test Process Maturity Model, the Project Effectiveness Maturity Model (PEMM), Luftman's Business IT Alignment model, and Nolan's growth model. Basically, all of these models describe process capability levels, expressing how well processes are performed.
- **Value chain maturity** – explain how well an organization is able to contribute to a value chain. A value chain maturity model is shown in figure A.11 and examples of this school are the KPMG world class IT maturity model and the INK management model (based on EFQM).

Combinations can also be found, e.g. in the Gartner Networking Maturity Model.

According to the quality model of EFQM (European Foundation for Quality Management, see figure A.9), the road to 'total quality' passes through the phases *product-focused, process-focused, system-focused, chain-focused,* and *total quality-focused* ('utopia'). This means that, before being able to realize a state of continuous improvement, the organization must first have control over a number of aspects. The phase in which the organization becomes skilled in managing *processes* is crucial in the maturity approach. The organization cannot focus on systems and chains until these processes are under control.

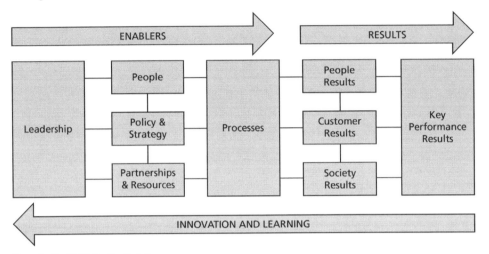

Figure A.9 The EFQM Quality Model[45]

The CMMI model (figure A.10) also deals with the extent to which organizations control their processes. The continuous representation, for instance, is expressed through the stages *Incomplete process, Performed process, Managed process, Defined process, Quantitatively managed process* and *Optimizing process.* The CMMI staged representation also defines maturity in terms of the extent to which the organization controls its processes.

Processes are *internal* affairs for the IT service provider. An organization that is still trying to gain control of its processes therefore has an **internal focus**. Organizations that focus on gaining control over their systems in order to provide services, are also still internally focused. The organization is not ready for an **external focus** until it controls its services and is able to vary them on request. This external focus is required to evolve into that desirable customer-focused organization. This is expressed in the value chain maturity model (figure A.11).

Because organizations can be in different stages of maturity, IT managers require a broad orientation in their discipline. Many organizations are now working on the introduction of a process-focused or still have to start working on this. Process control is a vital step on the road towards a mature **service-oriented** and – ultimately – **customer-driven** organization.

---

45   The EFQM Excellence Model is a registered trademark of EFQM

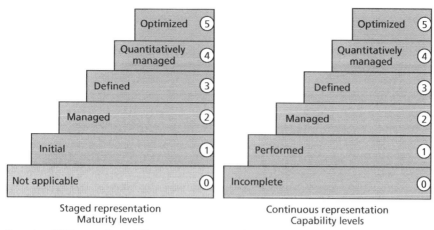

Staged representation   Continuous representation
Maturity levels   Capability levels

Figure A.10 CMMI, a maturity model for process management[46]

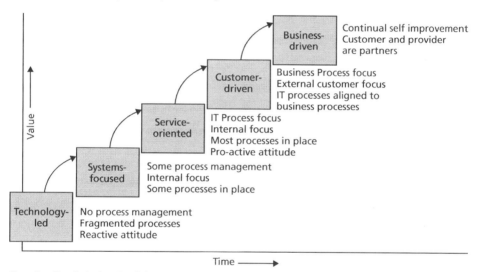

Figure A.11 Maturity in the value chain[47]

In the last twenty years, ITIL has made an important contribution to the organization of that process-focused approach. The development started in North-Western Europe and has made progress on most other continents in the last decade. On a global scale and in hard figures, however, only a minimal number of organizations have actually started with this approach – and an even smaller number have made serious progress at this point. The organizational change projects that were thought to be necessary to convert to a process-focused organization were not all entirely successful. The majority of organizations in the world clearly require access to good information and best practices concerning the **business processes of IT organizations**. Fortunately, that information is abundant. The ITIL V2 books provide comprehensive documentation on the most important processes, while ITIL V3 adds even more information.

---

46   Capability Maturity Model and CMMI are registered in the U.S. Patent and Trademark Office by Carnegie Mellon University.

47   Bosselaers, Theo, Mark Griep, Joost Dudok van Heel, Joachim Vandecasteele and Rob Weerts (2000). The Future of the IT Organization. In: J. van Bon (ed.), World Class IT Service Management Guide (2000). ten Hagen & Stam Publishers, The Hague.

A.11 Core processes of a service provider

ITIL V3 acknowledges the difference between functions and processes: functions (organizational capabilities) make use of processes (repeatable strings of activities). In ITIL, the description of such functions may cover *activities* that are not covered in the description of the relevant processes.

As explained previously, what ITIL calls a 'process' does not always follow the above mentioned definition of what a process is. One solution to this is to consider the twenty-six ITIL 'processes' as twenty-six ITIL 'practices'. For example, in ITIL Capacity management covers a range of activities that cannot be ordered as a logical and repeatable sequence of activities. As such, the ITIL context describes a capacity management practice (CMP) or function rather than a capacity management process.

By definition, the structure of a process is in fact a series of activities that are placed in a logical order: a **workflow**. This workflow is controlled by means of the **control activities**. These control activities make sure the operational activities are performed in time, in the right order, etc. (e.g. in the change management process it is always made sure that a test is performed *before* a release is put into production and not *afterwards*).

Like any other kind of service organization, an IT service provider has only a very limited set of **frequently repeated basic processes** or process groups:
- Four processes are concerned with **effectiveness**:
  a. **agreeing** with the customer what you will deliver ('*contract management*').
  b. **delivering** what you have agreed ('*operations management*').
  c. **repairing** anything that goes wrong ('*incident management*').
  d. **changing** your service if this is required by the customer or by yourself ('*change management*').
- Two processes are concerned with **efficiency**:
  e. **knowing** what you use to deliver your service with ('*configuration management*').
  f. **adjusting** (to) conditions that may prevent you to deliver tomorrow what you have agreed today, proactively eliminating risks that would prevent this ('*risk management*').

This goes not only for an IT service provider, but for other service management fields as well. Imagine a catering service provider, the national post, or any other service provider: they all will perform these same basic tactical and operational processes.

For an IT organization:
- **Contract management** will cover areas of responsibility such as service level management, supplier management, business relationship management.
- **Operations management** will cover the activities required to realize the operation of the IT service, when the service is not down or changed. This would normally cover the planning and execution of all operations activities, including the monitoring of all services and components, which is the bulk of the IT provider's activities.
- **Incident management** covers anything that needs to be done for the repair of services or components.

- **Change management** covers anything to be done for actually changing an IT service or component.
- **Configuration management** covers all activities for providing accurate information on all infrastructure components which the organization uses to deliver their services.
- **Risk management** covers all proactive management activities that make sure that the organization will be able to deliver all quality of service (QoS) parameters that were agreed with the customer (in terms of capacity, performance, finance, etc.), while conditions are continuously changing.

Of course, an IT organization will have some kind of **strategic process** above this list. However, strategic activities do not usually get caught in process descriptions. First of all, the frequency of these activities is relatively low, so the short term repetitive nature is missing. And second, C-level managers (CEO, CFO, CIO, etc.) in strategic positions do not usually consider their activities as being standard and commoditized. The Service Strategy book in ITIL is a good example: although many activities are described, you will not find a strategic process in the book (according to ITIL's definition of process). The set of *high frequency basic processes* is therefore limited to the tactical and operational level, and covers no more than six core processes.

A.12 Setting up functions in the service provider's organization

Looking at the provider's organization, and at documented best practices, we can recognize a large number of functions. Each of these functions uses one or more of the core processes. Functions can have different formats, including:

- **an infrastructure format** – focused on managing a part of the information system: e.g. the application, the network, the database, desktops, servers, mainframes, telephony, database, data, system software, middleware, power, climate, etc. Examples of well-known functions are application management (team), network management (team), database administration.
- **a service quality format** – focused on managing a quality aspect, e.g. availability, continuity, security. Relevant functions can be availability management (team), IT service continuity management (team), security management (team).
- **an activity format** – focused on managing one or more specific activities (processes). Relevant functions can be change management team, configuration management team, requirements engineering, service desk.
- **an organizational format** – focused on organizing responsibilities in departments according to criteria such as size, region, skills, specialty. Examples of functions can be the EMEA Business Unit, Team West, Corporate Headquarters.

A function can of course also be a mix of any of these – and other – formats. Finding the optimum organizational structure is a balancing act: which functions are most important to the organization, which processes are essential, how is management along the function dimension (also known as 'the line') and along the process dimension balanced?

You may now recognize the following examples of regular functions:
- **Capacity management** is an <u>infrastructure function</u> that uses a set of basic processes:
  - for realization of the capacity of the agreed services at the agreed rate/demand, this function uses *operations management*
  - for repairing capacity issues it uses *incident management*
  - for changing capacities it uses *change management*
  - for agreeing on capacity aspects it uses *contract management*
  - for proactive actions concerning capacity issues it uses *risk management*
  - for the knowledge of which capacity carriers are deployed in which parts of the enterprise infrastructure it uses *configuration management*
- **Security management** is a <u>service quality function</u> that uses a set of basic processes:
  - for realization of the security of the agreed services at the agreed rate/demand, this functions uses *operations management*
  - for repairing security issues it uses *incident management*
  - for changing security it uses *change management*
  - for agreeing on security aspects it uses *contract management*
  - for proactive actions concerning security issues it uses *risk management*
  - for the knowledge of which security measures are deployed in which parts of the enterprise infrastructure it uses *configuration management*
- **Service desk** is an <u>activity function</u> (call handling) that uses a set of basic processes:
  - for the operational support of calls (service requests) according to the agreed services at the agreed rate/demand, this function uses *operations management*
  - for handling incident calls it uses *incident management*
  - for handling change calls it uses *change management*
  - for agreeing on call handling performance it uses *contract management*
  - for proactive actions of call handling issues it uses *risk management*
  - for the knowledge of which service infrastructures are deployed in which parts of the enterprise it uses *configuration management*
- **Corporate Headquarters** is an <u>organizational function</u> that uses a set of basic processes:
  - for realization of the agreed services at the agreed rate/demand, this function uses *operations management*
  - for repairing service issues it uses *incident management*
  - for changing services it uses *change management*
  - for agreeing on service levels it uses *contract management*
  - for proactive actions on service issues it uses *risk management*
  - for the knowledge of which service infrastructures are deployed in which parts of the enterprise it uses *configuration management*
- Network management, application management, data management, financial management, workload management, print management, knowledge management, etc. will now all be recognized as variations to the themes above.

If these functions would be perceived as processes, this would require descriptions in terms of logical sequences of activities, inputs and outputs, feedback mechanisms, et cetera. The fact is that the functions listed above are not normally described in those terms, and that thus the interpretation as a function is more realistic than the interpretation as a process.

The number of functions that can be defined is endless: a function can be defined on each service attribute that is agreed upon. Common paragraphs in an SLA deal with familiar QoS's like availability, capacity, cost and continuity (see figure 1.1). As a consequence, we will find availability management, capacity management, financial management and continuity management functions in that organization. But if the organization also agreed to QoS's for performance, reliability, maintainability, scalability or others – you may expect to find functions like performance management, reliability management, maintainability management, scalability management and others. These functions would then all use the six basic processes for their activities.

Appendix B. Terminology and definitions

B.1 Acronyms used

ARM	Application Response Measurement
BCM	Business Capacity Management
BCs	British Computer Society
BFU	Business Forecast Unit
BMI	Business Metric of Interest
BSC	Balanced Scorecard
BU	Business Unit
CAB	Change Advisory Board
CASE	Computer Aided Software Engineering
CCM	Component Capacity Management – see RCM
CDB	Capacity Management Database – see CMIS
CDB/CMIS	To cover both extant versions of ITIL
CFIA	Component Failure Impact Analysis
CI	Configuration Item
CICS	Customer Information Control System (z/OS)
CIS	Configuration Management Information System – see CMDB
CMDB	Configuration Management Database – see CIS
CMDB/CIS	To cover both extant versions of ITIL
CMG	Computer Measurement Group
CMIS	Capacity Management Information System
CMM	Capability Maturity Model
CMP	Capacity Management Practice
CMT	Capacity Management Team
CPM	Corporate Performance Management
CPU	Central Processing Unit
CSF	Critical Success Factor
CSI	Continual Service Improvement
DB2	Database 2 (z/OS)
DB2 UDB	DataBase2 (Universal Database for distributed systems)
DES	Discrete Event Simulation
DSL	Definitive Software Library
ERP	Enterprise Resource Planning
ICT	Information and Communication Technology(ies)

IDEF	Integrated Definition (methods)
IEC	International Electrotechnical Commission
I/O	Input/Output
IT	Information Technology
ITI	IT Infrastructure
ITIL®	IT Infrastructure Library®
ITIP	IT Infrastructure Planning
ITSCM	IT Service Continuity Management
ITSM	IT Service Management
itSMF	IT Service Management Forum
J2EE	Java 2, Enterprise Edition
KPI	Key Performance Indicator
KBIS	Knowledge Based Information System
LAN	Local Area Network
LPAR	Logical Partition (z/OS, AIX, HP-UX, iSeries et cetera))
LVM	Logical Volume Manager
MIB	Management Information Base
MIS	Management Information System
MTBF	Mean Time Between Failures
MTTR	Mean Time To Recovery/Respond
NAS	Network Attached Storage
NUMA	Non-Uniform Memory Access
OGC	Office of Government Commerce
OLA	Operational Level Agreement
PC	Personal Computer
PE	Performance Engineering
PR/SM	Processor Resource/System Management (z/OS)
QA	Quality Assurance
QNM	Queuing Network Models
QoS	Quality of Service
RAID	Redundant Array of Independent Disks
R/CCM	To cover both extant versions of ITIL
RCM	Resource/Component capacity management – see CCM
RDBMS	Relational Database Management System
RFC	Request For Change
RFP	Requests For Proposal
RMF	Resource Measurement Facility (z/OS)
SAM	Service Assurance Matrix

SAN	Storage Area Network
SC&D	Software Control and Distribution
SCM	Service capacity management
SMF	System Management Facility (z/OS)
SIP	Service Improvement Program
SLA	Service Level Agreement
SLAM	Service Level Agreement Monitoring
SLM	Service Level Management
SLO	Service Level Objective
SLR	Service Level Requirement
SMP	Symmetric Multi-Processing
SNMP	Simple Network Management Protocol
SPE	Software Performance Engineering
SPEC	Standard Performance Evaluation Corporation
SPOF	Single Point Of Failure
TCP/IP	Transmission Control Protocol/ Internet Protocol
TP	Transaction Processing
UC	Underpinning Contract
UML	Unified Modeling Language
WAN	Wide Area Network
WFS	Workload Forecast Scenario

B.2   Models, frameworks and standards used

There is a lot of 'process speak' involved in this area with terms such as 'business process reengineering' and design frameworks such as SSADM for detailed process definition and other older management consultancy techniques such as Organization and Methods, Operational Science, Time and Motion studies, and standards for systems analysis and systems design et cetera. The current vogues are all well worth looking up in Google (and the cryptic notes below are only an initial individual reaction to them).

It seems that many people are hoping to find a prescribed solution rather than realizing these are mostly just different views trying to formalize IT infrastructure definition and its implementation, and require adopting and adapting as appropriate to fit into local circumstances. The definitions for standards are even more difficult to apply to people and organizations than to software and hardware, and even they have proved elusive. This set of notes is a limited view of matters – for a more formal and considered glossary see the one issued for ITIL V3.

BAM (Business Activity Management) – Essentially BAM is the activity of collecting rules for managing business activities by defining the process, deliverable and owner et cetera. BAM refers to the aggregation, analysis, and presentation of relevant and timely information about business activities inside an organization and its customers and partners.

BASEL II – The Basel Capital Accord (Basel II) was prepared by the Basel Committee on Banking Supervision with implementation in 2006. Instead of assessing risk in general, each loan commitment is analyzed individually.
Business capacity management is the application of business management practice to comprehend, communicate and control the performance of an organization effectively. It is also known as BPM (business performance management) or CPM (corporate performance management).

Business IT Alignment – bITa is the relationship between the business and IT, the understanding of the value the IT service provision brings to the business and ensuring that IT supports the business objectives.

BSC (Balanced Scorecard) – *www.balancedscorecard.org*
A definition of best practice for evaluating and improving business processes over a year or two's strategic management consultancy project. This is a top down business performance management tool developed in the early 80's to present value beyond traditional cost measurement approaches. It is based on financial and non-financial KPIs, with internal and external perspectives and assesses results compared with causes.

BS 15000 – the world's first formal standard for IT service management where ITIL provides most of the underpinning material definitions. It combines the guidelines of ITIL with the quality management concepts of ISO 9000-2000 to provide a level of quality specifically for ITSM which can be audited. This is a pass/fail test, now superseded by ISO/IEC 20000.

CMM (Capability Maturity Model) – http://www.sei.cmu.edu/ *software engineering institute/ Carnegie Mellon official site*
This has been around a long time, defined by various management or academic consultants in slightly different ways but typically five layers of process implementation from basic ad hoc introduction to 'repeatable' or 'reactive' to 'defined' or 'proactive' to 'quantitatively managed' through to 'optimized' effective implementation.

COBIT – see *www.isaca.org/cobit www.isaca.org www.itgi.org*
A high level umbrella for IT security/audit et cetera with key performance indicators: COBIT has been developed as a generally applicable and accepted standard for good Information Technology (IT) security and control practices that provides a reference framework for management, users, and IS audit, control and security practitioners. COBIT is 'Control Objectives for Information and related Technology'. Launched in 1996, it is based on the Control Objectives of the Information Systems Audit and Control Foundation (ISACF). The COBIT cube defines the quality, fiduciary and security criteria for effectiveness, efficiency, confidentiality, integrity, availability, compliance and reliability. This is defined for 4 domains, 34 processes and 318 controls for activities.

EFQM – *www.efqm.org*
The European Framework for Quality Management set up by the EU with 14 major European industrial companies. This is a business excellence model and incorporates the staff's perception of the internal processes and their key performance results for people, customers and society.

IDEF – This is a business process definition standards framework adopted by the USA DOD for Integration DEFinition. It contains five thick books, where page 72 of book one introduces drawing a vertical line with an arrow upwards to represent a feedback loop. A popular alternative approach is based on the Unified Modeling Language (UML).

ISO – *www.iso.org*
International Organization for Standards, maybe famed least for its OSI definition, and famed most for its ISO 9000 quality standard (with 14,000 other standards).

ISO 9000 – Quality management systems definitions, framework and processes standards

ISO/IEC 20000 – standard for IT service management largely derived from BS 15000.

ITIL (IT Infrastructure Library) – *www.itil-officialsite.com*
A high level descriptive framework for IT service provision, providing a set of guidelines for good practice as to what has to be done, not how to do it.

ITIL certification – A growing pipeline of education and training for individuals.

ITIP (IT Infrastructure Planning) – a view of the activities involved with establishing and improving the IT infrastructure as regards current and future performance.

ITSM (IT Service Management) – used as a high level embracing phrase for 'all 10 ITIL service delivery and service support practices'. See also www.itsm.org

KPIs (Key Performance Indicators) – Try *www.kpiusa.com* as a typical introduction. KPIs are used at the business level to indicate the progress of predefined subsets of the business. A concept comparable to the traditional Natural Forecast Unit for Workload Components used in capacity planning, but typically at a higher level and more enterprise-wide.

MOF (Microsoft Operations Framework) – *www.microsoft.com/mof.*
Microsoft Operations Framework v4 offers a lifecycle approach for IT services, with three ongoing phases (Plan, Deliver, Operate) and one foundational layer that operates throughout all of the other phases (Manage). On the web there are a number of extensive and detailed white papers on each of the components of MOF. In MOF v4 capacity management is part of the reliability service management function.

PRINCE2 – The long-established OGC published formalized project management technique.

PROMPT – A project management approach adopted by the CCTA but later superseded by PRINCE.

Six Sigma – *www.isixsigma.com.*
As its title implies, six sigma is to do with the quality control and reliability of items, more traditionally associated with quality testing on a production line, checking the number of defects and trying to reduce it to less than 6σ and achieve a near perfect production rate. 6σ levels are a fine target for mass production such as small parts turned on lathes, but for many IT related processes achieving 3-4σ levels may well be adequate. The essence is to be able to measure the local value of sigma and try to improve it.

Sox (Sarbanes-Oxley) – *www.sarbanes-oxley.com.*
New procedures defined post Enron to try to improve regulatory compliance with financial controls and tighten up on audit trails et cetera.

SSADM V4 – Systems design techniques underpinning application development promoted by the OGC. Other similar approaches include – IDEF – DSDM – RAD – UML – UPF – RUP with the unified modeling language perhaps dominant now, with the unified process framework perhaps replacing IDEF and the IBM rational unified process a growing commercial definition

TQM (Total Quality Management)
A philosophy and set of guiding principles. Essentially a quality initiative to do things right and document the process. Typically self-directed teams with little training focus on a single function on a quality oriented basis.

B.3   Glossary used

Analytical modeling – a technique using mathematical models to predict the behavior of computer systems typically using algorithms such as multi-class queuing network theory.

Business capacity management (BCM) – the activity responsible for understanding future business requirements and their likely impact on IT resources

Business driver – a measurable entity that influences directly the definition of business requirements for IT.

Business function – a business unit within an organization, e.g. a department, division, branch.

Business process – a group of business activities undertaken by an organization in pursuit of a common goal, usually depending on several business functions for support and inter-dependent with other business processes.

Business unit (BU) – a segment of the business entity by which both revenues received and expenditure are controlled and measured.

Business forecast unit (BFU) – or 'Natural forecast unit', being the essential business driver that determines the arrival rate of a transaction in terms meaningful to the user or the business (e.g. orders placed, invoices processed, customer enquiries, web site hits).

Capacity – the maximum throughput that a device can deliver whilst meeting agreed SLAs.

Capacity management – the function responsible for ensuring that the capacity of the IT services and infrastructure is able to deliver agreed SLAs in a cost-effective and timely manner. 'The provision of a consistent and acceptable end-user service at a known and controlled cost.' 'The right kit in the right place at the right time to do the right work at the right speed to meet the right business need at the right cost.'

Capacity management database (CDB) – database containing all the data required to support capacity management, known in ITIL V3 as CMIS.

Capacity management information system (CMIS) – containing all the data required to support capacity management, known in ITIL V2 as the CDB.

Capacity plan – used to manage the resources required to deliver IT services.

Capture ratio – defined as the amount of CPU time that is gathered by looking at process data versus the total system-wide CPU used. The difference is made up by processes that stop during the intervals between measurements. Since short lived processes may start and stop between measurements, and we don't know whether a process stopped immediately before a measurement or just after a measurement, there is always an error in sampled process measures. The error is reduced by using a short measurement interval, but that increases overhead.

Capture interval – the granularity of data collection for performance metrics, also known as the snapshot interval.

Capture period – the period of time of day during which data is collected and considered, also known as the capture window.

Component capacity management (CCM) – the process responsible for understanding the capacity, utilization and performance of devices providing the IT service, known in ITIL V2 as Resource/Component capacity management .

Customer – recipient of a service with responsibility for the cost and demonstration of business need.

Function – a subdivision of an organization that is specialized in fulfilling a specified type of work, and is responsible for specific end results. Functions are independent subdivisions with capabilities and resources that are required for their performance and results. They have their own practices and their own knowledge body.

Model – 'a simplification of reality built for a specific purpose'.

Peak period – a period of time of standard duration, for which resource usage will be planned or reported on such that the plan or report will accurately reflect the heaviest demand for resources on a typical day. The peak period will always be within the part of the day considered as important for the service(s) running.

Performance assurance – the assurance of an application's performance throughout its lifecycle by a combination of performance engineering and capacity planning processes making a total capacity management regime.

Performance engineering (PE) – the assurance of an application's performance by predicting its likely resource demands and affecting design and development where feasible. Also referred to (and largely introduced and promoted) as software performance engineering by Dr Connie Smith.

Process –a sequence of interrelated or interacting activities designed to accomplish a defined objective in a measurable and repeatable manner, transforming inputs into outputs

Resource – typically computer and related equipment, software, facilities or people. Resource/component capacity management – the activity responsible for understanding the capacity, utilization and performance of devices providing the IT service, known in ITIL V3 as component capacity management.

Server – typically a computer, a pool of computers or any combination of computers, usually connected to a network.

Service – a means of delivering value to customers by facilitating outcomes the customers want to achieve without the ownership of specific costs or risks. In ITSM, a service is usually made up of a number of applications or parts of applications.

Service capacity management – the activity responsible for understanding the performance and capacity of IT services.

Simulation modeling – a technique that creates a detailed model to predict the behavior of computer systems using a discrete event simulation engine.

Super-user – an expert user who may be able to act locally to deal with first line support incidents.

System – a group of, interrelating, or interdependent components that form a unified whole, operating together for a common purpose

User – the person who uses a service on a day-to-day basis.

Workload – generally a representation of the demands for resources made by a discrete business application.

Workload component – generally a refinement of the workload into components that represent different aspects of the workload that need to be controlled separately in that they have different business drivers for growth. Also often categorized by key attributes such as its type (interactive, batch), priority (mission-critical) et cetera.

Appendix C. Checklists

This set of checklists is based on experience over the years as to what is helpful in assessing the CMP at a number of sites and how best to improve it.

C.1 Capacity management objectives for assessment

This list of objectives is a generic outline of the typical objectives for capacity management. It is provided as a list of absolute statements that need to be qualified and clarified within each enterprise. They are not 'yes/no' statements so much as a target for improvement in terms of eliciting local objectives and constraints. There is a variety of similar 'self-audit' or 'self-review' forms available on the web (including an excellent one from OGC called ITSM Service Delivery: capacity management Self-Assessment Questionnaire 2001) which can act as a useful starting point. This list should be expanded into a set of statements clarified and modified to match the local situation and then used as a basis for 'gap analysis' and progress review. A popular mode of approach is to define the CMMI levels and then ask a variety of individuals within the enterprise to score the local performance of the capacity management team (or sometimes merely to score on a scale of 0 to 10). This will usually reveal a number of gaps and 'points of pain' as well as different perspectives from different teams within the organization. This can then be used as a basis for deciding on the objectives for process improvement as well as a subjective measure for assessing progress.

ITSM capacity management is in place:
• Capacity management is a mandatory inclusion in the ITSM practices with explicitly defined interfaces to quality assurance, development and testing as well as business and user units and also all the other ITSM practices. See section C2 for details of the ITSM interfaces.
• Capacity management determines the agreed services and workloads to be monitored, analyzed, reported on and planned in consultation with service level management and configuration management.
• Capacity management produces and maintains relevant capacity plans for all agreed services and servers which are then acted upon.
• A capacity management database (CDB/CMIS) is maintained to assist in developing and maintaining capacity plans for all agreed services and servers and for reporting on performance and is in alignment with the configuration manage management database (CMDB/CIS).
• Future capacity demand is forecasted based upon current workloads with consideration to the strategic plans (i.e. corporate and business unit plans), the development portfolio, pre-production load testing and pilot sites.
Capacity management activities are in place:
• Capacity management activities are in place for resource/component capacity management, service capacity management and business capacity management for all agreed services and servers.
• Capacity management activities (i.e. monitoring, analyzing and reporting of usage and performance, tuning recommendations, implementation and tracking, capacity planning and modeling, demand management and application sizing) are in place for all agreed services and servers for all three sub-practices, see section C.3 CMP map.

- BCM activities are in place and the organization is committed to a corporate capacity management plan which includes future business requirements:
  - there is a process to ensure future business requirements for IT services are identified and parameterized for incorporation into capacity management plans
  - business plans are analyzed to deduce likely workloads and ensure sufficient capacity in anticipated time-scales

- SCM activities are in place and there is a process to ensure there is sufficient capacity to support planned services:
  - end-to-end service response times are measured
  - required service levels and forecasts are used to define and size service elements
  - standard reports are issued regularly concerning service performance levels
  - the CMT provides information concerning infrastructure requirements to maintain service levels

- R/CCM activities are in place and the organization is committed to the proactive management of the capacity of the servers, networks and desk-top machines:
  - there are mechanisms for analyzing system usage and reporting on performance
  - the utilization of each resource is monitored on an on-going basis
  - variations, trends, patterns and deviations from plans are identified and analyzed in the utilizations of resources
  - standard reports are issued regularly concerning performance and the use and allocation of key resources

- A capacity management team (CMT) is in place with defined and documented activities and responsibilities clearly communicated, including deciding on hardware, upgrades, performance reports and alerts et cetera. – see section 4.1 CMP data flows.

Capacity management inputs are in place:

- Capacity management tools are in place and agreed metrics collected for hardware (servers and SANs), software, networking and agreed peripherals and workstations.

- Business units provide agreed information for company strategy, business plans, major projects, changes and volumetric data to the CMT.

- IT management provides information on commitments and plans for new technology.

- Development and testing provide application sizing data to the CMT.

- Finance provides budget and chargeback information.

Capacity management reports are in place:

- Capacity management activities provide regular and exception reports on an agreed basis to an agreed distribution for all agreed services and servers concerning:
  - resource utilization and infrastructure requirements for maintaining service levels
  - performance (against agreed service levels) and workload trends (against forecasts)
  - end-to-end service throughput and responses
  - service elements are defined, sized and reported on for new services
  - details of proposed new workloads from development and QA are reported
  - forecasts of new workloads and their resource requirements are reported
  - market testing of new and emerging technologies is reviewed and reported
  - recommendations based on technology trends/ emerging technology
  - variances between planned & actual utilization and performance
  - performance is reported on against agreed service levels on a regular basis for all services

- Key service level performance attributes (e.g. response time, throughput) have been identified in SLAs for all agreed services and are policed and reported on regularly.

- Capacity plans are issued for agreed services on agreed timescales, see section D for a capacity plan template and an example.

Capacity management interfaces with other ITSM practices are in place:

- See the ITSM interface checklist section C.2 for details.

Good practice is being observed:
• The purpose and benefits of the CMP have been disseminated within the organization.
• Standards and quality criteria relevant to capacity management activities have been developed, documented, and communicated – see section C.9 CMMI, section C.10 KPI and section C.11 Risks.
• Responsibility for capacity management activities are clearly defined and assigned to specific individuals who have the appropriate experience and training.
• Suitable tools to support capacity management activities have been implemented and are being appropriately utilized.
• Appropriate mechanisms are established for the CMT to be made aware of relevant activities such as production software roll-out, changes to standard builds, external changes to key metrics (e.g. DBA disk 'clean-up' releasing space and affecting trends).
User perception is measured:
• Feedback is collected and analyzed from customers and users to ascertain their level of satisfaction and perception of the service provided and the information is actively monitored and used to improve the service.

Table C.1 Capacity management objectives for assessment

C.2 ITSM interfaces to and from capacity management

Table C.2 shows potential data flows across the interfaces between ITSM functions and processes. These need to be defined and assessed within each organization and should include local guidelines as well as links to standard operating procedures.

To capacity management	From capacity management
From availability management	**To availability management**
Business processing and resilience requirements are passed to the CMT	Make availability management aware of potential non-availability of resources due to capacity issues
Availability technologies, both used and planned, are made available to the CMT	Feed regular performance, monitoring and alerting data to availability management
Component Failure Impact Analyses (CFIA) are passed to the CMT	Inform availability management of requirements for additional infrastructure needed for required level of resilience
From change management	**To change management**
Change requests are forwarded to the CMT to review capacity and performance implications	Provide predictions on the performance and capacity aspects of planned changes, and forward RFCs on planned capacity changes
Details of changes to existing workloads are forwarded to the CMT	Capacity management is represented on the CAB
From configuration management	**To configuration management**
The CMDB/CIS is accessible to the CMT for read and update with CI changes communicated	Input the capacity effects of changes to the CMDB/CIS
Provide details of IT components and workload deployment across them	Input the capacity details of newly available resources to the CMDB/CIS, in the course of a change

To capacity management	From capacity management
From continuity management	**To continuity management**
Business continuity plan and other service continuity considerations are passed to the CMT.	Provide updates on minimum configuration requirements as live processing levels change
Vital business functions and their minimum processing requirements are defined for the CMT	Incorporate all recovery options into capacity plan
Raise RFCs as live processing changes	Assess the impact of RFCs on recovery options
From financial management	**To financial management**
IT budget forecasts and actuals fed to the CMT	Capacity plans with recommended actions for next year fed to financial management
Chargeback regime agreed with CMT	Chargeback regime agreed with financial management
	Provide billing or capacity/usage reports against cost centers
From incident management	**To incident management**
Report capacity related incidents	Provide education as to how to identify capacity issues
	Resolve capacity related incidents, document solution and report to incident management
	Provide performance reports to service desk on agreed basis of metric detail, granularity and frequency
From problem management	**To problem management**
Report capacity related problems	Provide education as to how to identify capacity issues
	Resolve capacity related problems, document solution and report to problem management
	Provide performance reports to service desk on agreed basis of metric detail, granularity and frequency
	Report performance and capacity problems identified by the CMT
From release management	**To release management**
Release plans are passed to capacity management	Provide predictions on the performance and capacity aspects of planned releases
Suitable data for sizing new systems is provided at an early stage in the development process	
From service level management	**To service level management**
Performance and workload aspects of SLAs and OLAs made available and changes communicated	Help define performance targets in SLAs and OLAs that can be policed
Service level breaches passed to capacity management on a regular basis	Report current and potential future capacity breaches to agreed service levels, to SLM
Performance data provided for systems provided by external suppliers	Service level reviews include capacity management

To capacity management	From capacity management
Interdependencies within a service and between services are documented and passed to capacity management	
From operations management	**To operations management**
Monitoring and performance data are provided	Tuning requests that are not considered to be changes
Information on planned and scheduled activities are provided	Temporary monitoring requests in the course of risk investigation (problem studies)
From event management	**To event management**
Traps collected and resultant actions for alarms and alerts	Thresholds, patterns, correlations, alarms, alerts to SNMP traps
From demand management	**To demand management**
Requirements for service with associated needs such as business need, priority, budget, security, recovery, integrity, availability, continuity, performance, capacity	Quotas, limits, constraints, priorities, costs, charges, chargeback options

Table C.2 ITSM interfaces to/from capacity management

C.3 Capacity management map of sub-practices versus activities

Table C.3 shows the three sub-practices across the top and the major activities down the side and fills in relevant actions within each cell. These need to be defined and assessed within each organization.

Sub-practice Activity	Resource/Component	Service	Business
Monitoring			
	Metrics from all platforms, databases and applications collected and held in a CDB/CMIS; include metrics such as batch run times, backup run times and archive/tape utilization	Categories resources by the services they provide as in the Service Portfolio/Catalogue	Categories and weight services to reflect business significance in the light of business strategy and plans
	Thresholds defined for metrics to allow exception reporting	If response time or throughput is part of the SLA ensure relevant data is collected	Access and collect business metrics, business measures of interest and KPIs
Analysis			
	CDB/CMIS data is analyzed regularly at an agreed frequency covering an agreed period	Analyze response time to identify major contributor	Compare business drivers with achieved service levels and resource utilization levels

Sub-practice Activity	Resource/Component	Service	Business
	Average and maximum values are recorded for each period, with bottlenecks, patterns and trends analyzed	Check SLAs measurable and achievable and report exceptions to SLAs	Measure and report on BMIs and KPIs
Tuning			
	Areas where resource utilization can be improved are identified and proposed tuning activities modeled to assess potential benefit	Assess and model level of benefit of proposed tuning activities to the service	Assess relevance and accuracy of business drivers et cetera and feedback to the appropriate business unit
Implementation			
	Resource utilization figures are published to the agreed recipients	Publish achieved service levels to agreed recipients	Publish business volumes, KPIs and BMIs to agreed recipients
Demand management			
	Identify resource utilization of individual services to enable variable charging	Identify and agree services that provide business critical applications	Agree weighting of criticality with the Board
	Identify utilization patterns of individual services to enable off-peak scheduling	Identify mechanisms for variable charging on a per service basis	Agree charging mechanisms and options for workload smoothing
Modeling			
	Use trend analysis to assess likely resource utilizations per device	Use trend analysis to assess changes in service workloads	Use trend analysis to assess changes to meet new business demands
	Model systems behavior under varying workloads and provide tuning recommendations	Model systems behavior under varying business forecasts for workload changes	Model systems behavior under varying changes to meet business needs
	Adopt a modeling solution to analyze resource utilization data	Adopt a modeling solution to predict future service levels	Compare business driver forecasts with actuals and reports
	Identify business metrics (drivers) to use as input to forecasts	Use SLRs as target in modeling exercises	Use business drivers to assess impact on workload and hence service levels
Application sizing			
	Assess resource requirements for new applications or upgrades	Assess resource requirements for new services or upgrades	Assess business requirements for new critical services
	Feedback performance analysis about new projects to developers	Feedback achievable service levels for new projects to SLM	Feedback actual service levels for new projects to business units

Sub-practice Activity	Resource/Component	Service	Business
CDB/CMIS			
	Store collected resource data in CDB/CMIS and integrate with service and business data	Store target and achieved service levels in CDB/CMIS and integrate with resource and business data	Store business and financial data in CDB/CMIS and integrate with resource and service data
Capacity plan			
	Use regular utilization reports as input to the capacity plan and group resources in a way that is directly usable in the planning activity	Produce service capacity plans on an agreed regular basis (e.g. quarterly)	Produce consolidated datacenter/ enterprise capacity plan on an agreed regular basis (e.g. annually ahead of budget round)
	Track actual growth in utilization of devices against predictions	Track actual growth in service workload against previous predictions	Track actual growth in critical workload against previous predictions

Table C.3 Capacity management map of sub-practices versus activities

C.4   Metrics to collect

Table C.4 is indicative only. The terminology varies with the platforms involved and the metrics selected and the level of detail required or used.

For each metric group (CPU, memory, disk, workload, database, network, application), and for each environment (UNIX, Windows, z/OS, network, application, other): collect data in an agreed manner (ad hoc/regular, and if regular, specify the snapshot interval, data collection period and if it is to be used automatically to maintain a CDB/CMIS).

Group	Metrics
CPU	Number of processors, clock speed, total processor power such as selected TPC or Spec benchmark values
	Utilization (total; system; User; I/O wait; idle)
	Queue length
Memory	Available; utilization
	Page in rate; page out rate, swap in rate; swap out rate
	% reads cached; % writes cached
Disk	Utilization (total; by logical drive; by physical drive; by reads/writes)
Workload	Number of logons; concurrent users
	CPU total by user/ command/ process/ class
	Logical I/Os by user/ command/ process
Database	Number of users, sessions

Group	Metrics
	Cache effectiveness
	I/O profile (logical/physical) by user/ session
	Database size
	Long table scans
File system	% space free/ used and GB space free/used
Application	Number of users; number of transactions
	CPU usage by user/ transaction type
	Response times and throughputs by transaction type
Network	Router (load, path length/hop count)
	Bandwidth (available, utilization, packet size, proportion short to long)
	Quality (throughput, delay/latency, jitter, packet loss)
Response time	Collect measurements of user response time
Response time (cont)	Select method: application instrumentation, e.g. ARM or equivalent, robot' scripts/ terminal emulation, distributed agent software, passive monitoring systems, e.g. network 'sniffers', other
+ Partitions	CPU utilization by processor, memory in use plus other partition metrics
+VMs	CPU consumed, wait time for access to CPU plus other VM metrics
Thresholds	Set thresholds against key performance metrics at the R/CCM level:
Threshold metrics	Platform (UNIX, Windows, z/OS, Other), Network
Threshold conditions	E.g. single metric (e.g. CPU---}80%), or metric plus pattern (e.g. CPU---}80% for ---}1 hour) et cetera
Suitability	Identify the decision maker on what is a suitable threshold
Breaches	Identify who receives the reports and alerts when they are automatically generated as thresholds are breached
SLAs	Identify if thresholds linked to formal SLAs, OLAs or otherwise.

Table C.4. Metrics to collect

C.5 Capacity planning information required for new applications

Table C.5 is only indicative, as its detail will vary significantly with the development approach used. However, the basic concepts are fairly standard.

System summary:	
Outline description	A brief description of purpose of the systems
Environment	Batch, development or OLTP
	Software versions (e.g. OS, TP, database, development)
Timescales	Start development/system trials/ implementation

	Complete implementation or phases thereof
Development workload caused by this system	Number of programmers; number of terminals and also testing requirements
Service levels:	
Availability	How many days/week and which days
	How many hours/day and which hours
Central system serviceability	% uptime target; maximum recovery time
	Standby arrangements: hot standby, cold standby
Terminals/network	Mean Time between failures; acceptable repair time
	Need for standby, non-stop, alternative network access routes
Database	Transaction logging; Duplexing of database
	Currency – e.g. must the database be 100% up to date
	Frequency of security copying
Performance requirements	Define priorities for any single user or group of users
	Define priorities for any class of work
For on-line transactions:	Mean response time; 90% response time (where relevant and measurable)
	Number of simultaneously active users
For batch workloads:	Key deadlines for starting and/or completing jobs
	Any requirement to run concurrent streams of work
For development workloads:	Mean & 95%ile response times for a simple interaction
	No. of simultaneously active terminals
	Session throughput (sessions/hour)
Workload definition:	
Session characteristics	For each type of definable session:
	Type of user
	Number of sessions/day; typical session length
	No. of Tx per session; estimated think/type time
Transaction characteristics	For each type of definable transaction:
	Number of transactions/unit/time
	Number of screens per transaction/dialogue
	Av. no. of characters input and output/screen/layouts
	No. of rows/records read & written per transaction by file
	Volume of local and remote printed output.
Transaction characteristics (batch)	Number of transactions (Tx) per run
	Estimate of no. of rows/records read/written per Tx by file
	Av. no. of characters read/written for each I/O
	Volume of local and remote printed output

Database	Number of files; For each major file
	+ type of file e.g. master, transaction, work
	+ expected cache hit-rate
	+ volatility – rate of change
	+ number of records/items; + size of records/items
Volumes:	
Data is required (where relevant) for:	Number of active terminals by type
	Connectivity requirements
	Number of sessions by type
	Session length
	Number of transactions by type
	Size of database
	Time and duration of peaks e.g. daily/ weekly/ monthly; seasonal, pre Christmas peak hour, peak day et cetera;
	Size of each peak e.g. peak hour 10 transactions/ min, pre-Christmas peak daily load 1.5 times average
	Average load hourly/daily/monthly et cetera
	Growth rate; % linear, % compound and upper and lower bounds on growth
SITE:	
Configuration layout	Resources topology, terminal layout; communications network
File layout	Disk mapping across drives where relevant

Table C.5 Capacity planning information required for new applications

C.6   CMP data required for modeling

This list in table C.6 is indicative only.

SYSTEM LEVEL	for each server
	Number of processors, clock speed, total processor power such as selected TPC or spec benchmark values
	Total CPU utilization (i.e. system & user)
	CPU waiting I/O time, CPU idle time
	No. of physical transfers to each device
	Mean service time of each device
	Total numbers of paging and swap transfers (not available on some variants of UNIX)
	Average free memory
	For each network interface, the number of blocks/ packets transmitted/ received/ no. of errors/ collisions
WORKLOAD	for each instance of a command or process, or failing that, aggregated statistics by command or process:

	Start/end time
	If aggregated stats, the number executed and the total response time of those commands
	CPU time used (or CPU utilization)
	No. of page faults; average memory used
	Total no. of I/O transfers [ideally, if possible, broken down into user data I/O transfers, system related I/O (i.e. file management), paging/swap transfers; ideally, broken down by I/O device]
	Ideally, number of user transactions processed.
DATABASE	Any usage data collected about Oracle/SQL Server et cetera, broken down by database and session:
	Session start/end time
	CPU usage I/O, by device or file [divided into data I/O transfers and db admin I/Os; reads; writes; read hit rate %; write hit rate %]
	Frequency of lock requests and waits
	No. of user transactions processed
	Mean response time and preferably 95%ile response time [or some measure of the response time distribution]
	Av. memory used
CONFIGURATION	**for each server**
	Operating system type and version
	No. of CPUs
	List of I/O configuration, showing all devices by name, identifying controllers and associating devices with their parent controllers as well as a list of network interfaces

Table C.6 CMP data required for modeling

C.7 CMP deliverables

This table is indicative only. The requirements and detail will vary from site to site:

Workload forecast scenarios (WFS) – statements of requirements for capacity
Resource plans by equipment class showing capacity & usage over time derived from WFSs
Resource usage reports showing actual usage against plan to provide control
Resource inventory – list of equipment, topology, software and environmentals
Acquisition plans predicted changes to be applied in date order
Configuration diagrams – complete and up to date
Application design assessments – performance predictions, impact analyses, SLO evaluations
Designed and assured performance appropriate to the business requirements of the services
Optimum service/cost balance to ensure the best business outcome
Reports as listed in section C.8

Table C.7 CMP deliverables

C.8 CMP typical reports required

Table C.8 is indicative only. The requirements and detail will vary from site to site, but this list shows a representative starting point.

Analysis by System per node	
CPU by processor or total per interval:	% utilization (/system, /user, /IO Wait, /Idle).
Block device by device or total per interval:	% utilization, Read Write requests per sec, et cetera
IO per interval:	Logical reads & writes per sec, % cached, et cetera
Free memory per interval:	Free memory pages, pages freed/scanned/sec, et cetera
Paging/swapping summary per interval by CPU or total:	Page/swap faults per sec, physical paging IO /sec, et cetera
Process summary per interval by CPU or total:	Process switches/sec, processes running, et cetera
System calls per interval:	System calls/sec, system reads & writes/sec, et cetera
Analysis by user, user/command or command	
Per interval:	Username, elapsed time, No. commands, et cetera
Analysis per file system per interval:	
	Total/% inodes/blocks/KB available/used/free
Database analysis	
Overview (per interval):	CPU usage, current logons, reads/writes et cetera
File IO per file id/name per interval or over period:	physical disk reads/writes, response time, et cetera
Session analysis per session	Metrics, profile, table scans, redo log, latches
Alert summary	
Chronological list and exception reports to email et cetera	Of alerts, violations and severity; successful integration of major issues into relevant ticketing systems
Model reports:	
Per model	Response time per component (/cpu Busy/ Q et cetera)
	Device utilization & Q per device (/component)
	Memory residence & Q per component
Per scenario (per projection)	Response time analysis, throughput analysis, device utilization analysis

Table C.8 CMP typical reports required

C.9   CMMI stages and capacity management

Table C.9 suggests a list of activities that reflect the levels of maturity of capacity management as per CMMI. This is clearly subjective and requires local definitions.

#	State	Symptoms	ITSM	Capacity management
0	Inert	Frozen	Nil	Nil
1	Chaos Ad hoc	Undocumented Unpredictable	Multiple informal help options Minimal IT Operations User call notification Uncoordinated problem resolution Manual configuration of updates	Backup Ad hoc and post hoc monitoring & alerting
2	Reactive Tool leverage	Fire fighting Centralized IT operations Silo IT infrastructure (network, db, server, desktop)	Asset register/inventory discovery Simple problem management (trouble ticket) Simple event management Recovery/replication for storage Desktop software distribution Real time event monitoring	Simple alert management Simple uptime measurement Simple utilization threshold analysis
3	Proactive Operational process engineering	IT operations command centre Consolidated Service desk Defined process managers Identified escalation resources Ops-AppDev collaboration	Analyze workload trends Set local thresholds Predict problems Measure app availability Mature problem, incident, configuration, change and performance analysis processes Root cause analysis Change tracking and control Asset management within silos	Simple utilization trend analysis Availability management with component SLOs Establish performance management Event correlation with automation Proactive performance monitoring, thresholding and reporting Historical CDB/CMIS End-user transaction response time assessment Resource level capacity management
4	Measured Service delivery process engineering	Business IT alignment Service delivery process engineering Defined services and service quality Ops- appDev – IT architects collaboration Business service management	Relationship managers Service delivery managers IT service definition, classes, costs, service portfolio/catalogue, requests and delivery Configuration management and policies in CMDB/CIS Change management and compliance audit Process integration and automation across ITSM	Performance engineering Capacity plans End-to-end SLA reporting Capacity management Availability and SLA management with measurement and reporting App transaction profiling Service level capacity management

#	State	Symptoms	ITSM	Capacity management
5	Optimized Value-added Manage IT as a business	IT as strategic business partner IT and business metric linkage IT/business collaboration improves business process Business agility	Real time infrastructure Business planning CIO on executive Ops – AppDev – IT Arch – Business collaboration Automation of IT infrastructure Business oriented SLA policies Process integration and automation across ITSM and business processes IT service portfolio	Aggregated IT capacity planning as part of the business planning activities Business service management with business revenue impact analysis Enterprise dashboard reporting Corporate performance management Business-level capacity management

Table C.9 CMMI stages and capacity management

C.10 CMP KPIs

Note that many of these measures have to be refined in practice at every site, for example, to modify the word 'service' to read perhaps as 'all mission critical services' or 'all category 1 services'. CMT is used to indicate the capacity management team.

#	Practice	KPI	Measure
1	Capacity management: BCM	Involvement in projects/ services	% of projects/ services involved in at BCM
2	Capacity management: SCM	Involvement in projects/ services	% of projects/ services involved in at SCM
3	Capacity management: R/CCM	Involvement in projects/ services	% of projects/ services involved in at R/CCM
4	Capacity management – capacity plans	Deliverables published	% on target with capacity plans
5	Capacity management – performance reports	Deliverables published	% coverage of agreed performance reports
6	Capacity management – exception reports	Deliverables published	Number of appropriate exception reports and alarms raised via CMP thresholds
7	Capacity planning	Unforeseen purchases	# of deviations from capacity plan
8	Resource monitoring	Target machines in CDB/CMIS	% machines with resource data in CDB/CMIS
9	Service monitoring	Services in CDB/CMIS	% services with service metrics in CDB/CMIS
10	Business monitoring	Business metrics in CDB/CMIS	% services with business impact in CDB/CMIS
11	Incidents	Number of capacity related	# incidents agreed as CMT issues; % when CMT involved at project launch versus. % when not

#	Practice	KPI	Measure
12	Problems	Number of capacity related	# problems agreed as CMT issues; % when CMT involved at project launch versus. % when not
13	SLA breaches	Number of performance related	# due to insufficient capacity
14	Confidence in process	Assessment of maturity and risk	% of services at risk (assurance matrix)
15	Systems in reasonable use	Overall system average utilization minimum level	% CPU average utilization to be above an agreed minimum such as 50% during predefined production period (e.g. 9-12 & 2-5)
16	Systems with reasonable spare capacity	Peak system utilization	% CPU average utilization to be below an agreed maximum such as 80% during predefined production period (e.g. peak hour of week).

Table C.10 CMP KPIs

C.11 CMP risks

The Capacity Risk Matrix attempts to provide an objective view of the CMP. It is usually a large document (typically on A3 sized paper) with a lot of detail and this checklist merely indicates the sort of data already underpinning the CMT KPIs above.

The objective of the Capacity Risk Matrix is to provide a dashboard representing the level of control CMT has on the current status and evolution of service requirements and platform capacity

All parameters are defined and scored for critical services (with local significance weighting factors applied):

Entity	Attribute	Weighting	Score
Indicators	Business, service and resource KPIs with thresholds	33%	
Problems	Known performance problems	17%	
Confidence self-assessment	CMT view of infrastructure to support future change	21%	
Reporting capabilities	Automatic and exception reports	8%	
Capacity model	Existing models and/or application test results	8%	
Historic data	Availability of historic data on application performance	4%	
Infrastructure process and tools	For measuring and controlling on the application lifecycle	4%	

Entity	Attribute	Weighting	Score
Application owner	Available and well aware of the status and evolution of the application	4%	

Table C.11 CMP risks

This is laid out as a table and scored in the light of defined ratings and measures to yield a total % score per service.

Threshold values are determined to identify those services which are seen to be at risk and need particular attention.

Appendix D. Capacity Plan

D1. Capacity plan template

A standard practical layout, based on an amalgam of ITIL, MOM and others. The major local variants will lie in the scope (one server, one service, one datacenter, one enterprise) and the detail available, particularly on business level aspects and workload characterization.

Contents

0. Management summary
1. Introduction
   - Scope of the plan and background to the server(s), service(s) involved
   - What elements of the IT infrastructure are addressed in this plan
   - Current levels of relevant capacity in the organization
   - Problems being experienced due to under capacity
   - Degree to which service levels are being achieved
   - Outline of structure of plan, references to related documents and glossary
   - Changes since last issue of the capacity plan
   - Methods used to obtain information and business data sources
   - Workload forecasts and modeling techniques used
2. Assumptions made
3. Business scenarios
4. Service summary
   - Current and recent service provision
   - Current and recent resource usage
   - Service forecasts

List of corresponding workloads and workload forecast scenarios

5. Resource summary
   - Service forecasts
6. Options for service improvement
7. Cost model
8. Recommendations
   - Business benefits to be expected
   - Potential impact of carrying out the recommendations
   - Risks involved
   - Resources required
   - Costs, both set-up and ongoing

0. **Management Summary**

This is a summary of the main issues, options, recommendations and costs. It should not contain any equations (or any material that is not elsewhere within the report). Describe here, in non-technical terms, the current state of the configurations (how much spare capacity, how this compares to performance thresholds et cetera), expected changes in demand and their business drivers, predicted hardware changes and their related costs.

This should always be written with the utmost care as it will be the most frequently read part of the plan. It should be kept to a single page if at all possible.

1. **Introduction**

The contents of this section depend very much on the site and its maturity in the use of
capacity management. It is a good place to pave the way for the rest of the plan and make sure
all likely readers have a clear understanding of the nature of the report and its intended local
impact.

— *Scope of the plan*
  > What the plan covers (service, server, enterprise)
  > List and brief description of business services supported
  > List of elements of the infrastructure that are(and are not) addressed

  The potential scope of capacity management includes all items of hardware, software and
  human resources. This extends from PCs to supercomputers, routers to WANS, printers
  to scanners, shareware to SAP. Clearly the sensible thing to do is to concentrate on those
  few mission-critical applications (the 'loved ones') that get the lion's share of attention —
  indeed, those where problems may result in the service desk taking a call from the managing
  director or CEO.

  As it says in the ITIL Service Delivery book, "ideally, the capacity plan should encompass
  all IT resources". Again, for practical reasons it is often better to have several capacity
  plans, each encompassing a different business area or critical project. Often sub-groupings
  based on span of control is appreciated by local managers who can then hone in on their
  own territory (and possibly try to ensure they do not appear as issues on a higher level
  aggregated report for executive management).

  The best way to enumerate the current levels of capacity is therefore to list the mainframes,
  servers and network hardware that carry the weight of the mission critical processing, and to
  specify their current model names and power ratings by some agreed method (for example,
  the SpecIntrate ratings). Similarly, the capacity of the largest (newest, most expensive) data
  storage should be described, together with approximate amounts of space used and free.

  An alternative and entirely practical approach, which is widely adopted, is to maintain
  multiple capacity plans, typically one plan per major application or project.

— *Objectives*
— *Requirements, targets, constraints*

  The objectives of the plan should be to ensure that agreed SLAs are met both now and
  in the future. In the absence of meaningful performance targets, it is usual to list here
  the assumed SLOs such as 'no more than a 30% degradation from the current level of
  performance whilst supporting up to 50% more workload.'

— *Background*
  • Current levels of capacity in the plan
  • Problems experienced due to under capacity
    Under-capacity, of course, is a 'bad thing'. If the cause of the under capacity is the failure
    to invest as recommended in the last version of the capacity plan, now is the time to say so.
  • Degree to which service levels are being achieved
    For internal users, the real issue is the ability to process the necessary work in the
    available time. For online customers using a web-based application, the main issue is
    likely to be the ease of navigation and the layout of the screens, rather than the response
    time (although that is of course relevant). Perhaps the best advice here is to concentrate
    on the 'loved ones', using uncontroversial statistics such as the number of performance-
    related incidents that have been raised with the service desk.

- Changes since last issue of the capacity plan
  This should only be a summary, not a line-by-line comparison.
- *Format of plan*
  - Outline of structure of report
  - References to related documents (and maybe a glossary)
- *Methods used to obtain information*
  - Business data sources
  - Workload forecasts
  - Modeling

The capacity plan is likely to have significant financial implications. For each of the three sub-practices (BCM,SCM,R/CCM) you should state how the relevant information was obtained. Together with a specific list of assumptions, these statements give the capacity plan the required degree of credibility.

2. **Assumptions**

Identify here any major assumptions that are key to the business or technical case. Do not list all the detailed assumptions made about particular technical issues such as mapping I/O to devices, more a place to log the major caveats that are associated with the plan. Typical examples that should be included are clearly the source of business information, the lack of business drivers or SLAs or other areas where the situation is not as the author would have preferred.

3. **Business scenarios**

This gives the range of possibilities considered for how the business will develop over the lifetime of the plan. There may be several scenarios, with optimistic, likely, and pessimistic growth estimates. Identify here the key assumptions made in the alternative scenarios evaluated. Again identify the source of information and any risk analysis done on the likely impact of errors in the estimates. Essentially list the key scenario criteria and any estimates of tolerance in the accuracy of those parameters or risk analysis undertaken.

4. **Service summary**

The objective of this section of the capacity plan is to give detailed information about the services that are being supported:

- *Current and recent service provision*
  This should quantify the transaction volumes and consequent resource consumption of the services being considered in this version of the plan. Trending can provide retrospective information about how accurate last year's business forecasts were, and so how much faith to put in the new forecasts.
- *Current and recent resource usage*
  Explain how the services identified will use the available resources, and show how the service forecasts will affect the demand for resources.
- *Service forecasts of business volumes*
  Use this section to report on old services disappearing and new services arriving, as described in the business plans that have been used as input to this capacity plan. These numbers are key.
- *Corresponding list of computer workloads and resource requirements*
  The service may be reflected as a single workload or a set of workload components that need to be considered separately.

This section of the plan translates the business forecast into computing terms by combining the current resource usage with the additional resources implied by the BFU forecasts. The table must identify all workloads used by the above services.

Many plans consider in detail only the processor and disk requirements of the workloads. Other related resources (memory, I/O bandwidth, disk controller, cache, memory, networks et cetera) are often not dealt with at an individual workload level but system wide, as part of the configuration management process which is covered in the resources section below.

Define the process and disk storage capacity demands that are expected to be made on each of the servers within the scope of the plan over the planning period. For each server, list the individual workloads with their expected requirements. Use a 'remainder' or 'other' workload to refer to the resource usage that cannot be attributed to a specific business workload or are not of interest to the study. This includes system processes, overhead and resource consumption that cannot be uniquely identified. It may also be useful to separate other required maintenance workloads such as back-up or de-fragmentation processes so that these workloads can be better managed.

For each workload, the factors leading to the changes in resource requirements are quantified and an explanation of significant changes provided. The main three growth factor types are described below:

+ Business growth – resource requirement changes determined by changes in the expected business volumes. Normally, the BFU figures will appear in the service section of this plan. This information is collected from the relevant business areas or taken from the SLA, where it exists.

+ Application maturity – underlying growth, caused by such factors as growing historical data bases, increased user familiarity with the application (leading to increased transaction rates), incremental improvements to the environment et cetera. This growth factor is derived from an historical analysis of observed resource consumption trends.

+ Technical change – the impact of any proposed change to the application itself or to its environment is reflected in this factor. Changes included here might be increased application functionality, enhanced middleware or the implementation of a new software release. The change might increase or decrease resource requirements. This information is gathered from the relevant developers or support areas.

Note that, for processor requirements, all individual workload predictions relate to the predicted peak period of the server as a whole – details of the peak period, workload classification scheme, workload integration algorithm and capture ratio compensation used to produce the workload forecast scenarios which are input to the resource section.

– *Workload forecast scenarios*

Essentially an integration of all the relevant workloads into convenient aggregations for consideration in relation to the servers used or the services addressed. (If there are no such forecasts, it is necessary to fabricate one, such as a simple assumption that if the current recent peak traffic is X, then this can grow to N*X before suffering capacity/performance issues. In this way, if there are known blanket increases due to the planned growth of an entire division or business unit, that workload will also be assessed in the plan.)

- *Workload section, processor requirements, processor scenarios*
  Describe here how the peak period is defined, how the individual workloads have been combined to produce the peak overall demand, how the workloads have been classified and how capture ratios (if applicable) have been incorporated in to the calculations.
- *Disk storage requirements*
- *Business and technical drivers*
  Describe here the business and technical factors which are causing the major changes (usually increases) in demand – referring back to the relevant workload tables, as required.

  Note that you should repeat 'Processor scenarios', 'Disk storage requirements' and 'Business and technical drivers' sections for each server in scope.

5. **Resource Summary**

   Here, you explain how the services identified on the previous service summary section will use the available resources, and show how the service forecasts will affect the demand for resources
   - *Resource forecasts – account of impact of workload requirements*
     This section is crucial. The results of modeling or other similar studies are a key input to this section, which will show the likely resource usage required by the business applications, based on the service forecasts outlined earlier and thus the resources required to support the applications in a manner that will allow service level targets to be met. Typically there will be several technical options – here is the place to explain them, and if possible rank them in order of cost-benefit.

     Insert here details of any hardware upgrades required. This section might include resources that have not been dealt with earlier (e.g. controllers, cache memory et cetera) and the justification for these upgrades must be provided here. This should also include any factors such as network LAN or WAN or special considerations such as coding practice for multi-tier client/server architectures which may seem appear initially as network issues.

     N.B. Repeat 'Processor plan', 'Processor upgrade description', and 'Disk storage plan' for all servers in scope.

6. **Options for service improvement**

   In practice there are some overlaps between this section and the previous one. Whereas the previous section is looking at the expected future resource usage of existing and proposed new applications, this section is looking at ways of controlling or managing the resource usage for the general benefit of all applications. Suggested topics in the ITIL guide include:
   - *Server consolidation (though not in those exact words)*
   - *Network upgrades*
   - *Application or system tuning*
   - *Rewriting old applications*
   - *Upgrading hardware or software as new technology or to assist with sustainability or support of service*

   Between them, the sections service summary, resource summary and options for service improvement include the bulk of the real work involved in writing a capacity plan. Effort put into these areas will repay dividends in terms of the acceptability of the plan as a whole.

7. **Cost model**
   - *Quantifies financial aspects of resource upgrades*
   This is where you explain the costs associated with the various options that you have put forward. You should also document the ongoing costs associated with the provision of IT services and the support costs/ benefits for replacement whether it be new technology or supportability.

8. **Recommendations**
   - *Summary of previous recommendations*
   This should outline the recommendations made in the previous plan, and their current status. For example, they could have been implemented, rejected or planned for the future.
   - *List of new recommendations*
   This is where you explain which options you prefer, and why. The following information should be assessed for each of your recommendations
   - *Business benefits to be expected*
   For example, the ability to support new services, or process higher volumes of existing work
   - *Potential impact of carrying out the recommendations*
   For example, that more office space will be required to hold all the proposed new hardware
   - *Risks involved*
   For example, that new hardware or software may not function according to specification
   - *Resources required*
   Expressed in terms of staff, time and money
   - *Costs, both set-up and ongoing*
   Associated with all the above.

D2. Capacity plan example

This is a simple example based on a well instrumented application running on a simple configuration with clearly defined business drivers, users, services, SLAs and workloads. It is intended to provide a vehicle for understanding the content of a capacity plan rather than appreciating the problems of generating a plan in real life.

Metronix overview

An enterprise with a single line of business and simple IT configuration.

There are just three services involved and they are all included in an annual capacity plan.

There are three divisions, called sales, customer service and management-finance (or mgt-finance).

Their workloads can be related to the number of active users for each.

They all work a 9-5 day and most of the processing is on-line. There is a small amount of other work (primarily security dumps and data management) done in an evening shift. The peak hours are from 10-12 in the morning and 2-4 in the afternoon and the averages over this four hour period are used for all the SLAs et cetera. They work and report on a monthly basis and projection points are established as 12 monthly periods per year.

The applications are all packaged from an external supplier, exploiting an Enterprise Java Bean Business layer. Multiple concurrent Java Virtual Machines run with a managed thread limit. A standard RDBMS environment is used and is well instrumented with application transaction counts and response times.

The architecture is three tier, with a front-end server, an application server and a database clustered back-end. The business is small but very profitable and a few years ago when there were I/O problems, the managing director (MD) was persuaded by a hardware salesperson to invest in a SAN (which is now beginning to prove worthwhile). So there is both local disk and a SAN, but the applications have been already migrated to do as much I/O as possible to SAN without major rewrites (and the application provider has resisted such rewrites for some time).

Current configuration
The front-end server is a single server with two processors (RPI/CPU=15).
The application server is a single server with 4 processors (RPI/CPU=125).
The database server is a cluster of machines with 8 processors (RPI/CPU=300).
(The RPI used in this case is SpecInt2000).

Current users and throughput
There are 500 sales users achieving a total of 7200 transactions per hour (2 per sec).
There are 100 customer service users achieving a total of 4500 transactions per hour.
There are 60 mgt-finance users achieving a total of 2400 transactions per hour.

SLAs
The agreed SLAs for each line of business are simple and are expressed in terms of the averages over the peak hours for all the transactions for each group of users:
- sales 1.5 seconds
- customer Service 2 seconds
- mgt-finance 6 seconds.

Business plan
The business is going well. Sales can readily be increased by adding more sales users. The product is stable and the corresponding growth in customer service is proportional to the sales, but at about half the rate of increase. The management and finance is lean, automated and efficient and is unlikely to require any more staff. So the expected growth for next year (in line with the growth over the last few years) is 10% sales, 5% customer support and zero in mgt-finance.

Brief
A known and trusted consultant has been brought in early to do his regular annual capacity plan project. He has previously created a bespoke capacity management solution using Excel. He has been brought in early because the customer service users are complaining about the service, though neither sales nor management-finance have (and they both usually do as soon as there is a problem).

He has been asked to try to find and recommend a solution that will resolve the current issues soon and keep the system going for another year that minimize costs and do not incur changes to the applications package and that will meet the SLAs to an acceptable degree.

He has been told to produce the answer quickly so that any necessary immediate purchasing can be actioned in the next month or so. The MD does not want a lot of options but would rather have a clear-cut recommendation. Precise costing can be left to Metronix staff, just 'ballpark' numbers will suffice.

Metronix capacity plan

Even with the simple scenario defined and all the given metrics and the absence of costing detail, the production capacity plan is fifteen pages long and incorporates twenty-one figures. Formal production plans for just three services as in this case might well be longer, but should try not to be much more than twice as long.

Please note that this section includes its own set of figures and tables numbered MCP 1-8 and MCP 1-13 respectively.

Metronix Capacity Plan March 2009	
Document:	C:\Metronix\Capacity Plan.doc
Author:	Adam Grummitt
QA:	Stuart Baker
Date:	09 March 2009
Last printed:	09 March 2009
Version:	V0.1 – early and quick draft
Status:	This draft has been generated to meet an urgent request from the MD
Circulation:	Readers for comment
Contents:	Management summary
	1. Introduction
	2. Assumptions
	3. Business scenarios

	4. Service summary
	    – current and recent service provision
	    – service forecasts

	5. Resource summary
	    – current and recent resource usage
	    – resource forecasts

	6. Options for service improvement
	7. Cost model

	8. Recommendations
	    – business benefits to be expected
	    – potential impact of carrying out the recommendations
	    – risks involved
	    – resources required
	    – costs, both set-up and ongoing

Management summary

The service under review is that for Metronix as a whole. It provides the IT infrastructure and applications to support all three divisions, namely sales, customer service and management-finance. It is based on a three-tier architecture with a front-end server, an application server and a database clustered back-end.

All three divisions have established service level agreements (SLAs) which were established some years ago and were still being met in last year's predictions. However this report was requested in the light of complaints about the service from customer service. An initial review and baseline model of the current status revealed that the relevant SLA is not being met, to a significant degree. The required average response time for Customer Service transactions over the key four hour period per working day (10-12am and 2-4pm) is 2 seconds. The current observed level is 2.8 seconds. This is largely because of the success of the company, such that the number of sales and customer service users has grown more than predicted last year. The required service levels for both sales and management-finance are currently being met.

However, this plan is also looking ahead for the next year. After discussion with the managing director, it has been assumed that the business will continue to expand at a significant rate, more than doubling in total sales next year. As the sales have been directly related to the number of salesmen for some years, this plan assumes (as agreed) a growth rate in sales users of 10% per month, of customer service of 5% and management-finance of 0%. If these numbers are not certain, a separate exercise will be necessary to undertake a sensitivity analysis to these estimates and produce a risk analysis. This may be thought advisable in the light of last year's pessimistic estimates.

Based on these given numbers, all services will be worse than their required SLAs within three months and the system will be saturated within ten months. There are options to improve the service. These fall into three groups.

The SAN is proving to be a fine investment. But the local disk I/O is a significant issue already and will become more so. Sadly, the main option of moving more I/O to the faster SAN is not available as the application provider is not prepared to undertake this until a potential future release whose date has already slipped some years. However, an immediate and relatively cheap upgrade to smaller, faster disks (10,000 rpm rather than 5,400 rpm) will get the customer service back to its required SLA. As this will take a while to agree and arrange, it is assumed that this will happen in period 2.

Upgrades to the servers are also proposed. The database clustered server can be moved from 8-way to 12-way in period 5 to maintain service levels. This will be expensive.

A further upgrade to the application server at period 10 will be required which will be not so expensive as only the processor chips are involved (doubling their speed and power rating).

With these three staged upgrades, the service will be maintained throughout the year based on the agreed estimates for growth. There will still be three periods within the year when customer service will suffer performance worse than their SLA. The delay in delivery of the faster local disks will mean that in period one the response time will be 2.9 seconds. In period four it will degrade slightly to 2.1 seconds and again in period nine it will fall to 2.2 seconds. However, these numbers are all within what customer service has been experiencing and it may be that their SLA should be renegotiated to say 2.5 seconds.

Other options for upgrades have been considered, or trying to undertake these upgrades more quickly. All of these approaches have been assessed as either more expensive or unrealistic with the administration and infrastructure work involved with the current size of the ITSM team. However, what is recommended is a separate project to establish a more effective reporting and alerting regime to track utilizations and avoid SLAs being violated.

1. Introduction

This capacity plan covers the entire IT system for Metronix. Thus it incorporates all three tiers of server (front-end, application and database) as well as the locally connected disks and the SAN. It does not address the network (although utilizations are observed to be less than 10% such that there are no network issues likely for some time).

The business services incorporated are those for sales, customer services and management-finance.

The objectives for the services are set out in their SLAs with performance targets defined for average response times over the agreed four-hour peak period (10-12am and 2-4pm).
The applications are all packaged from an external supplier, exploiting an Enterprise Java Bean Business layer with Java Virtual Machine threads. It makes use of a standard RDBMS environment and is well instrumented with transaction counts and response times.

The architecture is three-tier, with a front-end server, an application server and a database clustered back-end. There is both local disk and a SAN, but the applications have been already migrated to do as much I/O as possible to SAN without major rewrites.

The capacity plan issued last year assumed a reasonable agreed growth in the business. In the event, the business has grown even more than expected and there have been shortcomings in the service in the last few months for customers services users.

Note that throughout this report, the monthly accounting periods (P1 – P12) correspond to the forecast projection points (PP01 – PP12).

This plan is designed to address that issue as quickly as practical (in P2) and to ensure that given the increase in business expected this year, the services will be maintained at the required levels.

The structure of this report is as per the standard developed within Metronix over the years and is largely in accord with ITIL recommendations.

The methods used to gather data have been essentially by interview with the MD for the business driver estimates and with Operations for all the statistics available from the application, servers and RDBMS.

The financial numbers are estimates based on an initial scan on the web to be supported with more detail from operations and finance.

2. Assumptions

The main assumptions incorporated within this plan lie in the business estimates of the potential growth rates in the numbers of active users. There is also the key issue of the lack of control over the application provider, in that if more I/O could be directed to the SAN it would have a major impact.

The current SLAs are taken as fixed. There may be a case to review the figure for customer services (a value of 2.5 seconds would yield a cheaper configuration solution). The current values for the average response time over the standard four hour peak period (10-12am and 2-4pm) are.

Sales	1.5 seconds
Customer service	2 seconds
Mgt-finance	6 seconds

Table MCP-1 SLAs per service

3. Business scenarios

The growth in sales over the next year is planned to more than double. It has been agreed that this will be reflected in the number of users as in table MCP-2.

Sales	10% per month
Customer services	5% per month
Mgt-finance	0% per month

Table MCP-2 Assumed growth rates for next year

It has been established in the past that the number of active concurrent users is directly proportional to the number of users and the workload itself is directly proportional to the number of active concurrent users. These estimates are key to the plan proposed and may merit further sensitivity analysis.

4. Service summary

The current activity has been analyzed and is presented in a baseline model as in table MCP-3.

Service	Sales	Customer-service	Mgt-finance
Active users	500	100	60
Hourly throughput	7200	4500	2400

Table MCP-3 Current activity per service

The servers in the three tier architecture are defined in table MCP-4.

Server	Processors	RPI per CPU
Front-end	2	15
Application	4	125
DBMS	8	300

Table MCP-4 Current processor configuration

Current and recent service provision

The services are currently not all achieving the required SLAs – Customer services is in violation (shown in ▇).

End-to-end response time	Sales	Customer-service	Mgt-finance
SLA seconds	1.5	2.0	6.0
Observed	1.4	2.8	5.0

Table MCP-5 Current SLAs

Current and recent resource usage

The servers involved have been measured and found to be reasonably busy currently (except for the lightly used front-end server).

Server	Sales	Customer-service	Mgt-finance
Front-end	5%	8%	7%
Application	18%	13%	24%
DBMS	25%	14%	25%
Server	Sales	Customer-service	Mgt-finance
Front-end	5%	8%	7%

Table MCP-6 Server % utilization per service

Note that 'other' includes a variety of identified system administration processes and other related system management work. These are an intrinsic overhead and have been accounted for in the model.

The I/O rates have been measured for the locally connected disks and the SAN and are currently quite high for the former.

I/O rates per second	Sales	Customer-service	Mgt-finance	Other	Total
Local disk	75	150	100	30	355
SAN	750	1250	900	10	2910

Table MCP-7 I/O rates per service

The application metrics have been analyzed to assess the related number of active threads and transactions per second. Also the database metrics have been reviewed to check the queries per second and the query time in msecs.

Service forecasts of business volumes

The business volumes are related directly to the number of active users so a simple table of workload growth is applicable with hourly throughputs as in table MCP-8 (using simple monthly increments of 10% for sales, 5% for customer-service and 0% for Mgt-finance).

Service	Base-line	PP1	PP2	PP3	PP4	PP5	PP6	PP7	PP8	PP9	PP10	PP11	PP12
Sales	7200	7920	8640	9360	10080	10800	11520	12240	12960	13680	14400	15120	15840
Customer-service	4500	4725	4950	5175	5400	5625	5850	6075	6300	6525	6750	6975	7200
Mgt-finance	2400	2400	2400	2400	2400	2400	2400	2400	2400	2400	2400	2400	2400

Table MCP-8 Forecasts of hourly throughputs per service per projection point (month)

5. Resource summary

Initial scenario with just workload changes applied and no upgrade actions

The response times for each service have been analyzed taking the baseline configuration and incrementing the traffic as above. Values in red (▓) are in violation of SLAs. (This simple example has a single threshold for violations; more complex sites would use at least two to enable a Red Amber Green (RAG) coding rather than just Red/Green.)

Initial scenario:	BASELINE	PP01	PP02	PP03	PP04	PP05	PP06	PP07	PP08	PP09
Sales:	1.35	1.44	1.55	1.68	1.86	2.11	2.49	3.19	5.07	64.03
Customer service:	2.77	2.89	3.02	3.19	3.40	3.67	4.07	4.76	6.51	59.42
Management-finance:	4.97	5.27	5.63	6.08	6.66	7.45	8.66	10.85	16.60	193.60

Table MCP-9 Response times per projection point (month)

Presenting this graphically shows the non-linear degradation in response time arising from the linear increase in the number of users. Note that the Y-axis has been cut-off at 10 seconds.

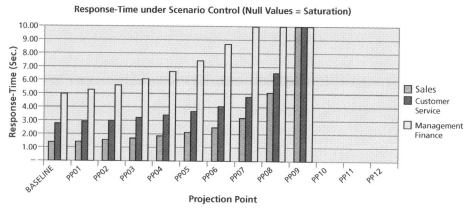

Figure MCP-1 Histogram of response times

The impact of queuing for devices is shown in table MCP-10. This is shown for PP7 when the responses are roughly double the SLAs. This shows the contribution of queuing and service at each logical device (each server CPU, disk, and SAN). The values have been normalized to % of each response time.

Service ID:	Sales	Customer svce	Mgt finance
Queuing at front-end	0%	1%	1%
Front-end CPU service	1%	2%	1%
Queuing at app server	14%	10%	16%
Application CPU service	4%	3%	5%
Queuing at DBMS server	40%	20%	34%
DBMS CPU service	6%	3%	5%
Queuing at local disk	13%	25%	15%
Local disk I/O service	18%	33%	20%
Queuing at SAN	1%	2%	1%
SAN disk I/O service	2%	3%	2%

Table MCP-10 Response time state analysis

This highlights the impact of the local disk queuing and service times to the response for customer-service. The same figures can be shown graphically:

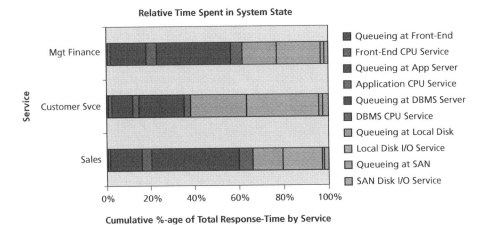

Figure MCP-2 Bar chart of response time state (normalized) at PP7

If there are no upgrades to the system, the SLAs will degrade even more than now. Currently the customer services SLA is the only violation with 2.8 instead of 2. Within three months, if no action is taken, all three services' SLAs will be in violation, within seven months they will all be about doubled and within 10 the system will be saturated. This is shown in the initial set of projections shown in table MCP-11, again just taking the baseline configuration and incrementing the traffic as in figure MCP-2.

The response times relative to their respective SLAs are:

Initial scenario:	BASELINE	PP01	PP02	PP03	PP04	PP05	PP06	PP07	PP08	PP09	PP10
Sales:	90%	96%	103%	112%	124%	141%	166%	213%	338%	4269%	sat
Customer service:	138%	144%	151%	159%	170%	183%	203%	238%	326%	2971%	sat
Management-finance:	83%	88%	94%	101%	111%	124%	144%	181%	277%	3227%	sat

Table MCP-11 Response times relative to SLAs

This shows the relative % response time by calculating response time *100/SLA. Under 100 good, over 100 bad.

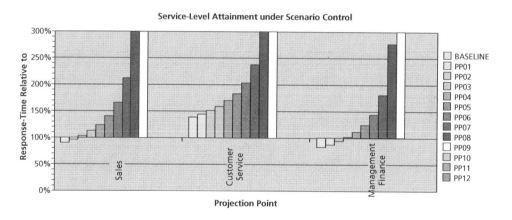

Figure MCP-3 Histogram of response times relative to SLAs

Relative response times as represented graphically in figure MCP-3, with a Y axis cut-off at 300%. This shows that both sales and mgt-finance are currently below the SLA (response time under 100% of the SLA) but rapidly degrade to double or treble the service level (200% or 300%) before the model saturates at P10.

The corresponding resource usages are as shown in table MCP-12 and figure MCP-4.

Initial scenario:	Baseline	PP01	PP02	PP03	PP04	PP05	PP06	PP07	PP08	PP09	PP10
Front-End:	23.0%	23.9%	24.8%	25.7%	26.6%	27.5%	28.4%	29.3%	30.2%	31.1%	32.0%
Application server:	65.0%	67.5%	69.9%	72.4%	74.8%	77.3%	79.7%	82.2%	84.6%	87.1%	89.5%
Database cluster:	71.0%	74.2%	77.4%	80.6%	83.8%	87.0%	90.2%	93.4%	96.6%	99.8%	100.0%
Local disk:	35.5%	37.0%	38.5%	40.0%	41.5%	43.0%	44.5%	46.0%	47.5%	49.0%	50.5%
SAN:	29.1%	30.5%	31.9%	33.2%	34.6%	36.0%	37.4%	38.7%	40.1%	41.5%	42.9%

Table MCP-12 Resource utilization per device

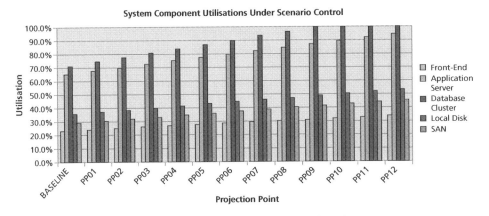

Figure MCP-4 Histogram of resource utilizations per device per projection point (month)

The resource usage for processors tends to degrade above 70% and become an issue above 85%. The corresponding values for locally connected disks tend to be around 35% and 45%. On this basis, attention is drawn immediately to the database cluster, the application server and the local disk.

Upgrade scenario with recommended actions applied
Many options were considered in the modeling of changes to the hardware. However, after analysis, the following scenario emerged as the most cost effective solution.

Processor upgrade options
The front-end processor configuration is small but supports the necessary throughput.
The DBMS cluster server needs an upgrade around P5 by when it will need to be upgraded from 8-way to 12-way. This should allow plenty of time for the procurement exercise which will be significant as the units are quite expensive.
The application processor configuration is adequate until around P10 when it will need faster chips (125 upgraded 150 RPI). This is a comparatively minor upgrade but will still need some preparation.

I/O upgrade options

The SAN is doing the bulk of the work and is performing well.

The remaining I/O which (sadly) has to be supported by locally connected disks presents an immediate problem. This could be addressed by adding more of the same disks, but these are already out-of-date technologically, and it will be more cost-effective to replace them by disks with approximately double the rpm (5,400 to 10,000 rpm). This should be done ASAP, but for the plan it is assumed not to happen until P2 (to allow for the paperwork and infrastructure administration and security involved).

Other upgrade options

Networks and memory have been reviewed and do not make a significant contribution to the service response times.

The above changes to CPUs and disks have been applied to the baseline model and the following table of relative service level achievement emerges.

Upgrade scenario	Base-line	PP01	PP02	PP03	PP04	PP05	PP06	PP07	PP08	PP09	PP10	PP11	PP12
Sales:	90%	96%	78%	86%	97%	68%	73%	78%	85%	94%	56%	58%	61%
Customer service:	138%	144%	91%	97%	105%	87%	91%	96%	102%	110%	76%	78%	81%
Management-finance:	83%	88%	69%	75%	84%	63%	67%	73%	79%	88%	49%	50%	53%

Table MCP-13 Response times relative to service levels with upgrades applied (compare with table MCP-11)

Graphically (and to the same scale as before):

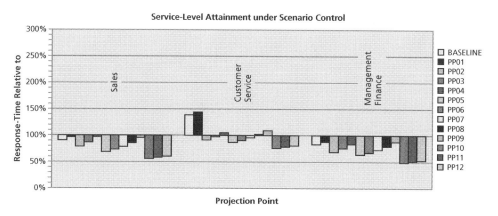

Figure MCP-5 Histogram of response times relative to service levels with upgrades applied (compare with figure MCP-1)

This shows that the only violations are for customer services and that they are marginal. After the initial baseline figure of 138% which degrades to 144% in P1 the SLA is then achieved until a slight violation in P4 at 105% and again in P8 at 102% and in P9 at 110%. These last three violations will scarcely be noticed by the users, especially after their recent experiences at 140% or so.

Sales and mgt-finance should sometimes notice that their service is somewhat improved but as soon as it starts to degrade towards their SLA it is improved again.

The utilization levels under this scenario are shown in figure MCP-6.

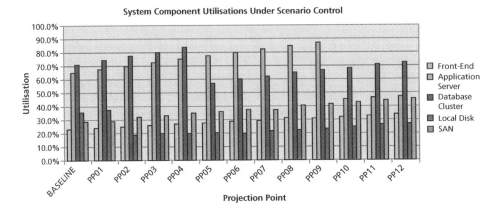

Figure MCP-6 Histogram of resource utilizations per device with upgrades applied (compare with figure MCP-4).

It could be that this report would be more clear if the irrelevant devices were excluded. This graph shows that the front-end is never an issue and the local disk is no longer an issue. However, the locally generated tailor-made reporting package does not readily enable the elimination of this visual noise[48].

The main conclusion of this report is that all is well, although the utilization of the DBMS cluster towards the end of the year may become an issue (especially if the growth assumptions prove pessimistic).

This is reinforced by looking at the queuing contribution at P12.

However, the response times overall look satisfactory as regards the SLAs. The absolute responses are shown in figure MCP-8 (on the same scale as before).

6. Options for service improvement

The options are considered above and a proposed plan is recommended:

1. faster locally connected disks at P2, from 5,000 rpm to 10,000 rpm with a service time improvement from approximately 10 msecs to 5 msecs
2. DBMS cluster upgrade from 8-way to 12-way at P5
3. faster CPU chips in the application server (125 RPI to 250 RPI) at P10

---

48   Visual noise is a term used by Edward Tufte who is a major advocate of effective graphics. See http://www.edwardtufte. com/tufte/

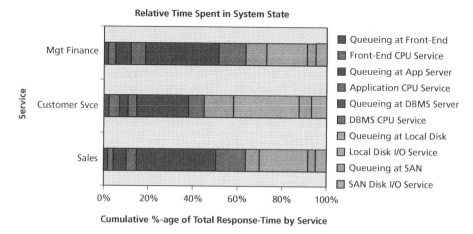

Figure MCP-7 Bar chart of response time state (normalized) at P12 with upgrades applied (compare with figure MCP-2).

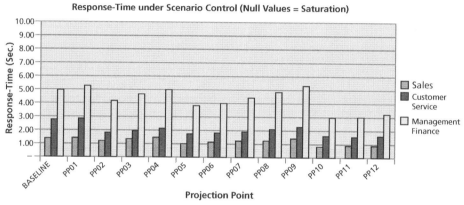

Figure MCP-8 Histogram of response time with upgrades applied (compare with initial figure MCP-1)

7. Cost model

This draft plans has been issued in response to an urgent demand for analysis. The precise costs have not been identified yet, but the upgrades selected have been recommended in the light of current procurement cost experience.

8. Recommendations

Summary of previous recommendations

- Last year's upgrades have all been actioned and have largely met the demands. However, in recent months the customer service demand has outstripped the resources available.

List of new recommendations

- The current recommendations are listed above in section 6.

Business benefits to be expected
- The main benefits will lie in the continued achievement of the required SLAs for sales and mgt-finance with only minor violations for customer services.

Potential impact of carrying out the recommendations
- The main benefit of carrying out the upgrades in this staged manner will be that the optimum cost-performance balance will be achieved.

Risks involved
- The main risks lie in the estimates for the business growth. However, the basic architecture of the current solution is scalable and can be modified again at reasonable cost to cater for whatever extra growth may emerge. The issue is to ensure that the relevant metrics are tracked and an early alert raised rather than waiting for user complaints. To this end a separate project to establish a more rigorous reporting and alerting regime is recommended.

Resources required
- As well as the actual upgrades (new disks, new processors, new chips) there will be the associated effort in terms of project management, CAB, administration, security et cetera.

Costs, both set-up and ongoing
- The costs have not been formally added to this report. A separate spreadsheet has been raised and submitted to the MD for consideration. It is based entirely on quick web-searched estimates to provide a yardstick for consideration and budgeting purposes. A more formal costing will be addressed internally within Metronix.

Appendix E. Knot ITIL

There is a possibility that many readers will decide there is too much emphasis on academic distinctions between differing interpretations of words extracted from different disciplines, such as systems analysis, operational research, business management and so on. In order to get feet back on the ground and be a little more practical, it is a good idea at this point to review the title of this book, *Capacity Management: A Practitioner Guide*. For many sites in the real world, it is not so much a matter of a selection of best practices or even just good practice but more an issue of avoiding bad practice. This was first observed and reflected on in a well-loved book popularly known as 'Not ITIL'.

An excellent ITIL 'complementary' book written by Brian Johnson and Paul Wilkinson is entitled "IT Service Management from hell – Based on Not-ITIL®". In honor of that book, this one will mention an alternative approach of "Knot ITIL". This is so-named in honor of the Gordian Knot, a legend associated with Alexander the Great who when faced with the intractable problem of undoing the Gordian Knot, solved it by a bold stroke of the sword, thus cutting the Gordian Knot. In this case, the knot is that involved with establishing ITIL practices and overcoming the related grumlins; the ITIL knot. The sword is this book.

Knot ITIL is mischievously proposed as it has the advantage of using words that are already well established in the IT world and are easier to remember and reflect the smaller number of six core processes.

As a variation to the information in section 11 of Appendix A, on the six ITSM basic processes contract management, operations management, incident management, change management, configuration management and risk management, a slightly different set of terms could be used – leading to the nice alphabetical structure of A-B-C-D-E-F. Rather than configuration management, 'Assets' is used to indicate not just an asset register but all the rest (topology etc) that is implied by configuration management. The incident management process would be replaced by 'Bugs', using that word to again imply not just software errors but all the bugs in documentation and related issues that the ITIL description covers. 'Change' is used to embrace the change management activities. 'Do' (or 'do it') is used to cover all the aspects of operations management. Proactive management of availability, continuity, capacity and all the related security issues in risk management are covered by 'Efficiency'. And 'Finance' would incorporate all the contract management activities.

Thus we have the same six core processes, with like ITIL practices merged where their descriptions are already quite similar. And they begin with the letters, A-F which aids the memory. This is not intended as a serious option but more as a point for discussion and to increase appreciation of the benefit that ITIL provides with a standard glossary.

In summary, Knot ITIL describes six core processes:

A	Assets	Both asset register and topology as in configuration management.
B	Bugs	Incidents, problems and events. Benign and malignant.
C	Changes	Changes and releases of controlled sets. Suppliers and access and information security.
D	Do it	Both continuity and availability. Both major ongoing disasters and minor disruptive disasters.
E	Efficiency	Availability, continuity and capacity management. Security.
F	Finance	Financial management and service level management. SLM includes service portfolio and catalogue.

This definition of six core processes (A-F) in Knot ITIL has an advantage in that six is both a perfect and virtuous number.
Perfect in that its factors add up to itself (1+2+3 = 6).
Virtuous in that both Buddhists and Hindus identify six virtues and it is only seven in Christianity if you accept temperance as a virtue.

This spurious argument was used in a paper given at CMG which derived a pseudo-theory based on all CMP issues being related to the perfect number six. This paper was drafted on 06/06/06.

Sources

Many different sources have been used in the development of this book. Acknowledgements are due to all the authors whose work has been referenced, either knowingly or unwittingly. Many of the ideas have been around for some time and have been reworked by a variety of authors. This book has merely attempted to summarize them and has also derived a lot of personal material from nineteen papers presented over the years at CMG (USA) by the author. Most of the major sources of inspiration are listed below, but a number of sources from the web have not been formally referenced or listed, largely as they emerged over time from the richly populated landscape that is Google. If there are any references missing, entering the key words into a good search engine is likely to reveal useful links to the topic and related discussions. For this reason, many of the footnotes and references in this book omit formal documentation as the likely website or search parameters should suffice.

Useful websites

A number of sites are quoted in context in the book. Key ones in this field are:
- **Groups**
  - www.cmg.org/CMG has lots of links to related sites
  - www.ukcmg.org.uk/UKCMG is an active international chapter of CMG
  - www.itsmf.com
- **Benchmarks**
  - www.ideasinternational.com/benchmark/bench.html is a gateway to benchmark sites such as spec, TPC et cetera
  - www.tpc.org/ is a link to the Transaction Processing Performance Council
  - www.spec.org/ is a link to the Standard Performance Evaluation Corporation and specint values et cetera
  - www.itsmf-benchmarking.com/ is an itSMF initiative covering various widely accepted standards
- **Education**
  - http://domanski.cs.csi.cuny.edu/ is an education in itself thanks to Dr Bernie Domanski.
  - http://en.itsmportal.net/ is a non-commercial source for ITSM knowledge
- **Examination**
  - EXIN: www.exin-exams.com/
  - TÜV SÜD Academy: www.tuev-sued.de/
  - BCS-ISEB: www.bcs.org/
  - APMG: www.apmgroup.co.uk/
- **Publications**
  - TSO for OGC: www.tsoshop.co.uk/
  - Van Haren Publishing: www.vanharen.net/
  - Inform-IT: www.inform-it.org/

Useful books

There is a vast range of books on the topic of capacity management and related disciplines. Some key ones are listed below:

- Smith, Dr. Connie (1990). *Performance Engineering of Software Systems*. Addison-Wesley.
- Menasce, Prof. Daniel (2004). *Performance by Design: computer capacity planning by example*. Prentice Hall, 2004.
- Menasce, Prof. Daniel (1994). *Capacity planning and Performance modeling*. Prentice Hall.
- Gunther, Neil (2006). *Guerilla Capacity Planning*. Springer-Verlag.
- Harrison, Prof. Peter (1992). *Performance Modeling of Communication Networks and Computer Architectures*. Addison-Wesley.
- Lazowska, Edward (1984). *Quantitative System Performance*. Prentice-Hall.
- Krzanowski, Wojtek (1998). *Introduction to statistical Modeling*. Hodder Arnold.
- Daintith, John & R.D. Nelson (1989). *The Penguin dictionary of Mathematics*. Penguin.
- Rowntree, Derek (1981). *Statistics without tears*. Penguin.
- Poole, David, Alan Mackworth & Randy Goebel (1998). *Computational Intelligence*. Oxford University Press.
- Hopgood, Adrian H. (1993). *Knowledge-Based Systems for engineers and scientists*. CRC Press.

Useful papers

Most of this book has been largely derived from a series of papers given by the author at CMG in the USA over the years:

- 1991 – *A Performance Engineer's view of System Development & trials*
- 1993 – *Cost-Benefit Analysis of Performance Engineering, management and capacity planning in Open Systems or IT infrastructure planning: Catch 22-29*
- 1994 – *Performance management of Client-Server systems* – awarded 'best CP paper'
- 1996 – *Client-server performance management: Evolution or revolution?*
- 1997 – *Performance tuning & capacity planning for Oracle on UNIX – A Case Study*
- 1998 – *Performance Management of distributed systems based on NT & Ethernet*
- 1999 – *Automated performance management advice using Computational intelligence*
- 2000 – *@2001 and all that. E Commerce Performance Management*
- 2002 – *Oracle Performance Management on major operating systems: WULZ*
- 2003 – *Performance assurance by capacity management: Experience refined through ITIL practice*
- 2004 – *Corporate performance management as a pragmatic process in an ITIL world*
- 2006 – *Six sensible steps towards implementing ITIL capacity management*
- 2006 – *ITIL capacity management appreciation workshop*
- 2007 – *The right mix of utility, consolidation and virtualization for optimum cost-capacity-performance*
- 2007 – *Who measures the measurers? KPIs and QoS for the capacity management process*
- 2007 – *Capacity management from A to A workshop*
- 2008 – *Knot not ITIL: How Not to Undo the ITSM Knot using "ITSM from Hell Based on Not ITIL"*

- 2008 – *Dash and Risk! Practical Experience in Implementing Capacity Management Process Audit at Euroclear*
- 2008 – *Mind the Gap – A Review of Gap Analyses of Capacity Management Practice in Various Enterprises*

However, some of this book is based on material derived from a large number of other authors over the years. The main ones are listed below. The papers are given at annual CMG/UKCMG conferences over the last 32/20 years or so. They have not all been properly acknowledged as the book would then have become unduly complicated by footnotes and references. We sincerely hope the authors who recognize any of their own work will appreciate the implicit complement so offered rather than resent it.

- For performance engineering, application modeling and software performance engineering try papers by Connie Smith, Alan Knight, Amy Spellman, Claire Coates, Adrian Johnson et al.
- For modeling algorithms try papers by Daniel Menasce, Neil Gunther, Jeff Buzen, Annie Shum et al.
- For the mainframe try papers by Cheryl Watson, Peter Enrico, Pat Artis, Glen Anderson, Frank Bereznay, Barry Merrill et al.
- For UNIX try papers by Ron Kaminski, Adrian Cockroft et al.
- For Oracle try papers by Tim Foxon, Gary Mulqueen et al.
- For Windows and virtualization try papers by Mark Friedman, Des Atkinson et al.
- For service management try papers by Alan Nance, Brian Johnson, Sherman Porter et al.
- For general papers on many topics try Dr Bernie Domanski, Adam Grummitt et al.

Index

A

Acronyms. 167
Activities 54
Amdahl's Law. .81
Analytical modeling 68
Application Services Library 20
Application sizing. 82
Arthur C. Clarke's three laws 102
Asimovs three laws of Robotics. 103

B

Basic processes 165
Benefits 47
Business capacity management 31
Business driver .35
Business forecast unit 35
Business information Services Library 20
Business process modeling 153

C

Capability Maturity Model. 15
Capacity. 27
Capacity management practice. 9
Capacity management pyramid 32
Capacity management team 9
Capacity manager. 102
Capacity plan. .89
Capacity planning 88
Capacity plan template. 191
Capacity Risk Matrix 189
Capture ratio 62
Central Computer and
    Telecommunications Agency 11
Changes. 63
Checklists. 175
Client-server and n-tier systems 81
Collection period 58
Compliance 117
Computational intelligence 144
Computer Measurement Group 13
Computer optimization
    client-server model 77

D

Consolidation. .38
Control 90
Correlation. 70
Cost 49
Cost-benefit analysis. 50
Critical success factors 133
Customer 99

Data archiving .42
Data flows 53
Data mining. .143
Data requirements 86
Data sources. 28
Deliverables 93
Demand management 18, 64
Deployment. .113
Design 108
Distributions 75

E

Employee 102
Enablers 117
End-user. 100
Erlang 75
Exponential distribution. 76
External focus. 160

F

Forced flow law 79
Forecasting. 65
Function 150

G

Governance .64, 90

I

Implementation guidelines. 118
Implement changes 63
Inputs. 90
Internal focus. 160
ISO/IEC 20000 154

ITIL 11
ITIL V3 lifecycle 154
ITOCO model 151

K

Kendall 75
Key guidelines 118
Key performance indicators 133
Key steps design .108
Kiviat 137
Knot ITIL 211
Kurtosis 96

L

Laws of thermodynamics 52
Linear trending 67
Line management 157
Little's law 72

M

Management 104
Management information base 28
Maturity 159
Measurement 129
Metrics 28
Model 30
Modeling 68
Modeling concepts 77
Monitoring 58
Moores Law 57
Multi-class model 79
Multi-processors .39
Myths 121

N

Natural forecast unit 35
Newton's laws of mechanics 45
Normal distribution 76

O

Office of Government and Commerce 11
Operational level agreements 94
Operational management 127
Organizational change 117
Outputs 91

P

Partitioning 40
Performance 27
Performance indicators 154
Pitfalls 119
Plan 107
Poisson 75
Practice owner .108
Procedure 155
Process 151
Process-focused .160
Process management 157
Process Management Matrix (PMM) 157
Process manager 151
Process model 152
Processor virtualization 40
Process owner 151
Process pathology 60
Provider 100

Q

Queuing 29, 71

R

Relations 94
Reporting 89, 144
Reporting system 130
Resource or component
    capacity management 31
Resources 25
Response time law 73
Risks 135
Roles 102

S

Sampling interval 58
Seasonality 62
Self-assessment .136
Server classification 36
Service 26, 149
Service assurance matrix 135
Service attribute 165
Service capacity management 31
Service level agreements 94
Service level management 94
Service lifecycle .43

Service management 150
Simple network management protocol 28
Simulation modeling 68
Six Sigma 95
Software development life cycle 1
Statistical techniques 69
Sustainability 2
System 150

T
Theory of Constraints 43
Three laws of CMP 103
Tool requirements 141
Trending 67
Tuning 62

U
Underpinning contracts 94
United Kingdom Computer Measurement
    Group 13
Utilization law 73

V
Value 149
Virtualization 38

W
Workload 27
Workload characterization 34